INSTRUCTIONAL MATERIALS CENTER
GRISSOM MIDDLE SCHOOL
Mishawaka, Indiana

973
Asi Asimov, Isaac

The birth of the United States

Dahlquist
154

33624702

THE BIRTH OF THE UNITED STATES

HISTORIES BY ISAAC ASIMOV

Ancient

THE GREEKS

THE ROMAN REPUBLIC

THE ROMAN EMPIRE

THE EGYPTIANS

THE NEAR EAST

THE LAND OF CANAAN

Medieval

THE DARK AGES

THE SHAPING OF ENGLAND

CONSTANTINOPLE

THE SHAPING OF FRANCE

Modern

THE SHAPING OF NORTH AMERICA

THE BIRTH OF THE UNITED STATES

INSTRUCTIONAL MATERIALS CENTER
GRISSOM MIDDLE SCHOOL
Mishawaka, Indiana

THE BIRTH OF THE UNITED STATES 1763-1816

by ISAAC ASIMOV

Houghton Mifflin Company Boston 1974

To Ben and Barbara
and Fred and Carol
and a million laughs

Library of Congress Cataloging in Publication Data

Asimov, Isaac, 1920–
The birth of the United States.

SUMMARY: This second volume of a history of the United States concentrates on the causes and events of the Revolution and the formative years of the new Republic.

1. United States–History–Revolution–Juvenile literature. 2. United States –History–1763–1816–Juvenile literature. [1. United States–History–Revolution. 2. United States–History–1763–1816]
I. Title.
E210.A84 973 73–19514
ISBN 0–395–18451–7

FIRST PRINTING C

COPYRIGHT © 1974 BY ISAAC ASIMOV
ALL RIGHTS RESERVED. NO PART OF THIS BOOK MAY BE REPRODUCED OR TRANSMITTED IN ANY FORM BY ANY MEANS, ELECTRONIC OR MECHANICAL, INCLUDING PHOTOCOPYING AND RECORDING, OR BY ANY INFORMATION STORAGE OR RETRIEVAL SYSTEM, WITHOUT PERMISSION IN WRITING FROM THE PUBLISHER.

PRINTED IN THE UNITED STATES OF AMERICA

CONTENTS

THE BIRTH OF THE UNITED STATES

1

THE GROWING ANGER

THE AFTERMATH OF VICTORY

In the year 1763 the Treaty of Paris ended a long series of wars with the French that had plagued the British colonials on the eastern seaboard of the continent for three quarters of a century. Those wars had ended with a total British victory.

The French were evicted from the continent. All of North America from Hudson Bay to the Gulf of Mexico and from the Mississippi River to the Atlantic Ocean was British. West of the Mississippi and to the south, North America was still Spanish, but Spain had been a declining power for over a century and she caused the British, and the colonists, too, little worry. This was especially so since the Spaniards had been forced to give up Florida, which had been their bastion for nearly two centuries, a stronghold from which they had harassed the southern colonies.

The great northwestern reaches of the continent remained as yet unclaimed and still a third power, Russia, sought for furs in what is now Alaska. But that was of no moment to the colonials in the east at that time.

And yet this total victory was the beginning of troubles for Great Britain. The defeat of their enemies began a train of events that led to the greatest defeat Great Britain was to suffer in modern times, and to the birth of a new nation destined in the course of two centuries to become the most powerful in history. It is with this tale that this book is to be concerned.*

The basic trouble was that the British colonists were coming of age, were gaining a self-consciousness which the British and their government were oblivious of and did not recognize.

The settled portions of the thirteen colonies had an area of about 250,000 square miles, nearly three times that of the island of Great Britain. By 1763, there were about one and a quarter million settlers of European origin in those colonies, to which might be added the unpaid labor of over a quarter of a million Black slaves. The population of Great Britain at the time was not more than seven million, so the colonial population was, even then, a respectable fraction of the British.

What's more, colonial society had grown to be distinctly different from the British. The colonial population was already quite mixed and in addition to men of English descent, there were also sizable numbers of people whose ancestral culture was Scotch, Irish, Dutch, German, or Scandinavian. The pressures of the frontier made colonial society far more equalitarian than that of the British and there was a contempt among many in the colonies for British titles and British subservience.

More and more the colonials thought of themselves not as transplanted Englishmen, either through descent or through adoption, but as Americans. It is by that name I will refer to them henceforward.

Nor had the recent association of British and Americans, as allies in the war against France, done the least to endear the two peoples to each other. Familiarity had led to contempt on both sides.

The British officers saw the Americans as a rude, uncultured population, undisciplined, untrustworthy, and barbaric, perfectly

* In my book *The Shaping of North America* (Houghton Mifflin, 1973), I carried the history of North America to the year 1763.

Thirteen Colonies in 1763

willing to trade with the enemy for the sake of profits. Since the Americans had no trained professional army and generally fought in a guerrilla fashion suited to the woods rather than to the tamed battlefields of Europe, they were considered cowardly by the British.

To the Americans, on the other hand, the British seemed overbearing, snobbish, and tyrannical.

Each side felt that it had won the war against the French without much help from the other, and even despite the other's positive hindrance. To the British, the war had been won by the regular army at the climactic Battle of Quebec in 1759. To the Americans, it was won by endless battles against the Indians, endless small skirmishes, and the suffering of a number of massacres of women and children. It was a war in which they had heroically won Louisbourg only to have the British pusillanimously give it back. It was a war in which the British had been disgracefully defeated at Fort Duquesne and were saved from complete annihilation only by the Americans.*

Until 1763, of course, Americans could not freely indulge themselves in complaints against the British. The French were the enemy and Great Britain's power was needed. But now the French were gone and the Americans, secure in their land, felt free to stand up against the British at last.

This was all the more true in that many Americans foresaw a glittering future. With France gone, all the land as far west as the distant Mississippi was open to American settlement, it seemed to them, and the colonies would continue to grow in area and population till they were a great power on the earth. Who would stop them?

But alas, the new lands were not empty. The French might be gone, but the Indians were not.

Nor were the Indians pleased with the settlement of 1763. The British were not as ready as the French had been to welcome the Indians into the forts on an equal basis, but had made their European sense of superiority distressingly obvious. They did not see fit

* For details on these matters, see my book *The Shaping of North America.*

to soothe Indian self-respect with fair words and presents, but somehow expected the Indians to recognize their own inferiority and to know their place.

What's more, the British were not interested primarily in furs. There were settlers on the coast who wanted land, who wanted to push the Indians aside and convert the wilderness into farms. And the French, as they made ready to depart, whispered all this into Indian ears and did not scruple to encourage them to resist, holding out vague promises of future help.

An Indian leader, named Pontiac, who had been born in what is now northwestern Ohio, and who had fought with the French, came to the fore. He formed a confederacy of the Indian tribes between the Appalachian Mountains and the Mississippi River, and arranged for surprise attacks on various western outposts in May 1763, barely three months after the Treaty of Paris had been signed and peace had, apparently, come.

The plan showed initial successes. Eight forts in the Great Lakes region were taken and their garrisons massacred. Detroit, however, held out against an attack led by Pontiac himself.

Fort Pitt (at the site of modern Pittsburgh) also withstood an Indian siege and to its relief there marched a company of 500 British regulars under Colonel Henry Bouquet. On August 2, 1763, the British encountered an Indian force at Bushy Run, twenty-five miles east of Fort Pitt. Bouquet defeated the Indians in a two-day fight, and though the British lost heavily, too, that was the turning point. Fort Pitt was relieved on August 10 and Pontiac was forced to lift the siege of Detroit in November.

Little by little, Pontiac's coalition broke down. The tribes deserted him and Pontiac himself was forced to accept peace on July 24, 1766. He kept the peace with the British thereafter but was killed in Cahokia, Illinois, in 1769 by an Indian of a tribe at enmity with his own, and one who may have been bribed for the purpose by an English trader.

It was a compromise peace, however. The British had no desire to commit themselves to endless wars against the Indians and to a constant effusion of blood and money in a wilderness three thousand miles from home. Nor were they particularly willing to see the irritating colonies grow without limit. They therefore agreed on their part to safeguard the Indian hunting grounds west of the Appalachians.

On October 7, 1763, a royal proclamation established a western boundary along the ridges of the Appalachians beyond which settlements might not be made. It was this, more than anything else, that broke up Pontiac's coalition and brought peace.

To the Americans, however, the "Proclamation Line" was an abomination. It had the effect of confining them to the coastal plain, exactly where they had been confined before 1763 by the French. Where, then (the Americans thought), was the point of defeating the French?

Restlessly, the Americans pressed against the Proclamation Line and learned to ignore, and therefore despise, laws made in Great Britain. The western settlers, the land speculators, the fur trappers, all learned to think of the British government as an enemy siding with the Indians.

In Virginia, the oldest and most populous of the colonies, the land hunger of the great plantation owners was particularly marked. It had been their desire to colonize the Ohio Valley that had been the immediate cause of the last war with the French, and many of them, despite their ties to English culture, became increasingly anti-British.

The most prosperous and influential Americans, however, were the merchants of the coastal cities and of New England particularly, men who had built fortunes on sea trade with the West Indies and with Europe. If Great Britain had managed to keep their loyalty, disaffection might have been held within bounds. The more conservative Americans might themselves have kept the ill-organized farmers and frontiersmen in line.

The failure to do this was Great Britain's greatest tactical mistake.

For a hundred years, Great Britain had been attempting to regulate American trade in such a way that British manufacturers and landholders might profit by it.

By the standards of that time, this seemed rational to the British. It had been British initiative which had seized and colonized the territory on which the Americans lived. It had been the British navy and the force of British arms that had continually protected them, first against the Dutch and Spanish, and then against the French. Since the Americans existed and thrived by the bounty of Great Britain, why should they not make some return for that?

It was almost as though Great Britain viewed the Americans as having rented their vast territory from the mother country, and expected them to pay rent gladly.

To the Americans, of course, it looked quite different. The colonies had been settled by men who had done the work with very little help from the British government, and in some cases because they had been driven from their homes by religious persecution.

It also appeared to the Americans that they had defended their homes against Indians, Dutch, Spanish, and French without much help from the mother country. It was only in the last war that Great Britain, her own interests threatened in Europe and Asia, had decided to take a vigorous part – and even then the Americans had helped tremendously.

Therefore, when the British attempted to control American industry and American trade in such a way as to channel money into the pockets of British merchants and landowners, Americans felt this to be unjust.

American merchants responded by carrying on illegal trade with other countries, or by carrying on trade without paying customs duties, or in other ways cheating Great Britain of the money she was trying to collect. Americans considered themselves not to be breaking the law so much as to be disregarding unrighteous and tyrannical restrictions.

It was over the matter of trade restriction and smuggling that the commercial interests of New England and the seaport cities grew increasingly anti-British.

THE NEW KING

In retrospect, we see that the British might have handled matters more wisely. If the Americans had been allowed to rule themselves to a certain extent, and if the more influential Americans had been allowed a share of the profits, the Americans might of their own accord have turned over more money to the British than Great Britain could have gained through coercion.

Added to the circumstances contributing to the British failure to see this was the sheer chance that a new king had ascended the throne; one who, by ill fortune, was precisely unsuited to the times.

On October 25, 1760, the British king, George II, had died after a reign of thirty-three years during which British dominions overseas had expanded greatly. Indeed, it is from this reign that one can truly speak of the British Empire.

His son, Frederick, who had been the heir to the throne, had died in 1751. It was Frederick's son, who was twenty-two years old at the time of his grandfather's death, who succeeded as George III.

The new King was not very bright. He had not learned to read till he was eleven and, late in life, he was to go mad. He never really had self-confidence in himself and, as sometimes happens, this was translated into obstinacy. He could never bear to admit he was wrong so that he persisted on his own way long after it was clear to everyone else that what he was doing was producing the very reverse of the results he wanted.

George III was no tyrant. He was a moral man who loved his family and who lived a perfectly respectable life with his wife and children. He was even lovable in some ways and was certainly a much better human being than the two Georges who preceded him had been.

He lived, however, at a time when elsewhere in Europe kings were absolute. That is, King Louis XV of France, who had been ruling nearly half a century at the time that George III succeeded to the throne, did as he liked. He had no Parliament to interfere with him; no Prime Minister to run the country without control; no elections to decide policy; no parties to squabble with one another; no politicians free to attack the King.

It was humiliating to George that he alone of all European monarchs was controlled and hounded by the landowning squires who dominated the Parliament. His great-grandfather, George I, and his grandfather, George II, hadn't cared. They had been German-born and had ruled over the German land of Hanover. They had been far more interested in Hanover than in Great Britain and were perfectly willing to let the British Prime Minister rule as he pleased. The first two Georges had, in fact, scarcely been able to speak English.

George III, however, felt differently. Though still ruler of Hanover, he was English-born and English-bred. He spoke English and felt English, and he had an intense desire to govern Great Britain.

During his teens, when he was heir to the throne, his widowed mother (whom he idolized) constantly urged him to take over the duties and powers that had once been part of the crown. "Be a king!" she had told her son, meaning a king after the fashion of the absolute monarchs elsewhere in Europe.

George III *did* try to be a king. He could not actually abolish the powers of Parliament and make himself into an absolute monarch. Had he tried this he would surely have been overthrown at once by a nation which had long since settled down to strictly limited royal powers. What he did, then, was to try to govern *through* Parliament by choosing those politicians who would be on his side and who would labor on his behalf. In this way, he did his best to place Parliament under his control.

He disliked William Pitt, for instance. Pitt (the minister who had taken over the direction of British policy in the dark years when the French seemed on the point of gaining victory, and who had led Great Britain to recovery and triumph) was the very epitome of what George III detested. Pitt was a powerful and resolute politician who behaved as though *he* were king.

After George III had been king for a year, he found means to force Pitt's resignation in October 1761. It was safe to do that, of course, since Britain's victory was by that time secure. With Pitt gone, the Treaty of Paris in 1763 reflected a kind of glory on George III. He was on the throne at the time and bore the credit of victory, even though it had been clinched before he had become king.

It was in the American colonies that George III could most nearly succeed in his ambition to "be a king." In the colonies, there was no Parliament to dispute control with him. There, at least, he could rule at his pleasure, appointing and discharging officials, setting policy, and clamping down on offenders. There were colonial legislatures, to be sure, but on the whole they had little power against the King.

George III did not exert his power in the colonies in any evil way for he was not an evil man. The American complaint was that he could do it at all, whether for good or evil, without consulting the Americans themselves.

The clashes began almost as soon as George III was on the throne, and they were over the matter of smuggling. Smuggling was always an evil in British eyes, but during the French and Indian War it had seemed absolutely insupportable. At least some of the illegal American trade was with the enemy, and it went to support the French and contribute to the deaths of British soldiers (and of American soldiers, too).

The British felt quite justified in making special efforts to put a halt to smuggling and to enforce the laws that Parliament had passed regulating American trade and commerce. This had been decided on by Pitt, in 1760, about the time George III had come to the throne, and in this case George III agreed with Pitt.

Enforcing the trade laws over a large, thinly populated land three thousand miles away, where the population generally was not willing to see them enforced, was easier planned than accomplished, however. Searching for smuggled goods and trying, once they were found, to prove them to have been smuggled was almost impossible without cooperation from the people on the spot.

For that reason, the British government decided to issue "writs of assistance." These were generalized search warrants. A customs official, possessing a writ of assistance, had the right to enter any building to search for goods. There was no need to specify the particular building or the nature of the goods being searched for.

Such writs of assistance were not a new thing. They had been issued as early as 1751. In 1761, however, when the new writs were issued, the Americans no longer feared the French and no longer felt dependence on British military help. They were more conscious of their rights and more ready to insist upon them.

The right and wrong of smuggling (and who could honestly condone trading with the enemy) was not at issue. The question was whether such writs of assistance were legal. Such generalized search warrants were illegal in Great Britain where it was an established axiom of the law that "a man's house is his castle." No matter how humble or ramshackle a man's house might be, it could not be entered by the King or by his representatives without due process of law involving a specific house for a specified purpose.

Why, then, was a man's house not his castle in the colonies?

In Massachusetts, particularly, where smuggling was rampant, there was enormous opposition, and the legality of the writs was called into question. On February 24, 1761, the case for and against the writs was argued in Massachusetts superior courts.

Against the writs uprose James Otis (born in West Barnstable, Massachusetts, on February 5, 1725), the son of one of the most respected judges in the colony. His argument, pleaded most eloquently, was that the rights possessed by Englishmen, in consequence of "natural law," could not be violated either by decree of the King or by act of Parliament. There was a basic "constitution" which, even if unwritten, embodied these natural rights and "an act against the constitution," he said, "is void."

In effect, Otis held that the British government in issuing writs of assistance was itself subversive, and that Americans in refusing to obey this particular law were, in so doing, upholding the basic principles of law. (He was preaching what we today call "civil disobedience.")

The British were not affected by this argument and continued their policy of issuing writs of assistance. To many Americans, however, Otis had raised a beacon of light that was to guide them onward and to justify them in rebelling against British law in the name of a higher law.

A similar event took place in Virginia, somewhat later.

In Virginia, it had been the custom, since 1662, to pay clergymen in tobacco. Hard money was scarce, and tobacco was a valuable commodity.

The trouble was that the value of tobacco fluctuated. Though its price was generally twopence a pound, there came a series of bad years in which the tobacco harvest was poor because of drought and the price went to sixpence a pound. This meant that if the clergy received their customary allotment of tobacco (17,000 pounds a year) their salaries would be, in effect, tripled.

The Virginia legislature, the House of Burgesses, which was controlled by tobacco planters, abandoned the tobacco payment in 1755 and established a money payment instead at the rate of twopence a pound. To this the clergy, of course, objected and took their case to the British government. On August 10, 1759, while George II was still king, the British government annulled the Virginia law and restored payment in tobacco.

The Virginians ignored the British ruling and finally a particular clergyman brought the matter up before the Virginia courts toward the end of 1763. The case was called the "Parson's Cause."

Arguing against the clergyman, and for the law as passed by the House of Burgesses, was Patrick Henry (born in Hanover county, Virginia, on May 29, 1736), the son of a Scottish immigrant. He had had little schooling and could not make his way either as a storekeeper or as a farmer. It was not until he tried the law that he found his bent, for he proved to be a remarkable orator.

In his speech against the clergyman's case, delivered on December 1, 1763, Henry did not concern himself with whether the law as passed by the House of Burgesses was wise or foolish, humane or cruel. The question at issue was whether the British government could, at its own will, cancel a law passed by the House of Burgesses. Henry argued that it could not; that again the "natural law" was violated by this arbitrary British action and that therefore that action was without force.

The jury was sufficiently moved by Henry's eloquence to award the clergyman just one penny in damages.

The notion of a "natural law" was an attractive one to the intellectuals of the time.

A hundred years before, the great English scientist, Isaac Newton, had worked out the laws of motion and of universal gravitation, and had shown how the workings of the universe could be expressed in these laws, which could be simply stated and clearly interpreted.

There followed all the enthusiasm of the so-called "Age of Reason" in which many felt, overoptimistically, that everything in the universe could be reduced to laws that were as general, as powerful, and as simply phrased, as Newton's law. There were even such laws governing society, some felt, that were as natural and as inevitable as the laws of motion, and as essentially unbreakable by governments.

The most outspoken and eloquent of those who believed in this "natural law" of society was a French-Swiss writer named Jean Jacques Rousseau, who was extraordinarily influential in his own time among the intellectuals of Europe and America. In 1762, he published his book, *The Social Contract,* in which he maintained that governments were instituted with the consent of the governed in order to bring about certain desirable ends more efficiently than could be brought about without government. Whenever a government proved, for any reason, incapable of bringing about those desirable ends or was not desirous of doing so, it had broken its contract. It was then the right of the governed to reorganize or replace the government.

It was this sort of thing which men like Otis and Henry had in mind, but the British King and his Parliament, quite oblivious to Rousseau's doctrines, went their own way.

THE STAMP ACT

As though to meet the growing evidence of anger in the colonies, the British government placed British soldiers on permanent duty in the colonies.

Prior to the French and Indian War, when the colonies were plagued by dangers from Indians, Dutch, Spaniards, and French, the British soldiers had been elsewhere. But now that all danger was gone, Parliament had voted, in the aftermath of the Treaty of Paris, to place a permanent force of 10,000 British regulars in the colonies.

This was distinctly more than was needed; and more than the British generals on the spot asked for. Moreover, the British soldiers were not placed on frontier posts where it might be argued they were needed against Indian uprisings or Spanish incursions. Not at all! They were placed in the larger and more comfortable cities.

Americans could and did argue, with considerable show of justification, that the soldiers were placed in America to give employment to those army officers who would otherwise be retired on half pay at the conclusion of the war; and they were so placed that they could be used against discontented Americans and against no other enemies of Great Britain.

The British government was deaf to these complaints. They had what seemed to them far greater troubles; financial ones.

In April 1763, George Grenville became Prime Minister and found himself with an insoluble problem on his hands. The British national debt had risen to 136 million pounds as a result of the war against France. That was an enormous figure for those days, and the day-to-day expenses of government had risen, too.

It was absolutely necessary to impose new taxes, but that is something that is never popular. Grenville's efforts to impose one tax or another was generally blocked by an unsympathetic Parliament (backed by an equally unsympathetic British public).

It finally occurred to the desperate Grenville that taxes might be placed on the colonies, instead. The national debt had, after all, arisen through a war that had been fought very largely in the interests of the colonies; it had been from *their* doorstep that the French menace had been removed. And the Americans had flourished and prospered during the war, largely through smuggled trade that had brought them profits at the expense of the British.

Why, then, should the Americans not bear a just share of the cost of the war now? In 1764, Grenville had Parliament pass a "Sugar Act" which raised the customs duties on sugar, wine, coffee, and textiles. These were "indirect taxes" paid by the importers, who then passed on the expense to the consumer. Despite everything the British could do, however, such indirect taxes were collected with difficulty and smuggling continued to place a large gap between the money that should be received and the money that actually was received.

Grenville also passed laws forbidding the colonies to issue paper money. Paper money was generally worth less than its face value in terms of gold. It was useful therefore for debtors to pay their debts in paper money. Since Americans were by and large debtors to the British, paper money was to the advantage of the colonies and to the disadvantage of British merchants.

What was really needed, however, was something more – a "direct tax." The individual consumer had to be made to pay some sum on specific occasions under such conditions that the payment was unavoidable.

The exciting notion arose of making all official papers illegal, without a special stamp – and then charging money for the stamp, with the money to go to the British government. The stamps could be put out in varying denominations from a halfpenny to ten pounds and every official transaction would require a stamp at a price suiting the case.

Anyone who went to court would have to file innumerable papers and, on each one, a stamp worth three shillings would have to be affixed. Anyone who earned a diploma would have to pay two pounds for a stamp to be placed on it or he wouldn't get the diploma. Various licenses would need stamps, so would bills of sale, newspapers, advertisements, playing cards, almanacs, and dice.

This was bound to be a lucrative tax, since there would be no way of avoiding it if transactions were simply illegal without a stamp. If, on top of that, severe penalties were placed for violations it was calculated that the tax might raise 150,000 pounds a year.

About the only concession made to American feelings was that the government agents who were to sell the stamps and collect the taxes were to be Americans, not British.

Parliament seemed satisfied with the notion. The "Stamp Act" was passed on March 22, 1765, and was to go into effect on November 1 of that year. Then, on May 15, 1765, Parliament passed the "Quartering Act." This provided that British soldiers could be placed in private houses if that were necessary.

The excuse for this was that there were insufficient barracks in the colonies to house the soldiers properly. It was quite obvious, however, that soldiers placed in a household against the will of the householder could be uncomfortable guests, and that if households were carefully selected, the power to quarter soldiers could be used as a way of punishing individuals with whom the government was displeased. Although there was no connection with the Stamp Act, Americans felt certain that the Quartering Act had been passed as a way of squelching protests against the stamps by placing soldiers in the houses of the more eminent protesters.

If the Quartering Act had been intended to keep the Americans quiet about the Stamp Act, it did not work. In fact, it is hard to imagine how any tax could have been devised that would be more instantly odious to the Americans.

For one thing, the Stamp Act was the first direct tax ever imposed on the colonies by the British government. It was the first time the individual American had to dig down in his personal pocket for a coin that was to go directly to the British King. That the tax picked his pocket was bad enough; that it was a *novelty* was much worse.

Then, too, it struck specifically at groups who were particularly articulate and influential — at lawyers who found stamps needed for every legal paper, and at newspaper publishers who found their products singled out for stamps. (At the time there were twenty-five newspapers in the colony, and these were widely read.)

What's more, the Stamp Act was universal in that it hit all the colonies alike and left the British unable to profit by turning one section against another. And it came in a postwar period of economic depression. *Everything* combined to make the Stamp Act completely unacceptable to Americans.

The Americans did not admit the justice of the tax in the first place. The British had incurred huge expenses in a war (they maintained) that was fought primarily in the service of British interests in Europe and Asia. In the portion of the war that was fought on the North American continent, the Americans themselves had contributed in men and money quite out of proportion to their population.

Furthermore, even if the tax were just, it was not acceptable in principle because it had been placed upon them without their consent, and this went against the "natural law" and the rights of Americans as free subjects of the crown.

James Otis found a phrase for it, one that swept the colonies and remained a clarion call to all who increasingly resisted the British government in the decade to come. He said, "Taxation without representation is tyranny."

In other words, an American Parliament might decide to enact just such a law as the Stamp Act and to donate the proceeds to Great Britain and that would be a legal action. Or American delegates might sit in the British Parliament and oppose the Stamp Act and it might be passed over their opposition and it would still be a legal action. To pass such a law without giving any American even a chance to discuss it or attempt to sway parliamentary feeling against it, was not legal but was an exercise of tyranny.

The British did not quite see it that way. At that time, only people possessing a certain amount of property could vote for representatives to Parliament. A majority of the British population had no vote and were not represented and yet they could be, and were, taxed by Parliament.

The Americans, however, saw this as a false analogy. The unpropertied individual in Great Britain, though he might lack a vote, could easily make his presence felt. He could shout, demonstrate, and riot, and if a law was unpopular enough, the turmoil to which it would give rise would give Parliament pause – especially after the experience, in the previous century, of King Charles I who was executed and King James II who was exiled.

On the other hand, who in Parliament would be in the least concerned over protests and riots taking place in a land three thousand miles away, far across an ocean?

And indeed, when Parliament passed the Stamp Act, it saw no occasion to be concerned over unrest so far away. It was up to Americans to find ways of forcing it to be concerned.

RESISTANCE!

Popular anger in the colonies rose steadily in the months after the passage of the Stamp Act.

In Virginia, Patrick Henry, who had just been elected a member of the House of Burgesses (largely through the fame he had gathered in the Parson's Cause), rose on May 29, 1765, to oppose the Stamp Act and to support certain resolutions maintaining the right of Virginia to make laws for itself.

Henry did not hesitate to point out what had happened to rulers in the past when they disregarded the rights of the people and brought upon themselves death at the hands of those who could find no legal redress.

Solemnly, he said, "Caesar had his Brutus, Charles I his Cromwell and George III ——"

It sounded as though he were going to threaten the reigning King with assassination or execution and some of the shocked and appalled burgesses cried out, "Treason! Treason!"

But Henry finished his sentence in a different manner altogether, saying "— may profit by their example."

In other words, George III might very well learn from the lessons of history how not to be a tyrant and might then rule beloved by his people. Henry finished ironically, "If this be treason, make the most of it," and walked out of the hall.

The House of Burgesses did not pass the resolutions but they were published in the newspapers for all to see.

Even before the Stamp Act was to go into effect, speeches had been translated into action. There were riots in the large cities; government officials were hanged in effigy; resolutions not to use the stamps were taken; and anyone who looked as though he might take the job as stamp agent was threatened and, sometimes, roughed up. Before the occasion came to use the stamps legally, every single American agent had resigned in terror and many supplies of stamps were destroyed.

In the fall of 1765, nearly one thousand merchants in Boston, New York, and Philadelphia banded together and organized boycotts of British goods in order to punish the British further by reducing even the customs duties. Courts announced plans to close rather than use the stamps on legal documents. It became a point of patriotism to use home-distilled liquor, homespun clothes, and home-manufactured objects of all kinds, even when they were not as good as those which could be imported.

The furor in America was not without its effect in Parliament. One fifth of the representatives had voted against the Stamp Act in the first place. Many were sincerely opposed to the policy of taxing the colonies without their consent, and others spoke in favor of the Americans as a way of registering their opposition to the King.

William Pitt, who was plagued by gout and was in general poor health, supported the American cause vigorously. So did Edmund Burke, who was to become a particularly renowned parliamentarian.

Isaac Barré was most notable in this respect, at least in the American colonies. He was born in Dublin, Ireland, of French parentage, but had fought loyally on the British side against France and had been wounded in the campaign against Quebec.

Defending the Americans in Parliament, he referred to them, emotionally, as "sons of liberty" and the Americans did not forget. A city in northeastern Pennsylvania, founded in 1769, was named Wilkes-Barre in his honor and in that of John Wilkes, another parliamentary opponent of George III. Barre, Vermont, which was just being founded at this time, is also named for him.

The howling opposition to the Stamp Act fostered the rise of still more radical viewpoints among the Americans. In Massachusetts, two men, Samuel Adams and John Adams (they were second cousins), came into prominence.

John Adams, the younger of the two (born in Quincy, Massachusetts, on October 30, 1735), was a brilliant lawyer, with all the unlovable virtues, and without any capacity for making himself popular. Though a man of strict integrity and rare intelligence, his vanity was his most noticeable characteristic. He wrote scholarly and effective articles against the Stamp Act, but Sam Adams took another route.

Samuel Adams (born in Boston on September 27, 1722) was a failure in life. He failed in law, in business, in anything he turned his hand to, until he found his life work in the year of the Stamp Act. It was then he discovered that he was a rabble-rouser and an effective one. He entered politics and made that his whole life, placing himself always on the side of radical action. He was the first American to come out openly for independence. He did not want Great Britain to mend its ways; he wanted it to go away altogether and it was to that he turned his mind.

Not only did Sam Adams organize riots against the Stamp Act, he also founded the so-called "Sons of Liberty" organization, taking the name from Isaac Barré's phrase.

The Sons of Liberty have been idealized in American legend, but in actual fact they were very close in their behavior to what we would call storm troopers today. They went about threatening anyone who bought stamps or traded with England and sometimes carried out the threats in terms of wrecking businesses or applying tar-and-feathers. They harassed stamp collectors and public officials to the point where even the governor was not safe. The house of the chief justice of the colony was looted while that of Thomas Hutchinson, a member of the governor's council, was burned down because he was thought (wrongly) to have approved of the Stamp Act.

Nor was James Otis idle. It seemed to him that this was a case for colonial cooperation. On June 8, he sent out letters to every colony, suggesting that they meet in New York City to decide on common action against the Stamp Act.

The response was enthusiastic and from October 7 to October 25, 1765, the "Stamp Act Congress" sat in New York City. Nine colonies were represented by delegates and the remaining four were absent through lack of opportunity to appoint delegates rather than through any lack of sympathy.

Prominent among the delegates was John Dickinson of Pennsylvania (born in Talbot County, Maryland, on November 8, 1732). It was he who drew up a declaration, voted by the Congress, to be presented to the King and Parliament, denying the right of any taxation without the consent of the colonial legislatures.

By the time November 1 arrived and the Stamp Act went into effect, it had already proved a complete fiasco. Nor did the months that followed show any improvement. The unavailing efforts to enforce the act cost far more money than was gathered, so that the net result was expense, not revenue.

Then, too, British merchants were beginning to be hurt by the grim American boycott and by January 17, 1766, were themselves petitioning Parliament for the repeal of the Stamp Act. Parliamentary opponents were becoming more and more firm in their opposition and Pitt, in particular, made tremendously effective speeches against it and in support of the American viewpoint.

Grenville's ministry had ended in disorder in October 1765, and the new Prime Minister, Charles Watson-Wentworth, second Marquess of Rockingham, was more disposed to listen to repeal.

Benjamin Franklin was in London at the time.* He had arrived in Great Britain in December 1764, hoping to persuade the British government to take Pennsylvania out of the reactionary grip of the Penn family, which then owned it as a kind of family estate, and make it a crown colony under the rule of the British government. He arrived in time to speak against the Stamp Act, but when it was passed by Parliament, he felt that it was the law, however unjust, and should therefore be obeyed.

For a while this made him extremely unpopular in the colonies. It was virtually the only time in his life that he badly misestimated popular feeling in America, perhaps because he was three thousand miles away at the time. Quickly recovering, he began to press for the repeal of the Stamp Act.

On February 13, 1766, he was questioned on the subject by a parliamentary committee and spoke eloquently in favor of repeal at just about the time the declaration of the Stamp Act Congress arrived. He detailed the great contributions made by Americans in the recent war and warned of outright rebellion if Parliament persisted. When Franklin's actions became known in the colonies, he was restored to American favor.

Parliament bowed to the inevitable and repealed the Stamp Act. George III signed the repeal on March 18, 1766.

When the news arrived in America, there was a hurricane of joy and every possible expression of loyalty and gratitude to the British government. George III's birthday, two months later, was celebrated deliriously and statues were raised to him.

It might have seemed that all was well again, but what few Americans noticed was that although Parliament had repealed the Stamp Act, it had not abandoned the right of taxing the colonies without their consent. It had, in fact, specifically maintained that right on the same day that the repeal had gone through.

All Parliament had done was to admit that the Stamp Act was the wrong way of going about the business. They would now look for other ways.

* Born in Boston, Massachusetts, on January 17, 1706, he was easily the most famous American of his time. His earlier career is described in *The Shaping of North America.*

2

THE ROAD TO REVOLUTION

THE SECOND ROUND

In July 1766, Rockingham, under whose leadership the Stamp Act was repealed, was dismissed by George III for reasons that had nothing to do with the colonies. From then on, Rockingham and those who followed him remained favorable to the American cause, but they also remained out of power.

George III, having been forced to back down, tried the experiment of a ministry which would represent a wide variety of views and accepted none other than William Pitt to head it. If Pitt had been a younger or healthier man, there might have been some chance for conciliation, but the fortune of history dictated otherwise.

Never really hale, Pitt, though still only in his late fifties, was a shattered man. He accepted an earldom and became first Earl of Chatham. This removed him from the House of Commons and put him into the easier atmosphere of the House of Lords. More and more, he withdrew from active leadership and for some years did not even appear in Parliament.

The Duke of Grafton, who succeeded him, had no capacity and the ministry he headed was really run, therefore, by the strongest man in it. This was Charles Townshend, a witty man who could speak eloquently, especially when he was slightly under the influence of liquor. All he lacked was judgment.

Townshend was Chancellor of the Exchequer (something like the American office of Secretary of the Treasury) and it was his duty to find the money to support the government. This remained a thankless task, and especially at this time when the colonies were all too conscious of their success in forcing repeal of the Stamp Act.

It did not occur to Townshend, or to any member of the government, to explore the possibility of having the colonial assemblies themselves impose taxes on the Americans. That would have seemed to them to be an intolerable admission of defeat and to have set a precedent that would lead inevitably to the total loss of control of Great Britain over the colonies. No, it seemed to the parliamentary leaders that Britain itself *must* tax the colonies.

But how?

On May 8, 1767, Townshend treated himself to a large helping of champagne, then, rather ebullient, delivered what was afterward called the "champagne speech." In it, he sparkled as effervescently as the champagne and heaped ridicule on those who opposed him; in particular, on Grenville, who was still buried under the disgrace of having passed the unlucky Stamp Act.

Stung into response, Grenville called out that Townshend might speak bravely but he dared not tax the Americans.

Hotly, Townshend refuted the charge and swore he would tax the Americans — and proceeded to do so.

He avoided the direct tax and went back to the indirect tax on American imports. The Americans had never officially objected to the British right to control trade and had been paying duties regularly — whenever they were caught, which wasn't often. It seemed to Townshend, therefore, only a matter of placing duties on new commodities, raising the duties on old ones, and improving collection.

By June 29, he had pushed acts through Parliament which placed duties on tea, glass, paper, and dyestuffs, effective as of November 20, 1767. Writs of assistance were to be issued and customs officials were to be granted wider powers in order to stop the smuggling. In this way, it was hoped that 40,000 pounds a year would be raised. This could be used, in part, to pay governors and judges in the colonies. This would have had the effect of placing the colonial executives and judiciary under parliamentary control since it would be Parliament, and no longer the colonial legislatures, who would hold the purse strings.

The so-called "Townshend Acts" were a miracle of poor judgment. The passage without colonial consultation, the projected manner of collection, and the announced purpose, all combined to exasperate Americans. In the mood in which the colonies found themselves then, the acts were merely provocations to new disorders, and the hornets were stirred up again.

Indeed, the hornets had not yet stopped flying and did not require the further irritation of taxation to make them troublesome. Although the Stamp Act had been repealed, the Quartering Act had not, and any American at any time could still be made the unwilling host of a soldier or soldiers, if the commanding general of the British troops in America saw fit to place him there.

The commanding general was Thomas Gage, who was not overladen with either tact or ability. He had come to America in 1755 with Braddock, had led the advance guard at the defeat at Fort Duquesne (see *The Shaping of North America*) and had managed to survive. He served in the later course of the war without particular distinction and, in 1763, with the rank of major general had become commander-in-chief of all the British forces in North America. It was he who had requested Parliament to pass the Quartering Act – which did not increase his popularity with Americans.

Gage's headquarters were in New York, and it irritated him to have the colonial authorities continually interfering with his efforts to place his officers and men in comfortable quarters. In a fury, he demanded that the New York assembly order enforcement of the Quartering Act. This the assembly stoutly refused to do and Gage put pressure on New York's governor to dissolve the body.

This was done on December 19, 1766, and Parliament later confirmed the act. A new and more conservative assembly was then elected, and it permitted quartering. All this accomplished, both in New York and elsewhere, was to increase popular hatred of the soldiers. The term "redcoat" became a term of insult and anger among Americans.

The news of the Townshend Acts and of the troubles with the New York assembly spread over the colonies together. It was clear that not only did the British government have no intention of working through the colonial assemblies; it was intent on making those same assemblies exist only at parliamentary pleasure. At this rate, Americans would soon be left with no self-government at all and would be subject to a pure parliamentary despotism.

The situation was made to order for Samuel Adams, who instantly began to beat the drums for a renewal of the boycott program that had done so much to force repeal of the Stamp Act. In September 1767, even before the Townshend Acts had come into force, public meetings in Boston were setting up nonimportation agreements. Adams wrote to radical leaders in other colonies, too, to spread the word, and Sons of Liberty everywhere began to make it hot for customs officials.

Adams was a brilliant agitator and made the most of his opportunities, but he could have done nothing without the help of British folly. So extreme was Adams in his views that most of the American leaders would surely have turned against him if they had had the chance to do so. The American leaders of the time were as aristocratic in their leanings as the British were, as confirmed in the belief that government should be handled by those men of better family who were also men of property, and as fearful of what we call "democracy" and what they would have thought of as "mob rule."

If the British had accepted the American leaders as their partners, there is every likelihood that there would still be a political relationship between the United States and Great Britain today (as between Canada and Great Britain). It was because Great Britain would not bend so far and persisted in a hard-line approach, that many American conservatives were forced into the arms of such radicals as Adams, Otis, and Henry.

An example of this was John Dickinson, who had dominated the Stamp Act Congress. He came of a well-to-do family, was a large landowner, had studied law both in Philadelphia and in England, and was a conservative man who was utterly pro-British in his feelings. And yet he could not agree that the British had the right to make laws for the Americans without any consideration whatever of any possible American say in the matter.

In the wake of the Townshend Acts, Dickinson took up his pen and, beginning on December 2, wrote *Letters of a Farmer*. Altogether, there were fourteen of these, which appeared far and wide in American newspapers through the winter of 1767–1768, and which were then published in pamphlet form.

In the *Letters*, Dickinson protested his loyalty to Great Britain, accepted the right of the British to regulate American trade, urged Americans to participate in no violent demonstrations, and refused to appeal to the doctrine of "natural rights."

Nevertheless, Dickinson expressed himself forcefully against the Townshend Acts and against the suspension of the New York assembly, as depriving Americans of their rights as Englishmen. (It was not their "natural rights" of which they were deprived in his view but of their specific rights under British law.) What Dickinson wanted, apparently, was limited self-rule for America; the kind of relationship that an American state has to the central government today.

A system of the kind Dickinson dimly envisaged and of the kind that was eventually (but only with a great deal of trouble) worked out in the United States, was completely unprecedented at the time. The British Parliament could not possibly see it. George III wanted no compromise and the parliamentary majority was strongly in favor of law-and-order policies. The Americans must be made to understand who were the masters.

FIRST BLOOD

The very focus of radical anti-British feeling was the city of Boston. There, Samuel Adams kept pushing the hysteria higher and higher. On February 11, 1768, he and James Otis persuaded the Massachusetts assembly to put their stamp of approval on a circular letter to all the colonies that the two had prepared.

The language of the letter was mild enough, but it called for common action on the part of the colonies in defense of their liberties, and the British considered it seditious. When the Massachusetts assembly refused to disown it, it was dissolved on July 1 by Hutchinson, whose house had been burned down during the Stamp Act disorders, and who was now acting governor of the colony.

About this time, too, John Hancock (born in Braintree, Massachusetts, on January 12, 1737) came into the news. He had inherited a large fortune and a prosperous business from an uncle who had died in 1764 and he was now one of the richest men in America. A great deal of the wealth he had inherited came from smuggling, so he was naturally completely against British regulation of trade and supplied much of the money that kept the Sons of Liberty going.

This made Hancock a marked man to the customs officials and on June 10, 1768, they seized one of his ships on the ground that it contained smuggled goods. It probably did, but it was an injudicious act just the same, for Hancock called on the Sons of Liberty and Boston was treated the spectacle of a first-class riot. The ship was rescued and the customs officials managed to make their way to safety only by an eyelash.

Great Britain responded by ordering two regiments of British troops from Halifax to Boston. They arrived on October 1, 1768, and at once there began a cold war between the Boston citizens and the redcoats.

But though Boston might be the site of the worst anti-British feeling, it was certainly not alone. There was plenty of rebellious feeling everywhere and however the Boston agitators worked to heat it up, that feeling was not their creation.

In Virginia, the House of Burgesses adopted anti-British resolutions prepared by George Mason (born in Fairfax county, Virginia, in 1725), a planter who was one of the great liberal thinkers of the time. The resolutions were presented by Mason's friend and neighbor, George Washington,* America's most distinguished soldier, who thus placed himself on the anti-British side. The House of

* Washington was born in Westmoreland county, Virginia, on February 22, 1732. For his early career and for some of the reasons for his anti-British attitude, see *The Shaping of North America.*

Burgesses was at once dissolved by the governor, but it met informally and organized a trade boycott against Great Britain.

And in the city of New York there were passions almost as extreme as those in Boston.

It was the custom of the more radical portion of the population to raise a "liberty pole" in some conspicuous spot in town. There the Sons of Liberty could meet, orate, drink, and generally make themselves noticeable. The usual policy of the British was to turn a blind eye to this and indeed that was the wiser policy since, by allowing the radicals to blow off steam, the revolutionary pressures were lowered.

Every once in a while, however, some British officer was bound to decide that what the rabble needed was a lesson. British soldiers had, for instance, cut down a liberty pole in New York in 1766 during the row over the Quartering Act, and that seemed to have done some good.

On January 19, 1770, some local commander was irritated into another demonstration of this sort. A detachment of soldiers chopped down New York's liberty pole, cut it in pieces and then, in deliberate provocation, piled those pieces in front of the headquarters of the Sons of Liberty.

Naturally, there was a riot, and several New Yorkers were slashed by British bayonets. The wounded were made martyrs at once and as the story went round concerning redcoats spilling American blood, new radicals were manufactured out of the uncommitted.

But the worst incident of this period occurred in Boston where the conflict between citizens and soldiers was sharpest. The Sons of Liberty did everything to harass the soldiers directly and, furthermore, to threaten and make uncomfortable any Bostonian who showed signs of fraternizing with the redcoats.

The result was that the British soldiers, who were, after all, not there voluntarily and who certainly wanted no trouble, found themselves in an untenable position. They were under strict orders not to fire on the citizens and yet those citizens felt no compunction about throwing stones at the soldiers.

On March 5, 1770, a group of idlers decided it might be fun to throw snowballs at a single British soldier standing sentry. The soldier did his best to dodge the snowballs and called for help. A detachment of twenty soldiers, bayonets fixed, came to his aid, but by that time the crowd of Bostonians had increased to several hundred.

As the soldiers were clearly under orders not to retaliate, the mob, among whom a Black named Crispus Attucks was conspicuous, grew bolder. After the insults and snowballs, came rocks and clubs. One of the soldiers, tormented beyond endurance, finally fired. Others followed. The crowd suddenly fled and behind them they left three dead and two wounded. One of the dead was Attucks who is sometimes described, therefore, as the first casualty of the Revolution.

Samuel Adams was ready. The event was called "The Boston Massacre" and fictional accounts of it were spread all over. The soldiers were described as having fired without provocation into crowds of respectable, peaceful citizens, killing without remorse or compunction. Bostonian anger at the highly colored tale grew so intense that Governor Hutchinson, in order to prevent much worse bloodshed, had to order the British regiments withdrawn from the town itself and placed on islands till matters cooled down.

The fact that the incident was not really a massacre can be shown by the fact that the soldiers were brought to trial and that John Adams himself (against whose American loyalties there can be no shadow of doubt) chose to defend them. He defended them so well and the real facts of the case were so notorious that the soldiers were acquitted of murder. Two were convicted of manslaughter and lightly punished, more as a concession to the crowd than to the truth.

It was not, however, the shouts and violence that most persuaded the Parliament that they were defeating themselves. It was the boycott. Again, as during the time of the Stamp Act, British industrialists and shippers were hurting badly as the American trade declined 40 per cent between 1767 and 1769. Pressure began to build again and Parliament was petitioned to back away from its taxation policy.

Townshend was not there to witness the failure of his policy. He had died, quite suddenly, on September 4, 1767, even before his Acts had come into force. He was succeeded as Chancellor of the

Exchequer by Frederick, Lord North, who was, and remained, a favorite of George III.

On January 31, 1770, when the Duke of Grafton stepped down, Lord North was chosen by George III to be Prime Minister, and, at last, the King had a Prime Minister he trusted and could rely on to be a faithful reflector of the royal views. Lord North was to remain in office for twelve years and between his incapacity and the royal stubbornness, America was to be lost to Great Britain.

North's first moves, however, were conciliatory. Within a month of the Boston Massacre (and with no connection with that affair) the new cabinet had decided to let the Quartering Act expire without renewal and to repeal the taxes imposed by Townshend – with one exception.

Carefully, Lord North kept the tax on tea. That was not for purposes of revenue particularly, but was simply a way of retaining the principle that the British parliament could tax the colonies without their consent. The hope was that with most of the taxes gone, the colonies would accept the apparent victory and abandon the principle. Then, presumably, at some less troubled time in the future, Great Britain would be able to tax more extensively.

To a certain extent, this scheme worked. The well-to-do conservatives among the Americans, who found it uncomfortable to be on the same side as the Sons of Liberty, were glad to accept Lord North's action as a gesture of peace and conciliation.

There was no wide jubilation as there had been after the repeal of the Stamp Act. That had proved to be but the prelude to a second round and this might be a prelude to a third. Nevertheless, Sam Adams found himself suddenly helpless as passions subsided among his countrymen. The boycott was ended, the colonies quieted, and it looked as though the crisis had passed.

SAM ADAMS AND TEA

Sam Adams had to wait for more incidents and for a while it seemed he would have to wait in vain. Two years passed in profound quiet and it seemed that Americans had won their immediate victories and had subsided into comfortable acquiescence to British policy.

In early 1772, for instance, it was announced that the governor of Massachusetts and the judges of that colony would be paid out of royal funds, thus making them independent of the colonial legislature – yet that hardly caused a ripple outside Massachusetts itself.

But then came a dramatic incident.

The various American harbors were patrolled by small British naval vessels on guard against the smuggling. Naturally, these were unpopular with those who smuggled and with those who were anti-British for any reason. One of them, the *Gaspée,* was particularly efficient at its job as it patrolled Narragansett Bay in the colony of Rhode Island and it was therefore particularly distasteful to the population of the coastal towns in the area.

And then, on the night of June 9, 1772, the *Gaspée,* while chasing a smuggler, unluckily went aground on a sandbank and came to a helpless halt.

The news spread and many Rhode Islanders were astounded at this stroke of luck and took quick action. Before the night was over, a mob had gathered, boarded the ship, maltreated the men aboard, hustled them to shore, and then burned the ship.

When the news reached Great Britain, the government was furious. It was the British fleet that protected the home island and the farflung interests abroad and no outrage could be permitted against any ship that was part of the navy, even if it was only a small revenue cutter.

A reward of 500 pounds (enormous in those days) was proclaimed for anyone who would identify any of those who had commited the outrage, and it was announced that any who were apprehended would be taken to Great Britain for trial.

The British, of course, had good reason to suspect that anyone committing an act on behalf of the right to smuggle would never be convicted in a colonial court, but it was nevertheless a serious error to announce a British trial for such malefactors.

For one thing, it did them no good, for despite the reward offered, not one person was turned in. Instead, the threat of a treason trial in Great Britain was played up everywhere. It was easy for anyone in the colonies to believe that no American accused of treason could possibly receive a fair trial in Great Britain. The accused would be far from home and would be surrounded by men alien to him and filled with anti-American prejudice.

Who could feel safe? Many Americans who were completely loyal to Great Britain had nevertheless made hasty remarks at the worst of the angry reaction to the Stamp Act and the Townshend Acts. If they were called to account for that and sent to Great Britain for trial, what then? And in the light of that, the royal payment of judges in Massachusetts began to look like an attempt to make colonial judges creatures of the British government.

The cry of British "tyranny" began to have a very personal terror about it.

Sam Adams was, of course, not asleep. He had found a man after his own heart in a bright and articulate physician, Joseph Warren (born in Roxbury, Massachusetts, on May 30, 1741), who had brought himself to the attention of the radicals by a fiery and effective speech he made on the occasion of the second anniversary of the Boston Massacre.

On November 2, 1772, Adams and Warren put their propaganda machine into high gear. Adams had long been sending letters to all points of the colonies, always urging united action, but now he and Warren formed "committees of correspondence" to handle the letter-writing procedure wholesale and to form a network of propaganda that would help unite the colonies in favor of the radical cause.*

Within three months, eighty such committees were established in the various towns of Massachusetts, and other colonies were beginning to take it up. In Virginia, for instance, the House of Burgesses officially established a committee of correspondence on March 12, 1773. Among the members of this group was Patrick Henry, of course. Also included was Thomas Jefferson (born in Shadwell, Virginia, on April 13, 1743) and Richard Henry Lee (born in Stratford, Virginia, on January 20, 1732). George Washington, who was anti-British but not radically so, was not among them.

Sam Adams, with a multi-colony-wide organization at his dis-

* James Otis was appointed to head the Boston Committee but he was drifting out of the real world. In 1769, he had been hit on the head in a brawl with a customs officer and had been passing into harmless lunacy ever since. He was sane only at lengthening intervals and he played no part in the conflict that was to come.

posal, waited for his next chance. It came from an unexpected direction and it involved the small tax on tea imports that had been left over from the Townshend Acts.

This tax on tea had continued to be maintained, and, on the whole, Sam Adams, despite all his efforts, had not been successful in rousing resistance against that one small tax, or in convincing people that they ought to fight for principle when things, on the whole, were prosperous and quiet. If Great Britain had left things at that, all might yet have blown over.

Unfortunately, though, the East India Company was in trouble.

The East India Company was a private firm, formed in 1600 to compete with the Dutch East India Company in trade with the far east. In its checkered history, the East India Company reached the peak of its fame when it established what was virtually an empire of its own in India during the mid-18th century.

In 1773, however, the East India Company was having financial difficulties over the matter of tea. India was a great tea-producer and the East India Company had millions of tons of tea at their disposal for which they had no market.

In the ordinary course of events, the East India Company would have had to put up the tea for auction in Great Britain, knock it down at dirt-cheap prices to British merchants who would then probably manage to sell it here and there at a profit.

The British government, anxious to save the Company, granted it the right to sell to British colonies directly and freed it of the necessity of paying taxes on the tea. This meant that the East India Company could sell the tea to the Americans at a considerably higher price than it would have received at auction and yet, thanks to the lifting of taxes, at a price cheaper than the Americans could obtain it elsewhere. Tea was a popular drink in the colonies and the East India Company was sure it would sell enough to pull itself out of the red.

But now it was no longer a matter of a mere tea tax. Various tea merchants in the colonies would be put out of business as the East India Company would use its own agents in an effort to cut down still further on middleman losses. Many tea smugglers would also lose a great deal of revenue since even through smuggling they would not be able to meet the competition.

Besides that, even to those who were not directly hurt, the mere notion that the Americans could be used to supply the money that would pull a British company out of the red was humiliating. It might be painless this time but what a dangerous precedent it would set.

Sam Adams's committees of correspondence got to work at once and found no difficulty in working up a storm of indignation against the new state of affairs. Plans were made to boycott tea and even to prevent tea shipments from being landed.

The East India Company, unaware of trouble, shipped off half a million pounds of tea to Philadelphia, New York, Charleston, and Boston. As it turned out, not a pound of it was sold. In Charleston, the tea was unloaded, stored in damp cellars, and was never bought or used. In Philadelphia and New York, matters didn't even go that far. The ships were not allowed to unload and were forced to go back to Great Britain with the tea still in their holds.

It was in Boston, predictably, that the situation proved worst. There the ships carrying the tea couldn't unload, but they refused to leave. They remained in the harbor, partly because two sons and a nephew of Governor Hutchinson had been appointed agents for the East India Company and stood to make a good deal of money if the tea could be landed and sold.

For three weeks the ships remained in Boston harbor, while Governor Hutchinson tried to get the colony to pay the duty and accept the shipment. Then Sam Adams took direct action.

On December 16, 1773, a group of Sons of Liberty disguised in Mohawk costume boarded the ships and dumped 342 chests of tea into the harbor. Nothing else on board ship was damaged. This came to be called the "Boston Tea Party."

BOSTON UNDER SIEGE

At last Sam Adams had hit the jackpot. For a decade he had, in his every waking moment, striven in every way he could to provoke the British government into doing something that would finally alienate enough Americans to make conflict inevitable. So far the British had never quite crossed the line of no return — but now they did.

The destruction of those chests of tea drove the King and his party into a blind rage. To them it was the last straw. It seemed to them that the colony of Massachusetts, and the city of Boston in particular, was the focal point of all the troubles of the past decade (and they were, to a large extent, right in thinking so).

Surely, it must have seemed to them, it was time to take firm measures with the contumacious city, to crush it and teach it a good lesson. Once Boston was cowed and made to understand who the master was, there would be no trouble with the rest of the colonies. At least, so the King's party reasoned.

On March 7, 1774, then, Parliament met to consider the colonial situation. An angry King George drove it on, and one by one a series of acts, designed to restrain or coerce Boston into better behavior, were passed. William Pitt and Edmund Burke opposed these "Coercive Acts" but the parliamentary steamroller passed over them.

The first of the Coercive Acts was the "Boston Port Bill" passed on March 31, to become effective on June 1, 1774. It amounted to nothing less than the shutting down of the port of Boston until such time as the East India Company was paid for the tea that had been destroyed. No ships might arrive or leave unless they carried military supplies for the British or vital food and fuel, in shipments that were cleared by customs officials. Everything else would have to use the port of Salem. This was clearly designed to destroy the prosperity of Boston, which depended almost entirely on sea trade, and, quite literally, to starve the city into submission.

The "Massachusetts Government Act" which was to go into effect on August 1, 1774, virtually deprived Massachusetts of all self-government. All sorts of officials who had previously been elected were now to be appointed by the governor, who was himself to be appointed by the King. Even town meetings could not be held without the approval of the governor. What's more, the governor would no longer be Thomas Hutchinson who, conservative though he was, was at least an American and a civilian.

Instead General Gage, a British military man, was to rule Massachusetts, and on May 13, 1774, he moved his headquarters from New York to Boston. The two British regiments in Massachusetts were increased to five, while a squadron of British ships was brought into Boston harbor. On May 20, the Massachusetts charter was nullified so that it was quite clear that the Coercive Acts had reduced Massachusetts to a territory under military occupation.

And to discourage resistance, an "Administration of Justice Act" provided that trials for treason be held in Great Britain whenever it was felt that it was unsafe to hold them in Massachusetts.

Surely Sam Adams, in his wildest fantasies, could have asked for nothing more. The Coercive Acts did in a moment what he could not do in ten years. It made Massachusetts the collective hero and martyr for all the colonies.

Massachusetts, and particularly Boston, and most particularly Sam Adams, had never been exactly popular with the rest of the colonies. There was a self-righteousness and a tendency toward bigotry in Massachusetts religion; a calculating, grasping unscrupulousness in Massachusetts traders and merchants; a violence in Massachusetts politicians; which grated on the respectable opinion-makers of the other colonies.

There were undoubtedly many influential Americans who felt that Boston was more responsible than the British for the conflicts of the last decade, and who felt that if only Bostonians would stop being so provocative and would cease making trouble, things would go on well with the British.

The Coercive Acts changed all that. The countermove to the Boston Tea Party was such an example of overkill that Boston was changed, in a twinkling, from a brash pain in the neck to a prostrate martyr. What the British called Coercive Acts, were called everywhere in America the "Intolerable Acts."

And the British government, as though in willful folly, went on to commit other acts that could only be designed to anger still more the colonies other than Massachusetts. On June 2, 1774, the Quartering Act was revived; not only for Massachusetts, which would have been bad enough, but for *all* the colonies.

Furthermore, in a move that had nothing to do with the Coercive Acts, the British, on June 22, chose this time to reorganize the government of Quebec, the Canadian province captured fifteen years before by the British but still largely occupied by French Catholics.

Quebec was placed under centralized rule by the British Parliament. The Quebec-French were used to this sort of distant and despotic rule, but the British colonists elsewhere viewed it as a dangerous precedent for themselves. The Catholic religion was given full toleration and was even allowed its usual privileges over other religions, something which American Protestants found detestable.

Finally, and worst of all, the boundaries of the province were extended southward to the Ohio River. This had been the situation in the days of French rule, and the French and Indian War, fought bloodily from 1754 to 1763, had been for the purpose of driving the French out of that region. Now the British were giving it back to the French.

This was all the worse since some of the colonies claimed the territory for themselves under the terms of their old charters. Massachusetts and Connecticut claimed portions of the territory in this fashion.

The British government might dismiss New England claims now that Massachusetts was being crushed, but Virginia, too, had claims to the territory. It had been her interest in the territory which had started the French and Indian War (see *The Shaping of North America*) and she did not wish to give it up. The Quebec Act displeased the powerful colony of Virginia even more than anything the British government did to Massachusetts.

Sam Adams, meanwhile, was working as busily as Parliament. He roused public opinion in Massachusetts so effectively that General Gage had control only over the ground his soldiers stood upon. Outside Boston, Massachusetts was virtually a colony in rebellion, ruling itself in defiance of Parliament.

Adams's committee of correspondence scribbled endlessly to all points in the other colonies calling for united action and for open demonstrations of support for Massachusetts.

Those demonstrations arrived. Gifts of food and money began to pour into Boston from everywhere, and Boston grew all the more intransigeant as it felt itself to be at the head of a colonial coalition.

Indeed, so clearly were the colonies united against the Coercive Acts that it seemed natural to call a meeting of delegates from all the colonies as in the days of the Stamp Act. The first move in that direction came from Virginia.

On May 24, 1774, when news arrived that the Boston Port Bill had been made law, the Virginia House of Burgesses, under the leadership of Patrick Henry, promptly denounced the act, saying that it placed Massachusetts under a "hostile invasion." They designated June 1, the day when the Boston Port Bill went into effect, as a day of prayer.

The governor of Virginia, who was John Murray, fourth Earl of Dunmore, promptly dissolved the Burgesses, put their meetings to an end, and sent them home. Before leaving, however, the radical members among the Burgesses instructed their committees of congresses to sound out the other colonies concerning a possible intercolonial meeting.

Sam Adams pounced on that at once, of course, and such a meeting was called. To signify the fact that colonies from all over the North American continent were represented, it was grandiosely referred to as a "continental congress." It is usually known in history as the "First Continental Congress."

Twelve of the thirteen colonies (Georgia was the exception) sent delegates, and fifty-six men assembled in Philadelphia on September 5, 1774. Peyton Randolph of Virginia (born about 1721) was chosen as president of the Congress (and ever since, the terms "president" and "congress" have been part of American politics).

The First Continental Congress included numerous men of distinction. Some were radicals, such as John Adams and Sam Adams from Massachusetts, and Patrick Henry, Thomas Jefferson, and Richard Henry Lee from Virginia. Conservatives were also present, however, such as Joseph Galloway from Pennsylvania (born at West River, Maryland, about 1731) and James Duane from New York (born in 1733).

The lines were drawn between the radicals and the conservatives at once. Patrick Henry wanted each colony to have a vote in proportion to its population. This would give a preponderant weight to the colonies of Massachusetts and Virginia, which were both populous and radical. The smaller colonies, however, insisted on a single vote for each colony, regardless of population. In order to keep the Congress from breaking up, the radicals gave in.

Then the question arose as to what to do about the Coercive Acts. Galloway of Pennsylvania urged a moderate course and wanted a conciliatory attitude toward Great Britain. He suggested that a kind of American Parliament be established and that laws over the colonies be required to have the approval of both the American and British Parliments.

Meanwhile in Suffolk county, Massachusetts (which included the city of Boston), Joseph Warren was at work. He prepared what were called the "Suffolk Resolves." These declared the Coercive Acts to be unconstitutional so that Massachusetts citizens were not bound to obey them. It advised the people of Massachusetts to form their own government, collect their own taxes, and to arm themselves as well, forming a civilian army of "militia." Finally, the colonies were once again to place a boycott on all trade with Great Britain.

The Suffolk Resolves were passed at a meeting of Massachusetts radicals and were then entrusted to Paul Revere (born in Boston on January 1, 1735), a skilled silversmith who had taken part in the Boston Tea Party and was heart and soul with the radical cause.

Spurring onward, Revere carried a copy of the Resolves across the three hundred miles separating Boston and Philadelphia. The Massachusetts delegates promptly began to press the Suffolk Resolves on the Congress.

The First Continental Congress endorsed the Suffolk Resolves on September 17, 1774, and then, on September 28, rejected the Galloway Plan by the narrow vote of 6 to 5. Galloway grumpily pointed out that in his view this combination of votes amounted to a declaration of war on Great Britain.

Finally, the Congress ended by drawing up a petition which, on October 26, was sent to King George. Another petition was sent to the people of Great Britain. Nothing was sent to Parliament, showing that the colonies still felt that the King was somehow being misled by bad advisers and would respond favorably if he could be reached over the head of Parliament.

The petition denounced all the wrongs inflicted on the colonies since 1763 and declared in favor of considering all colonists as having the various natural rights of Englishmen. On the other hand, the Congress did not try to deny the right of Parliament to regulate American trade.

The Congress also began to organize an American boycott of British goods as a way of putting teeth into their petition. It then adjourned on October 26, but not permanently. A "Second Continental Congress" was to meet on May 10, 1775, if by then American grievances had not been redressed.

On the whole, Galloway's view that the proceedings of the First Continental Congress amounted to a declaration of war on Great Britain was correct – at least in Massachusetts.

General Gage interpreted it in that fashion, but then he had been expecting the worst for some time. On September 1, 1774, even before the First Continental Congress had convened, he was doing his best to confiscate any supplies of gunpowder that the Americans might store away for use later. He sent soldiers into Cambridge and Charlestown, two towns just across the river from Boston, and seized both gunpowder and cannon. Armed colonists flocked into Cambridge but no one actually dared shoot at British soldiers.

In those days, Boston was located on a peninsula that was connected with the mainland by only a narrow neck. (Since then the rivers on either side have been partly filled in and what is now "downtown Boston" is connected with the more outlying parts of the city by a broad band of land.) General Gage set about fortifying this narrow neck and it was plain he was preparing himself for a siege.

As for the colonists, they organized a government of their own with John Hancock at its head and, in line with the Suffolk Resolves, began to form a militia. Special groups among the militia were to hold themselves ready for action at any minute at which a call might come, and they were called the "minutemen."

As 1774 drew to a close, both sides were clearly ready for open warfare. It needed only the spark – a few gunshots – to begin it.

3

THE ROAD TO INDEPENDENCE

THE REVOLUTION BEGINS

The fact that colonial readiness for resistance was increasing was made more clear each day. When it was learned on December 13, 1774, that Gage was going to put men in Portsmouth, New Hampshire, Paul Revere galloped northward with the news and on December 14, the colonials there broke into a local fort and carried off arms and gunpowder. There were no casualties, however, and the event did not represent actual war.

As 1775 opened, Parliament had to consider the actions of the First Continental Congress and weigh the American reaction to the Coercive Acts. It was not as though voices were lacking to point out the clear logic of the situation. Men like Pitt and Burke pointed out that it would be no use to continue with force; that in the long run the colonies could not be forced to accept a government they did not want; that it was wrong to try to make them do so.

All foundered on the rock of the intransigeance of the King and of his Prime Minister, Lord North. All Lord North would agree to do in the way of compromise was to offer not to tax any colony which turned over money voluntarily to the extent desired by Parliament. (To the colonies this was very much like having a bandit offer not to hold you up if you handed over your wallet voluntarily.) Even that much drew only a grudging consent from the King.

Indeed, Lord North placed a new Coercive Act before Parliament on February 27, 1775. This would forbid the four New England colonies to trade with any nation but Great Britain and the British West Indies. New Englanders were not to trade with the other colonies and were not to make use of the Atlantic fisheries — which were crucially important to the population.

It was clear that Great Britain was answering all appeals for relief by a further tightening of the screw so the Massachusetts colonials continued to prepare for war.

And General Gage continued to attempt to deprive them of the wherewithal to do so. On February 26, 1775, Gage sent his soldiers to Salem to pick up some military supplies there, but the city was swarming with angry colonials, and the soldiers turned back.

Again, no shot was fired in anger, no blow was struck. Yet surely it was only a matter of time. Even in distant Virginia, men waited breathlessly for news from the north, expecting with each post that word would come that the firing had begun.

On March 23, 1775, Patrick Henry stood up in the House of Burgesses to maintain the necessity of forming an armed militia in Virginia. He pointed out forcefully that war was about to begin. "The next gale," he said "that sweeps from the north will bring to our ears the clash of resounding arms! Our brethren are already in the field! Why stand we here idle? What is it that the gentlemen wish? What would they have? Is life so dear or peace so sweet as to be purchased at the price of chains and slavery? Forbid it, Almighty God. I know not what course others may take, but as for me, give me liberty or give me death!"

Those words rang through the colonies as for three weeks more, matters rested on a knife edge. What was in prospect, after all, was not a mere rebellion, but what amounted to a civil war of the English-speaking world. The colonies were a respectable size.

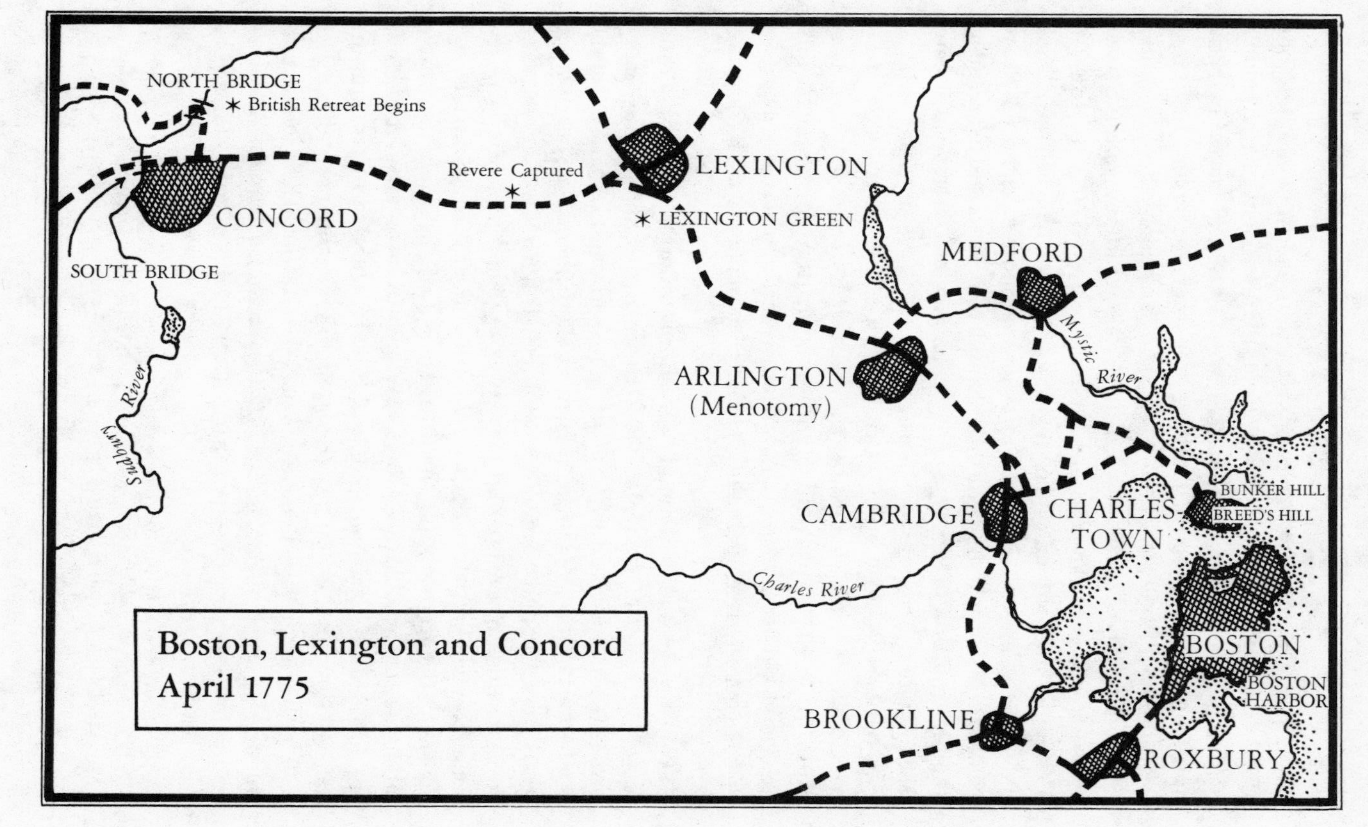

Boston, Lexington and Concord
April 1775

Their population was now about two and a half million, about one third that of Great Britain. The largest colonial city, Philadelphia, with a population of forty thousand, was the second largest English-speaking city in the world. Only London itself was larger.

And then it came ——

General Gage decided to escalate his efforts to disarm the Massachusetts colonials. The center of colonial resistance was the town of Concord, nineteen miles northwest of Boston. There the illegal Provincial Congresses met to rally and organize resistance. There the two radical leaders, Sam Adams and John Hancock, were to be found. And there a large supply of military stores had been accumulated.

Gage decided to send 700 British troops to Concord where they would either seize or destroy the military stores and where they were to arrest Adams and Hancock. Security among the British troops was poor, however, and there were few decisions made by Gage concerning which the colonials did not get early information.

Paul Revere and William Dawes (born in Boston in 1745) set out on the evening of April 18, 1775, to warn the countryside. They reached Lexington, a town eleven miles northwest of Boston on the route to Concord. Adams and Hancock happened to be sleeping there. Roused, and warned in time, they left hurriedly.

At Lexington, Revere and Dawes were joined by a young physician, Samuel Prescott (born in Concord in 1751). All headed for Concord but were stopped by a British patrol. Revere was arrested and was taken back to Lexington, where he was released. Dawes escaped, but turned back. Only Prescott went on to Concord, and carried through the vital task of warning that colonial center.*

The warning was effective. When the 700 British reached Lexington at dawn on April 19, 1775, they found a handful of armed minutemen, perhaps no more than forty, facing them. Major John

* Revere's part in all this was glamorized and expanded out of recognition by Henry Wadsworth Longfellow a century later. In his poem "Paul Revere's Ride" which is the version universally known to the American public, Revere rides alone and reaches Concord.

Pitcairn, who led the advance British contingent, called out to the minutemen to disperse.

This the minutemen ought to have done and probably would have done, for they were outnumbered nearly twenty to one, but from behind a stone wall there came a shot. Who it was who fired the shot no one knows to this day, but it was enough. The nervous British soldiers, without orders, fired pointblank at the minutemen, killed eight and left ten more wounded. The minutemen returned the fire briefly, then ran. The British marched on with a single wounded soldier as their only casualty.

To the British, at the moment, it might have seemed merely the brushing aside of a fly, but it was the first blood spilled in battle in what came to be called "The War of the American Revolution" or, more briefly, "The Revolutionary War."* Sam Adams, at least, thoroughly understood the significance of the event. Even as he was scuttling out of Lexington, he is supposed to have said exultantly, "This is a glorious day for America."

The British reached Concord and destroyed such stores as they could find (most had been removed in time) but, all around, the Massachusetts militia was gathering. At North Bridge in Concord, the British found themselves facing the gathering crowd of armed farmers. There was a sharp scuffle and there were fourteen British casualities. It was no longer a case of brushing aside a fly.**

By noon, the British had had enough and prepared for the march back to Boston. But now came the worst. The whole countryside swarmed with angry militia, four thousand of them according to some estimates. From behind every tree and every rock, it seemed, a gun-barrel gleamed and a bullet came speeding. There was rarely any easy target offered in return and the bewildered British troops

* To those who now think of the term "revolution" as somehow un-American, the fighting that began that day can be called "The War of Independence."

** This incident was immortalized by Ralph Waldo Emerson in 1837 in his poem "Concord Hymn" which begins:

By the rude bridge that arched the flood,
Their flag to April's breeze unfurled,
Here once the embattled farmers stood,
And fired the shot heard round the world.

staggered on, as one after another was hit. They might all have died before reaching Boston but for a strong relieving contingent sent to rescue them.

As it was, the trip to Concord had resulted in 99 British soldiers dead and missing and 174 wounded, some 40 per cent of the entire force, while the total American casualties were 93.

It was a small battle with relatively few casualties as battles go, but there has scarcely ever been a more important battle in history, for it marked the beginning of the birth of the United States.

It was now open war, for the first battle had been fought and the first casualties had been inflicted. The Massachusetts radicals made the most of the volley at Lexington to show that it had been provoked by the British. They also made the most of the picture of the British soldiers scuttling helplessly along the road to Boston under the galling American fire, so that American morale rose high.

The retreat from Concord was not merely a matter of British ineptitude, of course. It was also the result of a difference in arms that exerted an important, and even crucial, influence on events.

By the end of the French and Indian War a new weapon had appeared on the frontier in Pennsylvania and to the southward. It was called the "Kentucky Rifle" and was first introduced by the Pennsylvania Dutch who modified a European version so as to make it lighter and easier to load. It used a bullet smaller than the bore so that a greased patch was used to keep the fit tight. A rifled barrel (that is, one with spiral grooves on its inner surface) set the bullet spinning and made it move straighter and more accurately than did the smoothbore muskets used by the regular armies of the European powers.

This early American rifle could, in proper hands, hit a target the size of a man's head at 200 yards. It had the disadvantage of taking three times as long to load as did the musket, so that it wasn't adapted to the rapid volleys used in formal battles of the time. However, for a guerrilla fighter, safe behind a tree or rock, the Kentucky rifle was deadly. It meant that while American soldiers, lacking training and experience, lost most of the pitched battles they fought, they would nevertheless hold the countryside, and the British would rarely be able to control more territory than that on which their army stood.

FROM CONCORD TO BUNKER HILL

The Massachusetts radicals did not intend to let matters cool down. The Provincial Congress moved at once to place Boston under siege. By April 23, it had authorized the raising of an army of 13,000 men and placed them under Artemas Ward (born in Shrewsbury, Massachusetts, in 1727). He had fought in the French and Indian War and was the nearest thing to a professional soldier Massachusetts had at the moment.

The other New England colonies quickly sent contingents to join Ward's forces in Cambridge, across the river from Boston, so that the war now included all of New England. The news of the battle and its consequences spread over all the colonies. A party of hunters encamped in the Ohio wilderness heard the news and named their encampment accordingly. Around it grew up what is now the city of Lexington, Kentucky.

If the colonial forces were to have any hope of actually taking Boston, however, they needed artillery, and they had none. What they had to do was to take some from the British and the nearest place where they had a chance of doing so was at Fort Ticonderoga on Lake Champlain, the scene of much fighting in the French and Indian War.

The capture of the fort was suggested first by Benedict Arnold (born in Norwich, Connecticut, on January 14, 1741). He had joined the Massachusetts militia when it was first formed and now held the rank of captain. His plan was approved, he was promoted to the rank of colonel on May 3, and was told to go ahead with the venture.

In this, as in everything else, Arnold, however, had the breaks against him. He proved to be one of the best soldiers in America, but nothing ever turned out right for him. In connection with Ticonderoga, for instance, he was anticipated by someone who was closer to the spot.

Fort Ticonderoga was about 170 miles northwest of Boston. Just to its east, across Lake Champlain, was the region of the Green Mountains (now known as Vermont, from French words meaning "green mountains"). Living there was Ethan Allen (born in Lichfield, Connecticut, on January 21, 1738). He had fought in the French and Indian War and had come to the Green Mountain area in 1769. There he formed a group of militiamen who called themselves the "Green Mountain Boys" and whose chief aim was to see to it that the colony of New York did not succeed in establishing its rule over the area.

When news of Lexington and Concord reached him, it occurred to him at once that it might be a good idea to take Fort Ticonderoga just across the lake. Benedict Arnold hurried west to try to take over command but this Allen would not allow. Frustrated (as he was to be on many occasions) Arnold accompanied the party, nevertheless, and eighty-three men rowed across Lake Champlain on May 9, 1775. They achieved total surprise. The British garrison found itself unable to resist the sudden invasion of backwoodsmen and surrendered on May 10. Two days later, Crown Point, ten miles to the north, was also taken.

On May 10, the same day that Fort Ticonderoga was taken, the Second Continental Congress met in Philadelphia on schedule and found itself forced to take up the fact of actual war, at least in New England.

Peyton Randolph was chosen president again, but he died almost at once, and John Hancock was put in his place, an indication of the increasing radicalization of the body. Many of the delegates from the First Continental Congress were at the Second, too, and some additional men of prestige were included. Benjamin Franklin and George Washington, who were not at the First, for instance, attended the Second.

John Adams was the leading radical force in the Second Continental Congress and he labored mightily to get the colonies outside New England to make common cause with Massachusetts. He wanted the New England militia now besieging Boston to be recognized as an inter-colonial army, a "Continental army," to use the same view that called the meeting a Continental congress.

Adams knew that this would not be accepted if Massachusetts insisted on commanding the army and he hinted broadly that the delegate from Virginia, Colonel Washington, would be acceptable to Massachusetts as the commander-in-chief, and that the New England militia would be willing to serve under him.

It was a brilliant stroke. George Washington had fought in the early battles of the French and Indian War but had been frustrated in his attempt to play a more significant part by British anti-colonial prejudices. He was eager now to show what he could do. What's more, he was a rich planter who would serve without pay, and an enormously respected man of conservative character and known integrity. Men who would not trust the Massachusetts rabble-rousers, would trust George Washington.

So the Congress agreed. The Continental army was created on June 14, 1775, and George Washington was made commander-in-chief on June 15.

Under him were four major generals, of whom Artemas Ward was one. Another was Israel Putnam of Connecticut (born in Danvers, Massachusetts, in 1718) who, in a fever of patriotism, had ridden to take part in the siege of Boston the instant he had heard of the events at Lexington and Concord, even though he was pushing sixty. Then there was Philip Schuyler of New York (born in Albany in 1733) who was a wealthy landowner as respected and conservative as Washington was, and Charles Lee of Virginia, a British-born officer. All four major generals had, like Washington himself, seen service in the French and Indian War, but none of the four proved to have much military talent.

Even as the Continental army was formed, however, it was facing a showdown in Boston. The British had, as yet, no intention of giving in and more troops were landed in Boston on May 28.

On June 12, General Gage felt sufficiently confident in the strength of his forces to place Boston officially under martial law and to declare any American bearing arms, or aiding one bearing arms, to be a rebel and traitor. As an olive branch, however, he offered free pardon for any such rebel and traitor who was willling to lay down his arms – with the exception of Sam Adams and John Hancock.

The American answer to that was to make preparation to occupy and fortify the high ground in Charlestown, just north of the Charles River and just across the river from Boston. Like Boston itself, Charlestown was then located on a peninsula connected to the mainland by a narrow neck.

There were two hills in Charlestown, Bunker Hill and Breed's Hill, and either would have offered a commanding positon to place the artillery that was expected eventually to arrive from Ticonderoga. It was originally intended to fortify Bunker Hill only, but Breed's Hill was nearer to Boston and the plan was expanded to include it.

By dawn of June 17, 1775, 1600 Americans were on Breed's Hill. Gage might have sealed off the Charlestown peninsula by placing men on the neck and then have bombarded the hill from the ships in the harbor. The Americans could not have endured long, had this been done. Gage, however, was probably still smarting from the disgrace of the retreat from Concord. He felt the Americans needed a lesson and that their utter inferiority to the British regular must be demonstrated clearly.

He therefore ordered the fortifications on the Charlestown hills to be taken by assault and, for the purpose, sent 2400 men across the Charles River at noon on June 17. These were commanded by Sir William Howe, who had arrived with the most recent group of reinforcements.

For the British, it was a bad military situation. They would have to clamber up a hill, exposed to the fire of an enemy behind protecting ramparts at the top.* The only possible reason that could make a British commander order such an assault (other than invincible stupidity) was the feeling that the American militia could not withstand the sight of British regulars marching toward them and would simply flee.

Howe therefore ordered a contingent of his men to march up the hill, in perfect tight order, carrying heavy packs, and with their scarlet uniforms blazing in the sun. Behind their ramparts waited the Americans, in perfect position, except for the fact that they had virtually no gunpowder.

Their commander, Colonel William Prescott (born in Groton, Massachusetts, in 1726), dared not allow that precious gunpowder

* The hill was Breed's Hill, but the battle came to be known, for some reason, as the "Battle of Bunker Hill." Nowadays, what was once called Breed's Hill is called Bunker Hill in consequence.

to go to waste. Every bullet had to count, which meant that his men had to allow the British to come within short range, however frightening their approach might be to untrained farmboys.

"Don't shoot," he ordered, "until you see the whites of their eyes."

Up the hill went the British contingent, all the more confident since the lack of fire seemed to betoken fear on the part of the Americans. At the appropriate time, the Americans, who had held their fire until the soldiers were almost on them, let loose a volley in which nearly every bullet met its mark. The British line crumpled and the survivors staggered down the hill, leaving the area before the American redoubt red with blood and uniforms.

A second time Howe sent a British contingent up the hill and it met the same fate as the first. By now there was nothing to do but continue the same stupid game, since to quit and leave would be an enormous blow to British prestige.

So Howe sent up a third contingent, and it is a credit to British discipline that they moved at all. All that kept the third contingent alive was that the Americans were about out of ammunition. The third contingent of British troops reached the top of the hills, fixed bayonets and charged. The Americans, who had no bayonets either, had no choice but to get out of there. As rapidly as they might, they vacated Charlestown.

The British held the ground so they claimed the victory, but they had been too manhandled to attempt to pursue the Americans beyond Charlestown. Their casualties had been enormous, 1,054 killed or wounded, including 89 officers. One of the officers who was killed was the Major Pitcairn who had commanded the advance guard that had shed first blood at Lexington. The American casualties were only about 450 but one of them was Joseph Warren who had prepared the Suffolk Resolves the year before.

The British were badly disheartened by this too-expensive "victory" and seemed to be thrown into a lethargy. Having taken the Charlestown hills, they ought next to have occupied Dorchester Heights just beyond the neck that connected Boston to the mainland. Had they done so, there would then have been no place from which American artillery could have commanded Boston Harbor.

Prior to the Battle of Bunker Hill, it had been Gage's intention to do just that. After the battle, however, the stunned Gage did nothing. He had had enough and there was nothing to do but relieve him. He went back to Great Britain and on October 10, 1775, William Howe took over the command of the British forces in the colonies.

This, too, was an error. Howe would show himself over and over to be incapable of moving decisively against the Americans. One explanation is that he never had his heart in a war he felt unwise and unjust, but another is that he never recovered from that horrible hour of bloodletting on Breed's Hill.

Two and a half weeks after the battle, George Washington reached Cambridge and took command of an army that felt itself victorious at the Battle of Bunker Hill. Not the British, but their own lack of gunpowder, had defeated them. Not themselves, but the British, had been cut to pieces.

At once Washington set about supervising the training of the army and giving them some sense of order and discipline, as well as of victory.

BOSTON LIBERATED

Outside New England, there was still a vague hope that somehow the gradually deepening war might stop. The Second Continental Congress did not yet dream of independence and there was the cold feeling that the British would in the end triumph and that colonial leaders would be hanged as traitors.

A last effort was made, therefore, to urge peace. Dickinson of Pennsylvania drew up an "Olive Branch Petition" which the Congress signed on July 8, 1775, and sent on to King George. It protested the loyalty of the colonies and begged him for some concessions that would put an end to hostilities.

The petition didn't have a chance. On August 23, Parliament officially proclaimed that a general rebellion existed and on September 1, when King George was offered the petition, he refused it on the ground that he would accept no communications from rebels. It was clear that the British were going to bring the colonies back into line by force and would entertain no compromises.

There was, in any case, no feeling in favor of olive branches in New England. The euphoria that followed the Battle of Bunker Hill was such that the New England colonies began to think of offensive action. There was a rumor that the British were going to recruit Canadians to fight against the Americans, and it seemed that a bold attack against Montreal and Quebec might not only put a stop to this but bring the French into the fight against their old enemy, Great Britain, in the hope of regaining Canada.

The expedition was placed under Schuyler to begin with, but ill health temporarily retired him and his place was taken by another New Yorker, Richard Montgomery (born in Ireland in 1736), who had served in the British army.

Montgomery led his small contingent northward through the worsening fall weather, and when he approached Montreal, the British commander, Sir Guy Carleton, beat a strategic retreat to Quebec. Montgomery took the undefended city on November 13, 1775.

Meanwhile, Benedict Arnold, who had been disappointed of the command of the expedition against Fort Ticonderoga, was anxious to take part in this new adventure. He got Washington's permission, raised 1100 men, and made his way northward across Maine to Quebec. There he waited for Montgomery to come down the river from Montreal to join with him. By the time the junction was made there had been a considerable erosion of manpower and together they had something under a thousand men. Quebec was defended by twice that number.

On December 31, 1775, they ventured an assault in a snowstorm and it failed disastrously. Half the force was killed, wounded, or taken prisoner. Montgomery was killed and Arnold wounded. Arnold and the few hundred men who remained lingered near Quebec but there was no hope and after losing another skirmish they retreated the following June.

The fiasco was depressing to the American cause and was an excellent propaganda handle for the British. The colonials had claimed

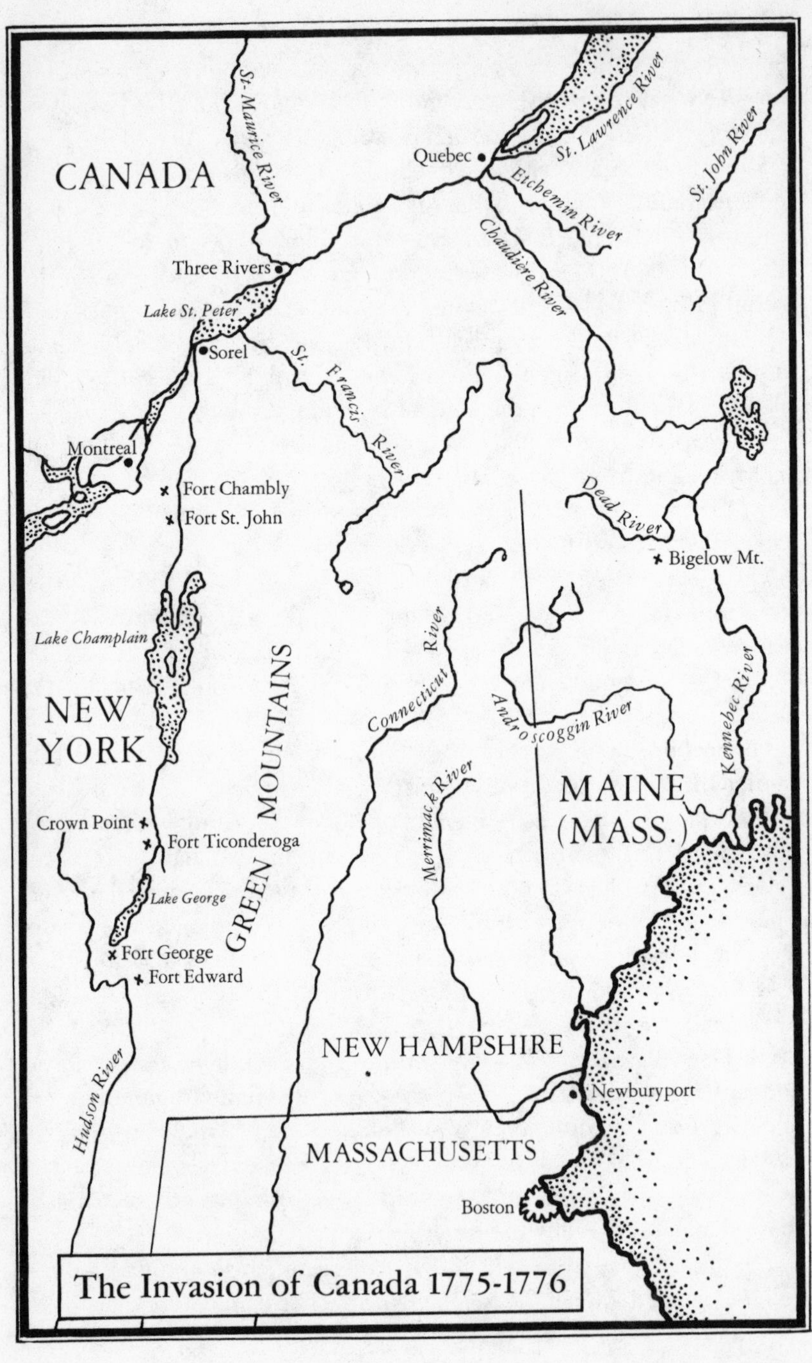

The Invasion of Canada 1775-1776

that they were only fighting defensively for their rights but now that could be countered by the statement that the Americans had attacked a peaceful province without provocation.

And still the conflict deepened. Georgia had joined the Second Continental Congress in September 1775 so that for the first time, all thirteen colonies were represented.*

Faced with an intransigeant Great Britain, the augmented Congress reluctantly took additional steps toward an expanded war. On October 13, 1775, it authorized the formation of a navy. There couldn't be true warships just at first, of course, but ships could arm themselves and carry on raids against British shipping.

In response, the British announced, on December 23, that all American ports would be closed to commerce as of March 1, 1776. The colonies were, in effect, placed under a blockade.

By the end of 1775, then, it was war up and down and yet *still* the spokesmen for the colonists generally avowed their loyalty to Great Britain. Only Sam Adams and a few ultra-radicals like him dared breathe the word "independence."

This changed, however, thanks to the work of Thomas Paine who, next to Sam Adams, himself, has a right to be considered the apostle of American independence.

Thomas Paine was born in England on January 29, 1739. He was the son of a Quaker, and remained throughout his life a thoroughgoing humanitarian, sympathizing not only with the needy and enslaved, but even with oppressed womankind. In November 1774, bearing a recommendation from Benjamin Franklin, he came to Pennsylvania.

Once there, he edited "Pennsylvania Magazine" and quickly came to the conclusion that independence was necessary for the colonies. For one thing, it was the only way that the colonies could

* There were actually more than thirteen British colonies in North America but the others, for one reason or another, did not take part in the Revolutionary War. Canada, still inhabited largely by French Catholics, preferred the rule of a distant Great Britain which would protect it against the energetic Protestants of New England. Nova Scotia, separated from the other colonies by sea, felt no common cause. The British West Indies were also separated by sea and, in any case, contained large numbers of slaves who, the white minority feared, could not be held down once revolutionary activity began.

set up a republic and free themselves of the tyranny of one-man rule and the waste of a hereditary aristocracy. Furthermore, he reasoned, it was only by declaring themselves to be fighting for independence that they could gain foreign aid.

Paine made many influential friends in the colonies, including Dr. Benjamin Rush (born near Philadelphia, in 1745). Rush was also of a Quaker family and was also a humanitarian interested in the same causes that moved Paine. Rush encouraged Paine to publish his views in a pamphlet and this was issued on January 10, 1776. It was entitled *Common Sense* and reviewed all the reasons for independence. Paine did not hesitate to push all unreasoning reverence aside and to lay the full measure of blame for Britain's repressive policy on George III himself.

Common Sense proved a bestseller. Its simple, straightforward, and highly dramatic style made it enormously popular. It, more than anything else, brought about the necessary switch in popular thought and turned independence into something demanded by enough Americans to make it politically possible. For one thing, it won over George Washington to the cause.

Whether independence would ever be militarily possible was the question, of course. That depended almost entirely on George Washington, who was waiting for the one thing that would make a forward step possible. That was the cannon from Fort Ticonderoga.

The responsibility for bringing those cannon he had placed on the shoulders of Henry Knox (born in Boston on July 25, 1750). Knox was a bookseller by profession and had learned a great deal about the technical side of artillery out of the books in which he dealt. He had been present on the occasion of the Boston Massacre, had joined the militia when it was first formed, was in the Continental Army now, and came to be one of Washington's closest friends.

He was the nearest thing to an expert in artillery in the army so Washington sent him to Ticonderoga for those cannon. It was a matter of 170 miles in a straight line, but was 300 miles by any practical route.

While he waited, Washington greeted the new year of 1776 by unfurling a new flag over his headquarters. It bore the thirteen red and white stripes, familiar to us today, one for each colony. In the upper left, however, there was still the Union Jack, made up of the crosses of St. George and St. Andrew, the patron saints of England and Scotland, respectively, and the well-known symbol of Great Britain.

Through the winter (and aided, rather than hindered, by the snow) Knox dragged those cannon along. On January 24, 1776, fifty-five pieces of artillery, averaging over a ton apiece in weight, were successfully trundled into the American lines.

By March 4, Washington was able to put those artillery pieces into place on Dorchester Heights, which Howe had recklessly continued to leave unoccupied. From that vantage point, the Americans could bombard any point in Boston and almost any ship in its harbor.

Howe recognized the danger and, having failed to prevent it, he now planned an assault on the artillery. He was delayed by heavy rains and by the time the weather cleared the Americans seemed too well entrenched and Howe had had time to bethink himself of Bunker Hill.

He decided that Boston had become too hot to hold on to and, on March 17, he evacuated the city, taking all the soldiers into the ships in the harbor. The fleet then sailed for Halifax, Nova Scotia, on March 26.

In little less than a year from the day of Lexington and Concord, the British had lost New England, and permanently. After Howe had left, the British never returned and from that day to this, Massachusetts has never felt the footsteps of a hostile army.

The evacuation of Boston was rightly considered a great victory for the Americans, but it was, on the whole, a wise move for the British.

New England was the most densely populated and rabidly radical part of the colonies and any attempt to take it by direct military force would be expensive and difficult. There were better strategies. For instance, New England might be isolated from the other colonies and then starved out. In the colonies outside New England the rebellious sentiments were far weaker and these, possibly, might be brought into line and New England beaten down at leisure.

The pro-British Americans were called "Loyalists" by the British and by themselves and were to be found chiefly (but not exclusively) among the propertied classes. According to some estimates, as much as a third of the American population were Loyalists, while another third were indifferent to political matters and merely strove to live as best they might. Only the remaining third were "Rebels" actively engaged in conflict with Great Britain. Loyalists were actually in the majority in the middle colonies.

To themselves, of course, the Rebels were "Patriots," while the Loyalists were "Tories," a name used for the British party which upheld the powers and prerogatives of the King.

The Revolutionary War was a civil war, then, as well as a war of national liberation. Even in New England there were Loyalists and a thousand of them were taken from Boston with the evacuating British. They feared for their lives if they remained behind and that fear was probably justified.

The Loyalists were very useful to the British throughout the war. Many of them served as espionage agents among the Americans. Others, up to 30,000 in number, actually served with the British troops. Their aid might have been decisive but the British always hesitated to use their services to the full. Had the British crushed the rebellions with the important help of the Loyalists, those Loyalists, once in control of the colonies, might have asked, as reward, just those concessions the British were refusing those Americans in arms against them.

THE DECLARATION OF INDEPENDENCE

The British evacuation of Boston did not fool Washington into thinking the war was over. It did not take very much penetration to see that the British, foiled at one point, would try at another and that the colonies' weak point was the middle region between radical New England and radical Virginia. Washington therefore led the main part of his army southwestward, arriving in New York on April 13, 1776, with 9000 men.

Meanwhile, between Paine's *Common Sense* and the excitement of the British evacuation of Boston, sentiment for independence was rising to record heights and the delegates at the Second Continental Congress could feel it in every despatch.

Oddly enough, it was North Carolina that stood in the forefront of the fight. As early as May 31, 1775, soon after Lexington and Concord, inhabitants of Mecklenburg county near what was then the western frontier of the state, drew up the "Mecklenburg Resolves" in which all British laws were declared null and void, and all British commissions useless. The resolves declared the intention of the signers to push for self-government, but did not actually use the word "independence." The event nevertheless gave rise to the legend of a "Mecklenburg Declaration of Independence."

A year later, the Provincial Congress of North Carolina, on April 12, 1776, officially instructed its delegates at the Continental Congress to push for independence. It was the first colony to do so formally. Virginia followed suit on May 15, and it was to be taken for granted that the four New England colonies would do so. What was needed, though, for independence was unanimity. Without that it wouldn't work. (One congressional delegate said nervously, "We must all hang together." Benjamin Franklin answered dryly, "Yes, or most assuredly we shall all hang separately.")

On June 7, 1776, Richard Henry Lee of Virginia put it to the test. He rose and offered a resolution to the effect that the colonies "are, and of right ought to be, free and independent States."*

The resolution was still too hot to handle and Congress delayed a vote by appointing several of its members to prepare a formal Declaration of Independence. Appointed to do this were Jefferson, Franklin, and John Adams, together with Robert Livingston of New York (born in New York City on November 27, 1746) and Roger Sherman of Connecticut (born in Newton, Massachusetts, on April 19, 1721).

It was Thomas Jefferson who did the major work in preparing the Declaration and he was obviously influenced by Rousseau and the doctrine of natural rights. He wrote that the colonies were to

* A "state," it must be remembered, is a sovereign region, one that rules itself and owes allegiance to no outside power. In the United States, today, a state is a nonindependent, subsidiary section of the nation, but that was not the meaning of the word in 1776.

assume "the separate and equal station to which the Laws of Nature and of Nature's God entitle them." He also said, "We hold these truths to be self-evident, that all men are created equal, that they are endowed by their Creator with certain unalienable Rights, that among these are Life, Liberty and the pursuit of Happiness. That to secure these rights, Governments are instituted among Men, deriving their just powers from the consent of the governed. That whenever any Form of Government becomes destructive of these ends, it is the Right of the People to alter or to abolish it, and to institute new Government, laying its foundation on such principles and organizing its powers in such form, as to them shall seem most likely to effect their Safety and Happiness."

Jefferson went on to draw up a long list of evils inflicted upon the colonies by Great Britain, placing them all clearly and specifically upon King George III; Parliament was not mentioned. This was, of course, necessary. No American felt any mystic loyalty to any legislative body, only to the King; and it was from the King that American feelings must be disentangled.

One evil listed by Jefferson was taken out at the insistence of those who didn't consider it an evil. Jefferson blamed the King for preventing Virginia from trying to regulate the African slave trade. The delegates from South Carolina refused to allow any derogatory mention of slavery at all, and out it came.

On June 28, 1776, the Declaration of Independence was presented to the Congress. It was difficult to push through. Some, like Galloway, were horrified. He said, "Independency means ruin. If England refuses it, she will ruin us; if she grants it, we will ruin ourselves." Galloway was an outright Loyalist, perhaps the most important in the colonies. He eventually joined Howe's army and finally left America in 1778. He lived out the final fifteen years of his life in Great Britain.

A number of the delegates who were not Loyalists and who were ardently in favor of American rights and of their self-government nevertheless felt that to push for actual independence was unwise; that it wasn't a practical goal. Prominent among these was Dickinson.

Nevertheless, colony after colony was won over to a vote in favor of accepting the Declaration. South Carolina's vote was won by eliminating the reference to slavery. Dickinson and another Pennsylvania delegate were persuaded to abstain so that the remaining delegates could vote Pennsylvania in favor. Delaware had two delegates present who were on opposite sides of the question but at the last minute, a third delegate, Caesar Rodney (born near Dover, Delaware, in 1728), having risen from a sickbed, appeared to cast the deciding vote for independence. Only New York did not vote, since its delegates were instructed to take no part in the debate. So, although the vote was unanimous, it was only 12 to 0, and the motion for independence was carried on July 2, 1776.

John Adams foresaw that throughout the indefinite future, Americans would celebrate July 2 as "Independence Day." He was right in essence, but wrong as to the date. Two days later, on July 4, 1776, the Declaration of Independence was signed by John Hancock, president of the Continental Congress, and it is that day which is now commemorated.

The Declaration of Independence was first read publicly in Philadelphia on July 8. On July 9, it was read in New York to General Washington and his troops, and the New York legislature, presumably ashamed of their attempt to duck the issue, voted to accept the Declaration, making it the full 13 to 0.

On July 19, the Congress voted to have the Declaration of Independence prepared in a beautiful copy on parchment (a copy that still exists as a treasured legacy of American history) so that all the delegates could sign. During the course of the summer and autumn of 1776, fifty-five signatures were added to that of John Hancock.

It was that signing which really laid it on the line, for every man who put his signature to the document was leaving written evidence to the effect that he was a traitor (if the British won). John Hancock, knowing this, signed nevertheless in a bold, free hand "so that King George can read it without his spectacles," and that has made his name an American slang term for signature.

When Charles Carroll of Maryland (born at Annapolis on September 19, 1737) signed his name, someone commented that his hand was trembling. Carroll, to show that this was not from fear, added the name of his estate so that he might more easily be identified. He appears as "Charles Carroll of Carrollton" on the document. Also among the signers are Samuel Adams, John Adams, Richard Henry Lee, Thomas Jefferson, Benjamin Rush, and Benjamin Franklin.

All of the signers are among the "Founding Fathers" of the nation and are semideified for that reason, although some of them are utterly obscure except for this one act of signing. The first among them to die was Button Gwinnett of Georgia (born in England in 1735). He died in 1777 and his signature (valuable because he was a signer) is so rare that its value is very high among collectors of such things.

Of the fifty-six signers, thirty-nine were of English descent, and all had at least one parent descended from ancestors somewhere in the British Isles. Thirty of them were Episcopalian (Church of England) and twelve were Congregationalists. There were three Unitarians (including Thomas Jefferson and John Adams). Benjamin Franklin, who refused to identify himself with any sect, called himself a "Deist." Charles Carroll of Carrollton was the only Roman Catholic among the signers.

4

HOWE VERSUS WASHINGTON

FOREIGN AID

July 4, 1776 is celebrated by all Americans as the date of the founding of the independence of the United States; the date from which our history as a nation begins; and the anniversary is celebrated in triumph every year for that reason.

The truth is, however, that the Declaration of Independence did not found, even in theory, a new and independent nation. It founded thirteen separate new and independent nations; nations with uncertain boundaries and with a great deal of hostility among themselves.

During 1776, various states adopted written constitutions, delineating their form of government, chose "presidents" and so on. Some did so even before the Declaration of Independence, the first being New Hampshire on January 5, 1776. The most important of the state constitutions was that of Virginia, adopted on June 29, just five days before Hancock signed the Declaration of Independence.

Included in it was a declaration of rights the state government might not violate – including freedom of press and religion, the right to trial by jury, the right not to be compelled to testify against oneself, and so on. This Bill of Rights, drafted by George Mason, influenced Jefferson in his writing of the Declaration of Independence and was the model for similar documents in other constitutions both in the United States and France. American concern for civil liberties as a legal right stems from this document.

The various former colonies, now busily organizing themselves as nations, were each jealous of its own identity and had each the full intention of ruling itself without interference from any of the other former colonies. Only the fact that they were united in war with Great Britain permitted any cooperation at all, however grudging.

And the cooperation was insufficient. The Continental Congress had no power to tax, no power to pass laws. It could only ask, and hope that the independent states might choose to give.

The states never gave enough. The Continental army was constantly in need of food, clothing, and ammunition, while the British, of course, always had enough. In fact, American farmers preferred to sell to the British who had hard cash to pay, rather than to the ragged Continentals who had no money except pieces of paper which represented promises to pay in gold eventually, *if* the rebellion were successful. (We still have the phrase "Not worth a Continental" referring to the paper money which the Continental Congress had begun issuing as early as June, 1775.)

The Americans, under these conditions, might keep up a guerrilla war for a long time, but there would be no hope of victory as long as Great Britain remained resolute. What was absolutely required was foreign aid; supplies, money, and naval help, if possible, to break the British blockade.

There was only one nation to which the Americans could turn and that was France. It was a difficult decision since for nearly a century France had been the enemy. To turn to them now against Great Britain was most distasteful and yet it had to be done. Only France could afford to help and only France would want to help and only France had the strength to defy Great Britain.

And yet France was not eager. It *did* want to help, not out of unselfishness, but out of a desire to weaken Great Britain. France had not forgotten the loss of its North American holdings less than twenty years before, and it was eager to do something to damage the British hold since that would offer it, perhaps, the chance to regain what was lost; or, at the very least, prevent Great Britain from growing too dangerously powerful.

On the other hand, the French government under Louis XVI (who had come to the throne in 1774 on the death of his grandfather, Louis XV) was an absolute monarch with no sympathy at all for the kind of representative government to which the British and the Americans were accustomed. Indeed, the French government was facing bankruptcy and increasing opposition from its own people and, rather than involving itself in foreign adventures, it ought, if it had had any sense (which it hadn't) to have been working on thoroughgoing and drastic internal reforms. There was also the consideration that an independent America might be (if it were too strong) as dangerous to French imperial dreams as a strong Great Britain might be, while if America lost the war, an enraged Great Britain might then turn on France.

So France hesitated.

Working in favor of the Americans was the fact that the Foreign Minister of France, Charles Gravier de Vergennes, hated Great Britain fiercely, and was always inclined to take a bit of extra risk in helping the rebelling Americans. A French playwright, Pierre Augustin Caron de Beaumarchais, famous at the time for his play *The Barber of Seville,* was an enthusiastic supporter of the Americans* and did his best to persuade Vergennes to take that bit of risk. On June 10, 1776, even before the Declaration of Independence was signed, Beaumarchais had persuaded Vergennes to agree to a quiet loan to the Americans. Spain, also eager to weaken Great Britain's hold on North America, matched that loan.

Naturally, the Americans wanted more and more help, unlimited help, in fact, from France. In order to plead this case, Congress on March 3, 1776, four months before the Declaration of Indepen-

* Although the French government was an absolute monarchy and, in theory, a foe of democracy, many French intellectuals had high democratic ideals and were what we would today call "leftists." The American Revolution was, in its time, supported by leftists everywhere.

dence, had sent a representative to France. This representative, the first American diplomat, was Silas Deane (born in Groton, Connecticut, on December 24, 1737). Unfortunately, he was incompetent. His best friend was a British spy, and Deane never knew this. Everything he did, then, was promptly reported to the British government.

Despite Deane's urgings, and Vergennes's impulses, however, France continued to take as few risks as possible. A vicious cycle was set up. The French would not really help until they were sure the Americans would win. The Americans, on the other hand, could scarcely work up a winning momentum without French help.

Oddly enough, the British also needed foreign help, but in another way.

The war was not popular in Great Britain. George III had a great deal of opposition in the nation and although he was powerful enough to keep those ministers he favored in office even when they lacked strong national support, he was not powerful enough to make the war popular. The British did not flock to the colors in order to be shipped three thousand miles to kill those whom many in Great Britain still thought of as other British subjects. In fact, there was some feeling that if George III defeated the Americans he would establish a kind of absolutism in America that might then be used as a precedent for the home island as well.

As a consequence, George III was forced to find foreign mercenaries to help flesh out his armies. He began doing so immediately after the Battle of Bunker Hill, and found them chiefly in the two small German states of Hesse-Cassel and Hesse-Darmstadt. The rulers of these vestpocket lands had absolute powers. Since they were in financial difficulties, they simply detailed thousands of their subjects for service with the British in return for generous payments which went, of course, to the rulers and not to the soldiers — though the soldiers received regular pay from the British once they served.

Altogether, perhaps 30,000 Hessians (as they were called) served in the British armies. The Americans used their presence in the British forces as a way of rousing indignation among their own people. It was one of the complaints against George III mentioned in the Declaration of Independence, for instance. And, indeed, recruiting was improved as Americans joined to fight, indignantly, against the foreign mercenaries.

The Hessians were good soldiers, it must be said, and committed no particular atrocities; nor were they mistreated when taken prisoner. Indeed, many of them remained in the country after the war was over and became American citizens.

STRUGGLE FOR NEW YORK

General Washington in New York had little leisure to debate matters such as foreign aid or independence. He was waiting for the British army which, he was sure, would come.

And it did. Three months after the evacuation of Boston, Howe brought his army to the vicinity of New York, where he could count on far less anti-British feeling among the population than was true in Boston.

On July 2, 1776, even while Congress was adopting the Declaration of Independence, Howe landed 10,000 men on Staten Island against no opposition at all. Howe's brother, Admiral Richard Howe, arrived ten days later with a strong contingent of ships. Further reinforcements under Henry Clinton and Charles Cornwallis arrived from Charleston (where they had been assailing the city with no success) on August 1.

By August, then, Howe had under his command 32,000 trained soldiers, including 9000 Hessians. Washington had only 18,000 men and these were largely poorly trained, short-term soldiers. (The Americans, unused to long campaigning and acutely aware of their farms and families at home, would sign up for only a few months. By the time the rudiments of training had been forced into them, it was departure time for them. The turnover was terrific and Washington never had as many men in actuality as he seemed to have on paper.)

Washington realized that New York would have to surrender if Howe seized Brooklyn Heights, just across the East River. He

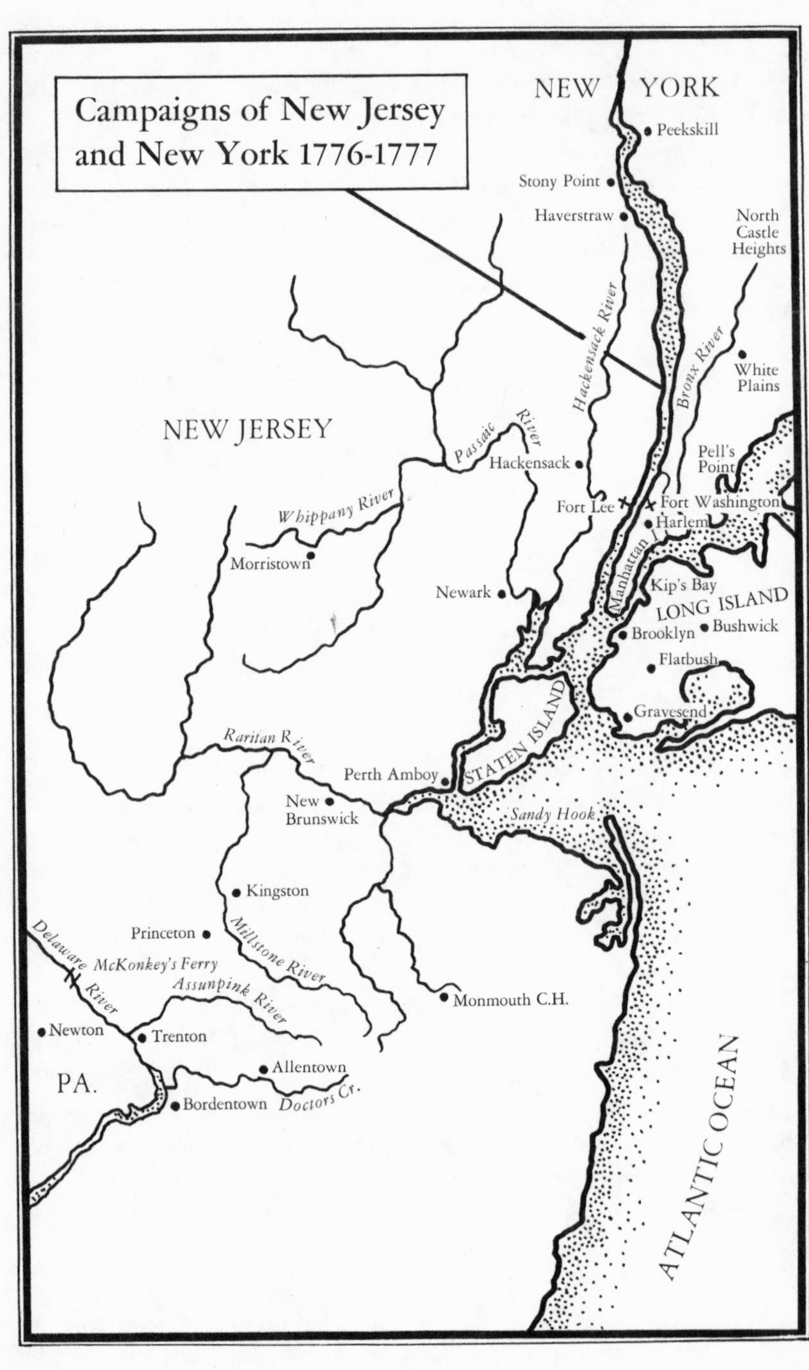
Campaigns of New Jersey and New York 1776-1777
NEW YORK
Peekskill
Stony Point
Haverstraw
North Castle Heights
Hackensack River
Bronx River
White Plains
NEW JERSEY
Passaic River
Hackensack
Pell's Point
Fort Lee
Fort Washington
Harlem
Whippany River
Morristown
Manhattan I.
Kip's Bay
Newark
LONG ISLAND
Brooklyn
Bushwick
Flatbush
STATEN ISLAND
Gravesend
Raritan River
Perth Amboy
New Brunswick
Sandy Hook
Kingston
Princeton
Delaware River
McKonkey's Ferry
Millstone River
Assunpink River
Monmouth C.H.
Newton
Trenton
Allentown
PA.
Bordentown
Doctors Cr.
ATLANTIC OCEAN

therefore placed one third of his forces across the river to try to hold off the British.

Between August 22 and 25, Howe shipped 20,000 men across the Narrows to what we now call the borough of Brooklyn. (What followed is usually called the "Battle of Long Island," and strictly speaking it did take place on Long Island. However, it took place on the westernmost part of the island where Brooklyn now is. The site would be clearer to modern ears if it were called the "Battle of Brooklyn.")

The Americans had unwisely placed forces south of the fortifications on Brooklyn Heights and thus invited a fight in open country which they could not possibly win. The British attacked them on August 27. Fighting was hot on the wooded hills of Flatbush, when a British contingent which had been sent far eastward came smashing in to the rear of the American forces, who were forced into a retreat to Brooklyn Heights. Both sides lost about 400 in killed and wounded, but the British took 1200 prisoners, and only half the American force managed to make it back to the safety of the Heights.

The next step, ordinarily, would have been for Howe to storm the Heights. A smashing victory would have probably destroyed the morale of Washington's forces and done dreadful damage to the American cause.

Here, however, came the ghost of Bunker Hill. Howe could not bring himself to send his men up the slopes in the face of American fire. Not again. Instead, he prepared to lay siege to the Heights and starve the Americans out.

Washington, however, felt he had won all he could in Brooklyn. His men had fought the outnumbering enemy as well as could be expected and there was no use in sacrificing more. Howe's failure to storm the Heights was a kind of victory in itself. It showed the British respected the Americans now, as they had not before Bunker Hill, and that was enough.

On the night of August 29, Washington directed the evacuation of Brooklyn Heights and the operation was achieved without loss. The next day, the British found themselves facing emptiness.

Of course, the loss of Brooklyn Heights meant that New York City could not be held, but for a while Howe held off from assaulting Manhattan island, for he was hoping even now, with the Declaration of Independence two months old, for a peaceful settlement.

He had taken General John Sullivan (born in Somersworth, New Hampshire, on February 17, 1740) prisoner during the battle in Brooklyn and he used him as an emissary. Off went Sullivan to Philadelphia carrying a message from Howe suggesting a peace conference be held.

Congress obliged. Three signers of the Declaration of Independence, Benjamin Franklin, John Adams, and Edward Rutledge (born in Charleston, South Carolina, on November 23, 1749) agreed to take the chance of going to Staten Island and placing themselves within the grip of a British general to whom they could only be traitors. On September 6, they met Howe, who was the soul of courtesy.

It came to nothing, though. Howe explained that there could be no discussions until the Americans agreed to revoke the Declaration of Independence. It was far too late for that. Anything short of independence would no longer do, so the conference came to an end. Howe, disappointed, made preparations for the occupation of New York.

On September 15, he ferried his troops across the East River to Kip's Bay on the eastern shore of Manhattan, well to the north of the city, which then occupied only the southern tip of the island. It was his hope that he would trap the American army to the south and force its surrender.

In this he did not succeed. Although Washington did not have the force with which to win victories and though he was not a great general, he was a shrewd and cautious one, and that is sometimes almost as good as being great. He had anticipated the British move and had evacuated the city and retreated to the northern portion of the island where he fortified Harlem Heights.

Howe pursued but again, after an indecisive skirmish, chose not to order a direct assault. Again, there was the vision of Bunker Hill.

For a month, Washington remained in Harlem Heights, trying to guess the next British move and for a month Howe remained in New York trying to decide on one.

It was during this interval that an incident took place, unimportant in itself, which has gained a hallowed place in American folklore. It involved Nathan Hale (born in Coventry, Connecticut, on June 6, 1755), a school teacher who had served in the siege of Boston and had attained the rank of captain. He now volunteered to act as spy behind the British lines. He was detected, captured, and condemned to be hanged on September 22, 1776.

Hale was a graduate of Yale and may have read Joseph Addison's *Cato* (published sixty years earlier) about a Roman patriot who died while fighting stubbornly for his city's liberties. Addison makes him say, "What pity is it that we can die but once to save our country." It's easy to have someone say so in a play, but Hale felt it in real life. On the gallows, his last words were, "I only regret that I have but one life to lose for my country."

Something else took place while Howe waited irresolutely in New York; something far less dramatic, but of crucial importance just the same.

Congress decided to strengthen its representation in France and sent Arthur Lee (born at "Stratford," Virginia, on December 21, 1740) and Benjamin Franklin to join Silas Deane. Lee was as incompetent as Deane and the two quarreled and intrigued against each other, doing far more harm than good to the American cause. Franklin made up for it, however, for he was ideal for the post. He was renowned in Europe as a scientist and as the inventor of the lightning rod. He was known for his writings and admired for his shrewd philosophy. He became the rage of the French aristocracy and, playing up to them for all it was worth, he glamorized the American cause to all of France.

RETREAT ACROSS NEW JERSEY

Howe's delay ruined the overall British strategy. Had he acted quickly after occupying New York, had he struck with the decisiveness and daring of a great general, or at least a bold one, he might easily have smashed Washington's small farm-boy army, and then followed through with an advance up the Hudson River to Albany.

British forces in Canada, which had already defeated an American force the previous winter, might have come south to join him and cut New England off from the remainder of the colonies. This would very likely have forced the Americans to some sort of compromise short of independence.

Indeed, the British forces were pushing southward from Canada already. Sir Guy Carleton, who had successfully defended Quebec the previous winter, was collecting ships to carry his men down Lake Champlain. Opposing him was Benedict Arnold still clinging to his scheme of Canadian conquest. Between October 11 and 13, however, Carleton's fleet smashed Arnold's hastily gathered and haphazardly manned ships and sailed down the lake to Crown Point, well toward its southern tip.

Carleton, however, received no news from Howe that would lead him to think he could expect cooperation. He did not wish to suffer through an Adirondack winter without hope of a union of forces. On November 3, therefore, he retired to Canada and Britain lost its chance.

It was on October 12 that Howe moved but his aims were limited. He sent his army up the East River and landed it at Pell's Point, in northern Bronx. His plan was to move to the Hudson and cut Washington off in northern Manhattan.

This attempt to defeat Washington by maneuvers alone failed again for Washington was well ahead of him. Leaving a contingent at Fort Washington in Manhattan's northern tip, he took his army into Westchester and marched for White Plains. Howe followed and at White Plains there was a small battle on October 28 in which the British drove Washington from a key hill, but in which they lost 300 men to an American loss of 200.

Howe again paused, finding it impossible to face blood, and waited for reinforcements. Washington at once slipped away to North Castle, five miles to the north, where, on November 1, he entrenched himself in an even stronger position.

Howe decided not to pursue the elusive Washington and, after another delay, turned on the American force holding Fort Washington. This and Fort Lee, just across the river on the New Jersey shore, were under the command of Nathaniel Greene (born at Potowomut, Rhode Island, August 7, 1742). Washington had advised the evacuation of both posts while there was yet time but Greene unwisely thought he might be able to hold them.

On November 16, Howe sent 13,000 men (mainly Hessians, and fighting under a Hessian commander) against Fort Washington and forced its surrender. On November 19, he followed up his victory by sending a body of troops under Cornwallis across the Hudson.

Fort Lee was taken, too, but here at least it was not a surrender. Greene managed to get his men out safely but was forced to abandon valuable supplies.

The loss of Fort Washington and Fort Lee was a bad blow to Washington, but he feared there was worse to come. The push across the Hudson meant that Howe might advance on Philadelphia. Ninety miles southwest of New York, Philadelphia was the largest American city and was the seat of the Congress so that it could, in a way, be considered the capital of the United States. At all costs, Washington felt, Philadelphia could not be given up without a fight.

Washington therefore left 7000 men at North Castle under Charles Lee and took 5000 men farther north to Peekskill. There, on the night of November 10, he crossed the Hudson River and raced southward to cover the route to Philadelphia. Washington joined forces with the beaten Greene at Hackensack, New Jersey, soon after the forts had been lost.

Cornwallis was advancing on them and there was nothing to do but retreat. Washington sent urgent messages to Charles Lee at North Castle to bring his men across the Hudson to join him. If there was a battle with the British, Washington would need all the men he could get.

Charles Lee, however, thought little of Washington and much of his own abilities. It was his intention to win some kind of amazing success which, when contrasted with Washington's continuing retreats, would net him the post of commander-in-chief. He therefore coolly disregarded Washington's orders. It wasn't till December 2, when he felt that nothing was going to happen at North Castle and that all the fighting would take place in New Jersey, that he led his men across the Hudson River.

By that time, Washington and Greene had been chased to New Brunswick and were still retreating quickly. They managed to reach the Raritan River and cross it while the slow-moving British lost their chance to get to a crucial bridge first and trap the Americans. (Indeed, Howe used part of his army on an utter side issue, sending it to capture Newport, Rhode Island. This the army accomplished on December 8, but it was a waste of effort since what Howe's aim should have been was the destruction of Washington's army. All else ought to have waited on that.)

As it was, Washington and Greene had reached Trenton, New Jersey, on December 11, and crossed the Delaware River into Pennsylvania, just ahead of the British. Cornwallis, making a decision worthy of Howe, decided to pursue no further at this time. He placed his men at Trenton and in some of the surrounding towns and got set to wait out the winter.

Charles Lee was still loitering in New Jersey, but on December 13, he got himself captured by a British patrol and taken out of action. It was the best thing he could have done for the American cause. Sullivan, who had been taken prisoner in Brooklyn, had been exchanged and now he took over Lee's command. He brought the soldiers into Pennsylvania on December 20, and joined Washington's forces.

The half year since Howe had come to New York had been a trying period for the Americans. After all the American successes in New England, Washington had lost New York, had been driven from one point to another, had been sent scurrying across New Jersey. Now Philadelphia itself was in danger; so clearly in danger, in fact, that the Continental Congress hastily cleared out of Philadelphia, and left for Baltimore, placing all power in Washington's hands.

Thomas Paine, who was serving in the army under Nathaniel Greene, published a series of pamphlets called *The American Crisis* in which he lifted failing American spirits, urging his fellow countrymen to see matters through the dark days.

The first number was published on December 23, 1776, and began:

"These are the times that try men's souls. The summer soldier and the sunshine patriot will, in this crisis, shrink from the service of his country; but he that stands it *now,* deserves the love and thanks of man and woman. Tyranny, like hell, is not easily conquered; yet we have this consolation with us, that the harder the conflict, the more glorious the triumph. What we obtain too cheap, we esteem too lightly: 'tis dearness only that gives every thing its value. Heaven knows how to set a proper price upon its goods; and it would be strange indeed, if so celestial an article as *Freedom* should not be highly rated."

COUNTERATTACK ACROSS THE DELAWARE

The situation as 1776 waned to its close was not as bad as it might have seemed. Thanks to Howe's slowness and his utterly unimaginative style of fighting, and thanks to Washington's skillfully handled retreat, the American army remained in being, and its morale had not been destroyed by any catastrophic defeat. Indeed, in what fighting there had been, the Americans had acquitted themselves respectably and it was British preponderance in numbers and supplies that had defeated the Americans, more than any lack of spirit among themselves. (Though it must be admitted that the Americans could not have done it without the help of Howe's incompetence.)

And now Howe, inert as usual, had gone into winter quarters. He had brought the bulk of the army back to New York, but left garrisons along the Delaware, at Trenton, particularly, to keep an eye on Washington. Howe was prepared to loaf through the winter, certain that the Americans on the western side of the Delaware River would do the same.

Washington was determined that the American would *not* do the same. It was necessary that the American army show itself to *be* in being and to possess an offensive spirit despite its long retreat. He therefore planned to strike back.

He chose Christmas night for the purpose. In Trenton, there were 1400 Hessians who would surely be sleeping off a thoroughgoing Christmas celebration. It should be possible to take them by surprise.

At 7 P.M. on December 25, then, Washington, with 2400 men, crossed the dangerous, ice-choked Delaware River at a point nine miles north of Trenton.* Two other smaller parties were supposed to cross farther south, but they didn't make it.

On the eastern bank, at 3 A.M. of the 26th, Washington's army was divided into two columns, one under Greene, and one under Sullivan. Both marched hastily toward Trenton by different roads.

While this was happening, the Hessian commander in Trenton, blissfully unaware of anything untoward, was spending the night drinking and playing cards. There is a tale that a Loyalist spy brought word of the impending American attack but was not allowed in. He sent in a note which the commander thrust into his pocket and forgot about. (Since almost identical stories are told about other surprise attacks in history, this tale may not be true.)

At 8 A.M. the American columns met in Trenton and attacked with Knox's artillery banging away. The Hessians, tumbling out of bed, didn't have a chance. The commanding officer was killed, along with thirty others, and over 900 of the Hessians were captured. The American forces suffered only five casualties altogether. Washington then led his army back to the west bank of the river, but when the British didn't react at once, Washington crossed the Delaware again and, on December 30, 1776, occupied Trenton.

It wasn't much of a battle taken by itself, but it meant that Washington and his army were very much alive. All American patriots took heart at the news and recruits flooded into Washington's army.

Howe realized the blow to British prestige and saw that it might be reversed if Washington's army could be taken in Trenton. On January 1, 1777, therefore, he bestirred himself to an unwonted activity and sent Cornwallis, with 7000 troops, hastening southward to make the catch. On January 2, Cornwallis reached Washington's army camped east of Trenton. It was late in the day, however, and

* This episode, so important to the American cause, was immortalized in a huge painting, "Washington Crossing the Delaware," painted in Germany in 1851 by the German-American, Emanuel Leutze. This is probably the best-known painting to be inspired by an incident in American history, and is exceeded in popularity only by the nonhistorical "The Spirit of '76," painted in 1876 by Archibald M. Willard.

Cornwallis felt it would be time enough the next day to do the job; "to bag the old fox," as he said.

The old fox was not so easily bagged. He left behind just as many men as were necessary to make the kind of sounds that one would expect from an occupied camp and the rest of the army slipped away before dawn. When Cornwallis woke, Washington was near to Princeton.

At Princeton, Washington narrowly defeated a British force, then marched northward to Morristown, New Jersey, which he reached on January 7. There he finally went into winter quarters. He felt he had done enough. The British thought so, too. Cornwallis went into winter quarters at New Brunswick, twenty miles south of Morristown.

One result of Washington's success was that by March 4, 1777, Congress had returned to Philadelphia from Baltimore. Their concern was still chiefly that of obtaining foreign assistance. Although on a large scale this still had to wait for a more solid success than Washington was able to obtain at Trenton, individual volunteers were beginning to come to America.

Of these, by far the most important was Marie Joseph de Motier, Marquis de Lafayette. Born on September 6, 1757, he was only nineteen years old when, in December 1776, he made up his mind to go to America and serve in its army. He was rich, happily married, and had every opportunity of leading the gilded life of a French courtier. This, however, he did not wish to do. He was a young idealist, full to the brim with notions of military glory, and with the theoretical notions of liberty of the French intellectuals.

He managed to get the American representatives in Paris to give him the rank of a major general and off he went, even though his father-in-law and King Louis XVI were against the notion. The Americans weren't overjoyed at his coming, either, feeling that he was going to be a fancy Frenchman who would demand special treatment and would despise the backwoodsmen he found himself among.

Quite the contrary. Lafayette intended to use his own money. The ship that brought him was his own. He would take no pay, and he asked no command. He asked only to serve. What is more, he met Washington and the two instantly struck it off well. It was a lifelong friendship almost as close as that between a father and son. (Washington was twenty-five years older than Lafayette.)

Lafayette's mere presence did wonders for morale. It somehow represented France's interest in the new nation, and Lafayette's unassuming manners and loyal service put France in a good light. No foreigner has ever been enshrined in American hearts and legend as Lafayette was to be.

Other notable foreign volunteers also arrived. There was Johann Kalb, a German of peasant derivation (born on June 29, 1721), who insisted on calling himself Baron de Kalb. He was a warrior of many years experience and was to die in action fighting for America.

There was also a Prussian soldier, Frederick William von Steuben (born September 17, 1730), who had fought with distinction under Frederick II of Prussia. He came partly because he was having financial difficulties (a chronic situation with him). The French paid his way over.

A Polish volunteer, Tadeusz Kosciuszko (born on February 4, 1746) was among the first to arrive. He helped fortify Philadelphia, while Washington's army was retreating through New Jersey and it looked as though Philadelphia would soon be attacked.

Another Polish volunteer was Casimir Pulaski (born on March 4, 1747), who had fought Russia on behalf of his native land with courage and tenacity. Poland was defeated, however, and he came to America to fight another battle for freedom. Like De Kalb, Pulaski was fated to die in action.

The new year saw another evidence of renewed optimism when, on June 14, 1777, Congress resolved on a national flag to be designed with thirteen alternating red and white stripes as in the flag of the Continental army. In the union, however (the rectangle in the upper left), there was to be, in place of the Union Jack, thirteen stars, one for each state. It was not specified how the thirteen stars were to be arranged, but a circular pattern came to be accepted.

This was the first national flag, and has been kept ever since with minor changes as to the numbers of stripes and of stars. June 14 has been celebrated unofficially as "Flag Day" ever since.

There is a legend, dear to the hearts of all schoolchildren and their teachers, that a certain Betsy Ross (born in Philadelphia in 1752) made the first flag, and even that she fixed the stars as five-pointed by showing how easily a five-pointed star could be made by properly folding cloth and then making a single cut. However, the story was first told in 1870, a century after the event, and there is no contemporary evidence that it happened.

5

THE TURNING POINT

BURGOYNE'S INVASION

In Great Britain, General John Burgoyne was planning British victory for 1777. He had been in Boston under Howe, and then he had been with Carleton when the latter had made his abortive strike down Lake Champlain.

Burgoyne felt quite grim about the manner in which that campaign had been handled. It was, he felt, the key to crushing the American rebellion; the means of separating the two rebel centers, New England and Virginia. Such a push down and up the Hudson, should have been carried through at all costs, in his view, and was not something that should have been abandoned so lightly.

He placed his plan before the British government. He himself, according to his plan, would take a strong army from Canada southward along Lake Champlain and the Hudson River, while Howe was to take his army from New York City northward. They were to unite in the vicinity of Albany, while a third army coming east from Lake Ontario would join them also. All New York would then be under effective British control and New England would be isolated.

The British government agreed to the plan but, as is usual in such cases, granted Burgoyne only half the number of men he felt to be necessary for the task. Burgoyne decided it would have to do.

On June 1, 1777, with 4000 British troops, 3000 Hessians, and 1000 Canadians and Indians, he set off southward. Going down Lake Champlain was easy and on July 1, he reached Fort Ticonderoga, which had been in American hands since Ethan Allen's exploit, two years before. There was no chance of the Americans holding it against Burgoyne's army, so the garrison wisely retreated. Burgoyne took the fort on July 6 and then moved on to Skenesboro at the southern tip of the lake.

He now had only seventy miles to go, but it was a hard seventy miles because it would have to be overland through thickly forested country. What's more, as the Americans retreated, they destroyed bridges and chopped down trees to block the road. Burgoyne's rate of progress was cut down to about a mile a day, partly because he insisted on dragging along a huge supply train. Still, by July 29 he was at Fort Edward, only forty miles north of Albany.

The American position was grave but, even with Burgoyne biting into upper New York State, the Americans found time and occasion to squabble over command.

Since the campaign was being fought in New York, it seemed natural that the highest ranking New York officer, Philip Schuyler, should command the American forces. On the other hand, Benedict Arnold, still seeking some post commensurate with his merits, wanted the command. He had been fighting gallantly along the Canadian border for a year and a half, and although he had been defeated, he had nevertheless handled his small and inadequate forces very well.

Interstate rivalries were crucial, however. If Arnold were to lead the force he would have to be made a major general, and there was no room left for further major generals from New England. On the other hand, the New England troops flatly refused to serve under Schuyler. Not only was he an aristocrat without the knack of im-

Campaigns of Upper New York 1777

pressing the common soldier, but most of the New England fighters were from the Green Mountain area and they considered New York as dangerous an enemy as Great Britain.

In an attempt at compromise, both Schuyler and Arnold were passed over and, on August 4, the command was given to Horatio Gates (born in England about 1727). In 1772, he had emigrated to America and settled in western Virginia. He joined the Continental army in 1775 and took part in the retreat from Canada in 1776.

He had shown no signs of greatness, but the New Englanders were at least willing to serve under him. Arnold had no choice but to serve under him, too, but Congress's refusal to give him the command, which he deserved, rankled within him. He did not forget.

What kept the Americans from losing the campaign while they squabbled was the fact that Burgoyne's slow progress was placing him in serious trouble, for he had about run out of food. The countryside was empty of anything to eat and something had to be done.

He expected supplies to arrive with Colonel Barry St. Leger, who was leading his contingent up the St. Lawrence River to Lake Ontario and then eastward across the width of New York to join Burgoyne. It was a roundabout path but, in theory, it would outflank American forces facing Burgoyne, who would suddenly find themselves attacked on the side and rear. It was the sort of thing that is very nicely done on the map, but with hundreds of miles of wilderness to cover and a possibly hostile countryside to plow through, matters become questionable.

St. Leger made it to Lake Ontario and disembarked at Oswego, New York, on July 25, about when Burgoyne was approaching Fort Edward. With a total force of 1700 men, St. Leger moved eastward across the width of Lake Oneida.

He was crossing Iroquois territory. The Iroquois for over a century and a half had been firmly on the British side against the Dutch and the French (see *The Shaping of North America*). They were never a numerous people, having always made up for their lack of numbers in daring and in skill at guerrilla fighting.

All through the 18th century, however, while they bled in war and could barely maintain their strength, the settlers all around had multiplied and spread. By the time of the Revolutionary War, the Iroquois could no longer dominate the region. As if that were not bad enough, they were disunited for the first time in their recent history. Some of the Iroquois tribes favored the American settlers, some the British army. On neither side were opinions wholehearted.

Loyal to the British army was the Mohawk chief, Joseph Brant, and he was with St. Leger. On August 3, 1777, the British force reached Fort Stanwix, about 70 miles east of Lake Ontario and still about 100 miles short of the place where Burgoyne was waiting south of Lake Champlain. The garrison holding Fort Stanwix refused to surrender and St. Leger settled down to a siege.

There were settlers in the vicinity, however, who were gathering to fight the invaders. Under General Nicholas Herkimer (born near what is now Herkimer, New York, in 1728), 800 of them marched to relieve the fort. They were trapped by Brant's Mohawks at Oriskany, ten miles short of their goal and were badly cut up, with Herkimer himself mortally wounded. The fight was fierce, however, and the Indians did not come off lightly. Feeling they had done enough and that it would be wise to conserve their manpower for another day, the Mohawks gradually slipped off into the forest.

Benedict Arnold, leading another small force of about 1000 men, marched westward in Herkimer's tracks. He deliberately encouraged the spread of rumors to the effect that his army was much larger than it really was. St. Leger, without his Indians, dared not risk a battle. On August 23, he abandoned the siege of Fort Stanwix and marched hastily back along the route by which he had come.

Burgoyne was thus left in the wilderness north of Albany with no chance of receiving help and supplies from St. Leger. Nor was there any hope that the victorious march of a British army from the west would rally the Iroquois and Loyalists of the area against the American rebels.

While St. Leger was stalled before Fort Stanwix, the food problem had forced Burgoyne to send a troop of men eastward with instructions to raid the New England countryside and bring back horses, cattle, and grain. About 700 men, half of them Hessians, the other half Canadians and Indians, were detailed for this.

Their first objective was Bennington in the Green Mountain area and there the Green Mountain Boys to the number of 2600 were waiting under Brigadier General John Stark (born at Nutfield, New Hampshire, on August 28, 1728). Stark had been in almost every important engagement in the Revolutionary War up to then, having fought at Bunker Hill, at Quebec, and having been with Washington during the retreat across New Jersey.

On August 16, 1777, Stark met the invaders at Bennington and led his men in a wild charge against them, crying out that victory would be theirs "or Molly Stark's a widow." Victory was theirs. The invaders, surprised and outnumbered, were killed or captured (except for a few Indians who managed to slip away). A reinforcing brigade sent out, too late, by Burgoyne, was driven off with a third of its number gone.

The Battle of Bennington was a shattering defeat for Burgoyne, quite beyond the numbers of men lost. It meant he was not going to get his food and supplies. Furthermore, news of the victory brought more men flocking to the American colors, so that Burgoyne found himself surrounded by growing forces.

He was going to have to fight or starve and every day the odds against him increased.

BURGOYNE'S SURRENDER

But where, meanwhile, was General Howe, who, according to Burgoyne's plan, was supposed to bring his army up the Hudson River and thus catch the Americans in the destructive jaws of a nutcracker?

Incredibly, Howe had decided to go off in another direction altogether. Even for Howe, this passes belief.

There is a legend that places the blame on Lord George Germain, the British cabinet member in charge of the colonies, who directed overall strategy in the war. He had accepted Burgoyne's plan and he was supposed to have informed Howe of exactly what his part would be. He is thought, however, to have gone off on a long weekend and, in his hurry to do so, to have shoved the message to Howe into a pigeonhole, planning to send it off when he returned. But then, when he returned, he had forgotten all about it.

This seems unlikely. While it is perfectly possible for a cabinet member (or anyone) to be careless in even the most important matters, Howe ought to have known even without instructions that he should go northward to meet with Burgoyne.

Apparently, Howe did understand that – but there was something else on his mind. He understood perfectly well that his handling of the war, thus far, had been abysmally bad. Bunker Hill was a continuing nightmare to him and now his 1776 campaign in New York and New Jersey was another nightmare. Even though he had taken New York and had inflicted several defeats on Washington, those defeats had not been crucial. Washington had slipped out of his grasp again and again, and had then made an utter fool of him with the coup at Trenton.

Howe was bent on making up for past mistakes by some brilliant military stroke that would crush Washington. Joining up with Burgoyne might end the war, but the credit would then go to Burgoyne. Howe seems to have convinced himself that if he took Philadelphia, he might force an American capitulation that way, with the credit all his own; especially since he would take Philadelphia and *then* race northward to join Burgoyne. Somehow, Howe managed to convince Lord Germain of this and that fool, having told Burgoyne Howe would come north to meet him, then gave Howe permission to go elsewhere.

So on July 23, 1777, while Burgoyne was sweating and panting his way through the forests south of Lake Champlain, Howe, who ought to have been moving up the Hudson River, calmly put 18,000 men on ships and sailed southward. He had no intention of taking the overland route through New Jersey where Washington was watching him. Instead, he was going by sea southward to the mouth of Chesapeake Bay, then up through the Bay to land just a few miles south of Philadelphia and catch it by surprise.

There was, of course, nothing to stop him at sea and on August 25, 1777 (after that Battle of Bennington and St. Leger's retreat had already left Burgoyne in a desperate position), Howe placed his

army ashore at what is now Elkton, Maryland, about forty-five miles southwest of Philadelphia.

Washington, who had naturally expected Howe to march toward Albany (who could foresee the full extent of Howe's stupidity?) had been drifting northward, but on receiving word of Howe's arrival at the head of Chesapeake Bay, he marched his 12,000-man army rapidly southward. Since Howe moved as slowly as always, Washington managed to reach the British at Brandywine Creek, about halfway between Elkton and Philadelphia.

On September 11, 1777, the Battle of Brandywine Creek was fought and Howe, fighting with the greatest care (for it was the ambition of his life, now, to crush Washington), executed excellent flanking maneuvers. He pinned the American army with a frontal attack and then sent columns to either side. Washington did not have the kind of trained soldiery who could be trusted to counter well-executed enemy maneuvers and at this battle he was completely outfought. He lost a thousand men and had to retreat as rapidly as he could to Philadelphia. General Greene kept the retreat orderly and prevented worse disaster.

There was nothing to stop Howe now from marching into Philadelphia. Again Congress left town hurriedly. On September 19, they met in Lancaster, Pennsylvania, sixty miles west of Philadelphia, and by the next day, they moved on to York, fifteen miles farther west.

On September 26, 1777, Howe took Philadelphia and, with the feeling of victory sweeping over him, he became the old Howe. He made no attempt to pursue Washington.

Washington, on the other hand, felt that it was impossible to allow Howe to remain in control of Philadelphia without some attempt to dislodge him. Howe's main encampment was in Germantown, seven miles north of Philadelphia and, on October 3, Washington attacked it in a very complicated fashion. The attack involved columns attacking from different directions and coming to each other's support in some pretty intricate maneuvering.

Unfortunately, Washington's untrained troops could not march and countermarch with the proper precision. Besides, the morning on which all that maneuvering was to reach its climax turned foggy and some American detachments, hopelessly lost, fired on their own side.

Washington ended by losing nearly another thousand men and had to retreat again, with Greene once more handling that part of the job admirably.

After that, Howe settled down in Philadelphia for the winter. The area had been cleared and Washington would not dare disturb him. Philadelphia society greeted him gladly and British officers had never been so comfortable in America before.

To be sure, Burgoyne was at his last gasp far to the north. Did Howe worry about that or feel a twinge of guilt at not making at least a gesture of marching to his help? Perhaps not. He had retrieved his reputation, in his own eyes at least, by defeating Washington handily in two battles and by occupying the rebel capital. He might even have kidded himself into believing that now, with himself ensconced in Philadelphia, the Americans would sue for peace.

Certainly from the condition of Washington's army, Howe might have seemed correct. After the double loss at Brandywine and Germantown, Washington took up winter quarters at Valley Forge, Pennsylvania, twenty miles northwest of Philadelphia. This placed his army between the British in Philadelphia and the Congress at York.

For the Americans the winter was horrible. It was unusually cold, with snows beginning early. The countryside was bare and the farmers would sell nothing to the small American army which had only worthless Continental currency with which to pay. The farmers sold instead to the well-heeled British in Philadelphia.

The ragged soldiers froze through the winter, with scarcely any food, virtually no warm clothing, and with a shortage even of shoes. Some three thousand died of privation and others deserted. That the fading ghost of the army held together and remained in being was almost entirely due to the commanding presence of Washington.

But at least the American army, suffering badly, *did* remain in being. Burgoyne's army, to the north, was in worse case. With the Battle of Bennington lost, with Americans swarming to Gates's army, Burgoyne nevertheless forced his way forward. He managed to reach and pass Saratoga. Gates had fortified Bemis Heights, seventeen miles south of Saratoga and only about twenty-five miles north of Albany and now he faced Burgoyne's approaching army.

Gates had 7000 men and on September 19 (eight days after Washington had lost the Battle of Brandywine Creek) Gates sent 3000 of these forward to engage Burgoyne's forces. These were under Benedict Arnold and Daniel Morgan. Morgan (born in Hunterdon County, New Jersey, in 1736) had been with Arnold at Quebec and had fought well there.

The fighting at Freeman's Farm, one mile north of the fortified Heights, was not particularly scientific. Both sides simply plowed forward. Morgan's sharpshooters wrought havoc among the British but the Americans were outnumbered and Gates, though his own numbers were growing rapidly, refused to send reinforcements.

The Americans fell back and Burgoyne held the ground, which

he then fortified. Technically, it was a British victory, but the British had had the greater casualties, and Burgoyne's forces were shrinking as Indians deserted, while Gates's forces continued to increase.

By that time, there simply *had* to be a move from New York, Howe had not left the city entirely denuded, but had kept a small force there under Clinton. Under the circumstances, Clinton took some men up the Hudson and on October 6 managed to take two forts just north of Peekskill.

Burgoyne, still waiting at Freeman's Farm, knew he could not possibly sit there waiting for Clinton to arrive. He had to either retreat or attack and if he attacked it had to be at once. The American forces had by now risen to 11,000 in number and were still increasing.

Meanwhile, Gates's officers were going quietly mad over the fact that Gates was not himself attacking. His lack of courage had cost them a smashing victory at Freeman's Farm. In his reports, moreover, he displayed an underhanded meanness when he failed to mention Arnold who was easily the most brilliant officer in the army. When Arnold protested, he received the usual dirty deal Fate handed him every time, for Gates relieved him of his command.

On October 7, Burgoyne made his move with a reconnoitering force intended to locate the exact disposition of the American troops. Fighting began, but under Gates's command the Americans pushed forward cautiously.

Arnold, condemned to remain out of the fight, could stand it no more. Storming in, he took over command of the center, quite illegally, and sent them charging forward. He charged with them and was badly wounded in the right thigh, breaking the bone. But the Battle of Bemis Heights ended in a smashing British defeat, thanks to Arnold's initiative, and now Burgoyne could do nothing better than stumble back to Saratoga.

The case was hopeless. Every day, more Americans arrived and added to the forces that now surrounded him. On October 15, Clinton had reached Kingston, about eighty miles south of Saratoga and, meeting resistance, gave up and returned to New York. Even if he had kept marching northward, he would not have arrived in time; and even if he had, the forces he would have brought with him would not have been enough to alter the result.

On October 17, 1777, Burgoyne finally gave up. There were now 20,000 men surrounding him, outnumbering him four to one, so he surrendered his army. Three hundred officers (including six generals) and 5500 men gave up, agreed to surrender their arms, march to Boston, go back to Great Britain, and take no further part in the war.

This event, which took place two weeks after Washington's defeat at Germantown, cancelled out Howe's victorious campaign with plenty to spare. Howe may have defeated Washington, but Washington had saved his army once again, and still hovered about Pennsylvania. Burgoyne, on the other hand, had *surrendered.*

The surrender of a British army on the field of battle was a most uncommon event under the best of conditions, but to have one surrender to a bunch of backwoodsmen who had been so heartily despised by British regulars scarcely bore thinking of. It was a stunning humiliation for Great Britain before the eyes of all the world.

THE FRENCH ALLIANCE

Benjamin Franklin had taken French society by storm, when he had arrived in France in December, 1776. Four years earlier, he had been elected a member of the French Academy of Sciences and now French scholars rushed to meet the aged philosopher from the west.

Franklin deliberately dressed very simply, like a Quaker. He didn't wear a wig, or powder, or a sword; he carried a stout staff instead. The French aristocrats were enchanted with this simplicity. Franklin, who had always had an eye for (and a way with) the ladies, knew exactly how to charm the fashionable beauties of French society.

Thanks to Franklin, the French aristocracy at the court of Louis

XVI were all for help to the Americans, and the favorable climate of opinion had made it possible for the French government to send supplies to the Americans in a discreet way. France also allowed American ships to use French ports in the course of their raids on British shipping. Carefully, however, France had refrained from doing enough in this direction to bring on an enraged British reaction.

But then, on December 7, 1777, news of Burgoyne's surrender reached Paris.

The French government was galvanized into activity when, for the first time, it looked to them as though the Americans might actually defeat Great Britain. If so, it would never do to let them achieve their independence without feeling properly grateful to France. It would be very useful for France to have an ally on the American continent. If the new nation could be converted into a kind of French auxiliary, the score might yet be evened with Great Britain.

Then, too, if the French didn't move swiftly, Burgoyne's surrender might drive Great Britain to make concessions which the Americans would accept. Britain's empire in North America would be reconstituted and the British and Americans might then celebrate their reconciliation by turning on a common enemy, which could only be France.

(As a matter of fact, the British *did* make concessions to the Americans after Burgoyne's surrender. Hastily, and almost abjectly, they gave in to all the demands of the Americans but one – they would not grant independence. Had they taken this attitude three years earlier, there might have been no war and today's world might have been entirely different. The British could not turn the clock back, however. The Americans would take nothing less than independence now. Since Great Britain could not bring itself to accept that, the war went on.)

The French, anxious to encourage the Americans to resist rumored British offers, now granted an outright alliance.

On February 6, 1778, the alliance between France and America was officially established. Generous terms for trade were set. American independence was recognized by France and official diplomatic representatives were exchanged. Franklin was no longer head of an unofficial commission; he was the American minister to France.

Such an alliance meant war between France and Great Britain, of course, and France was resigned to that. On June 17, 1778, there was a clash between ships of the two nations and war between them was a fact.

One of the first fruits of the French alliance was that supplies began to reach Washington's shivering army at Valley Forge. Baron von Steuben, the Prussian volunteer serving with the American forces, arrived at Valley Forge on February 23, 1778, and began to put the army through its paces, training it in the Prussian style. This was not done easily and Von Steuben was forced to call upon his entire supply of German invective in order to tell the clumsy Americans what he thought of them. In fact, there is a story that when he had finally exhausted himself, he ordered an aide to swear at the soldiers in English.

But when warm weather arrived, the American army was in better shape, and more nearly like a professional fighting force, than it had ever been before.

Washington had to weather another difficulty, too, in the wake of Burgoyne's surrender. It seemed to some Americans that Gates was a great general who had destroyed a British army. (Actually, Gates had done nothing, and what credit could be assigned to a single person, should have gone to Benedict Arnold, who was, as seemed his inevitable fate, once again ignored.) In contrast, Washington seemed a failure and there was considerable feeling in Congress that Gates ought to replace Washington as commander-in-chief.

There has grown up a legend that there was an actual conspiracy to this effect headed by Thomas Conway, an Irish-born soldier who had served in the French army and had come to the United States only in 1777. Against Washington's recommendation, he had been appointed inspector-general of the Continental army.

If there was indeed such a "Conway Cabal," it was extraordinarily inept. Gates lacked courage in political infighting as well as in military affairs, and, when pressed by an indignant Washington, he quickly and cravenly disowned any part in the matter. It turned out that despite the events at Saratoga and at Philadelphia, Washington's popularity with his officers, soldiers, and Americans generally could not be withstood. Congress found itself forced to support him, but did so as half-heartedly as possible. Conway resigned and was replaced as inspector-general by Baron von Steuben.

If Washington's record and personality kept him in office, Howe's most certainly did not.

With the spring of 1778, the British government decided it had had enough of William Howe. By then, it was quite clear that his move to Philadelphia was a colossal blunder. He had not even succeeded in destroying Washington's army and had made no attempt to do anything to it when it was reduced to skin and bones at Valley Forge. His whole record was one of such ineptitude that it is hard to avoid the conclusion that he did more for the American cause than any American general, with the exception of Washington himself.

On May 8, 1778, Howe was relieved of his command and was succeeded by Clinton, who had at least made the effort to move up the Hudson Valley and succor Burgoyne.

Clinton found himself facing a serious escalation in the war. France was in it now and France had a fleet. France's ships had always been defeated by the British in the course of the French and Indian War, but it wasn't safe to count on British naval victories as certain. There were reports of a French fleet heading across the Atlantic and Clinton dared not allow his forces to be spread out too thinly.

He therefore prepared to evacuate Philadelphia (for the sake of which Howe ruined Burgoyne) and to concentrate his forces in New York. On June 18, the British left Philadelphia and began the northeastward march across New Jersey. (On July 2, Congress returned once again to Philadelphia after an absence of nearly nine months.)

Washington was no Howe. He at once broke camp at Valley Forge and set off in pursuit of the British. It was his intention to strike at the British while they were strung out in the march and for that purpose he sent off a detachment of 6400 men under Charles Lee to race ahead and catch the British.

This was the same Charles Lee who had been insubordinate at the time of Washington's retreat from New York. He had been taken prisoner then but by a colossal stroke of bad luck for the

Americans, he had been exchanged and returned to the war. Washington made one of his rare errors in judgment by trusting him with a command.

Lee apparently thought he was still with the same army that had reeled across New Jersey nearly two years before and had no appreciation of the new professionalism that had entered its ranks. He was certain that any attack by the Americans would merely lead to defeat. Therefore, on June 28, 1778, when he finally caught up with the dispersed British at Monmouth Court House, New Jersey, about fifty miles northeast of Philadelphia, he attacked only in gingerly fashion. His orders were confused, as though he were laboring to see to it that any ill-fortune that followed would be blamed on the incapacity of his subordinates and not on himself.

Then, when Clinton began a rapid concentration of his own forces, Lee hastily ordered a retreat. By that time, Washington, with the main army, arrived. Horrified at the sight of the Americans retreating without any signs of an adequate battle having been fought, Washington let Lee know his thoughts in full. It was a new side of Washington. Those who had been aware only of his stately reserve and gentlemanly calm, listened with awe as Washington turned the air blue with his comments. (Lee was court-martialed on July 4 and was found guilty on August 12. His military career was over and it is now known that he was actually a traitor who had secretly been working with the British.)

Washington ordered the retreat halted and the forceful Von Steuben reformed the columns and sent them forward again, but the chance of overwhelming a section of the British army and panicking the rest was gone. It was now a full fight between the two main armies, roughly equal in numbers.

The Americans showed their mettle by resisting the British attacks and by holding firm. Neither side was driven from the field and there were equal casualties on either side, about 350 each.

During the night it was the British who slipped away so it might be considered an American victory. However, the British were trying to get to New York and succeeded in doing so without serious losses despite Washington's effort, so it might be counted as a British tactical victory. The best solution might be to consider the Battle of Monmouth a draw.

Washington could only lead his army to White Plains, which he had left nearly two years before, and from there keep an eye on the British in New York. He lacked the strength to attack them there.

THE WAR ON THE FRONTIER

During the better than three years from April 1775 to June 1778, the major battles had been fought near the great cities of the New England and middle states: Boston, New York, and Philadelphia. There was, however, the western frontier, and the war was fought there as well.

The frontier was alive with settlements and Indian hostility was important. Through all the gathering disputes between the Americans and the British, and despite the Proclamation of 1763, the westward push had kept on. If one man can be said to embody this fact, it was Daniel Boone (born near what is now Reading, Pennsylvania, on November 2, 1734).

While Boone was still young, his family moved to the western borderlands of North Carolina. From 1767, Boone trapped and hunted beyond the Alleghenies and on April 1, 1775, he established a fort he called Boonesboro in what is now central Kentucky. He brought his wife and daughter there and they were the first American women to live in Kentucky.

Where Boone led the way, others followed. Land speculators even attempted to form new colonies along the western borders. A colony named "Vandalia" was formed in 1769 (and was approved by King George in 1775) in the area that is now West Virginia. In 1774, most of the area of Kentucky was organized as "Transylvania" by Richard Henderson (born in Hanover county, Virginia, in 1735).

These colonies were stillborn. The older colonies would not permit their existence. Virginia insisted that all the territory on which Vandalia and Transylvania were organized (and more beside) belonged to her.

Still, whether the land of the Appalachian mountain range and to the west belonged to the seaboard colonies or not, they were being settled. It is estimated that by the time of the Revolutionary War, 250,000 settlers had poured into the backwoods.

The westward push did not fail to meet resistance from the Indians. The Shawnee tribe, whose center was in what we now call the state of Ohio, considered the lands south of the Ohio River to be part of their hunting grounds.

Lord Dunmore, the governor of Virginia, sent out armed parties in 1774 to counter the Shawnees and what followed was called "Lord Dunmore's War." After one such party was ambushed by the Shawnees, Lord Dunmore gathered 1500 of the settlers on the western frontier of Virginia, put them under Colonel Andrew Lewis (born in Ireland in 1720) and sent them to the Ohio River. Lewis encountered an Indian force at Point Pleasant (a name given the site in 1770 by George Washington himself) on the Ohio River about 160 miles southwest of Pittsburgh, and on the western border of what is now the state of West Virginia.

There Lewis defeated the Shawnees on October 6, 1774, ending Lord Dunmore's War and making the area south of the Ohio River reasonably safe for white settlement. This was the last colonial war against the Indians. Within less than a year, Lord Dunmore was forced to flee Virginia and the colony had become an independent state.

The Revolutionary War, however, brought a new increase in Indian troubles; and a very dangerous one, in fact, for the British formed alliances with the Indian tribes and encouraged them to engage in raids in which noncombatants were slaughtered indiscriminately. In fact, some American Loyalists were worse in this respect than the British were.

A notorious example was John Butler (born in New London, Connecticut, in 1728). In 1777, he recruited Loyalists and Indians and formed an alliance with the Mohawk leader, Joseph Brant. On July 4, 1778, "Butler's Rangers," as they were called, defeated a party of settlers led by Zebulon Butler (born in Ipswich, Massachusetts, in 1731, and no relative) in the Wyoming Valley of Pennsylvania. What followed was an indiscriminate massacre. The small town of Wilkes-Barre was totally burned and 227 scalps were collected.

On November 11 of that year, a similar massacre was carried out by Butler and Brant at Cherry Valley, New York, about sixty miles west of Albany. Forty scalps were collected there, taken from settlers who had already surrendered.

Farther west, in Fort Detroit, the British commander, Henry Hamilton, supplied surrounding Indians with knives and paid bounties for American scalps. He was called "The Hair Buyer" in consequence.

The Americans, turning what strength they had against the British, seemed helpless to counter this raiding in the west, but a plan was developed by George Rogers Clark (born in Albemarle county, Virginia, on November 19, 1752). He had fought in Lord Dunmore's War and had been active in the exploration and settlement of Kentucky.

Now he suggested that he lead a force forward to take posts in the Ohio Territory; posts that had belonged to the French twenty years before and were now held by French settlers under British officers. He reasoned that the French settlers were not overfond of their British overlords and that with France in alliance with the United States, the French in the Ohio Territory would be ready to change sides. In that case, only a small force of Americans might be sufficient to catalyze that change.

Patrick Henry, now governor of Virginia, approved the plan and gave Clark the rank of lieutenant colonel. Clark collected 175 men and set down the Ohio River on May 12, 1778. By the beginning of July, he was on the upper Mississippi River and took the settlements of Kaskaskia and Cahokia without any trouble as the French did indeed change sides. The fort at Vincennes, 100 miles east of the Mississippi, also defected from the British and acknowledged Virginian sovereignty. (*Virginian* sovereignty, not American. Clark was fighting on behalf of his state.)

Hamilton the Hair Buyer reacted. He swooped down from Detroit with 500 men (half of them Indians) and on December 17, 1778, took Vincennes.

Clark led his small force from Kaskaskia to Vincennes in February 1779, across what is now southern Illinois, making his way through flooded lowlands in freezing weather. They shivered their way onward and on February 25, 1779, struck Vincennes. The British, caught completely by surprise, gave it up.

What Clark did with a bare handful of men was of first importance. While the British were fighting over a stretch of seacoast, Clark insured American control over vast areas in the interior. America was growing faster than the British could subdue it.

And if the Americans were winning the backwoods, they were also making terrific nuisances of themselves on another frontier, the sea. There was a Continental navy as there was a Continental army. The American ships had no hope of really defeating the British navy but they could prey on British commerce, and they did. Hundreds of British merchant ships were taken.

The most successful of all the American sea captains was John Paul Jones, who had been born in Scotland on July 6, 1747, and who arrived in the United States only as the Revolutionary War was breaking out. He had been at sea from the age of twelve, and his experience insured him rapid advance in the Continental navy. On August 8, 1776, he achieved the rank of captain.

He took merchant ships with gratifying regularity and it was he who carried the official news of Burgoyne's surrender to France. (The news got to France, unofficially, before him, however.) Upon his arrival on this occasion, he received a salute from French ships on February 14, 1778. This honored the flag of the United States, which his ship flew — the first actual demonstration denoting the recognition of the United States as an independent nation by anyone outside the United States itself.)

In the spring of 1778, Jones ranged through the waters around the British Isles, wreaking havoc on such shipping as he could find, landing on the Scottish coast, and, on April 24, actually taking a British warship named *Drake* after the great British seaman of two centuries before, who had been the John Paul Jones of his day (see *The Shaping of North America*).

In the summer of 1779, Jones was at the head of a small fleet with himself in the flagship, *Bon Homme Richard* (an old ship, refurbished for use and named in honor of Benjamin Franklin who had used "Poor Richard" — or "Bon Homme Richard" in French — as a pseudonym). He again made for British home waters.

On September 23, Jones encountered a squadron of British merchant ships, guarded by warships, of which the largest was the *Serapis.*

Counting on the superiority of his small arms fire, Jones brought the *Bon Homme Richard* alongside the *Serapis* and lashed them together. For three hours on a moonlit night, the two ships fought gun to gun.

The *Bon Homme Richard* was sustaining serious damage and the cry came from the *Serapis:* "Do you surrender?"

John Paul Jones, according to a story first told about forty-five years later, called back sturdily, "Surrender? Why, I have not yet begun to fight."

And it was the *Serapis* that surrendered, even though the *Bon Homme Richard* was in a sinking condition and its crew had to be transferred to the British ship.

Jones's depredations did not seriously damage the British economy and could not of themselves have defeated Great Britain. Nevertheless, his feats humiliated the British. It was of their navy that the British were most proud and here was an American seaman prowling their waters at will, taking warships, and, worst of all, showing himself to be more of a bulldog than the British salts.

The British people might be unmoved by fighting going on three thousand miles from home, but with Jones at their doorstep they could see that the war was not going well. So could other European powers, who, finding that the Americans were not afraid of British seapower, began to wonder why they themselves should be.

6

THE ROAD TO VICTORY

FRANCE TAKES PART

Despite the brightening outlook in the west and at sea, Washington knew that the war was not likely to end without an actual defeat of the British on the seacoast. For that, his own forces were helpless.

In 1778, the British were in firm control of the ports of New York City and of Newport, Rhode Island. While they controlled the sea, they could reinforce their armies in either city at will and from those as bases strike anywhere along the shore. If Washington could only break the line of British ships, either or both cities could be laid siege to and starved out, and the British would very likely have to quit the war.

But the destruction of the British fleet could only be done, if at all, by the French fleet and the French faced up to this. Soon after the alliance with America was ratified, France sent a squadron of seventeen ships westward under Charles Hector D'Estaing. These ships arrived in the neighborhood of New York on July 8, 1778.

By that time, though, the British had evacuated Philadelphia (precisely because they had heard a French squadron was on its way) and were concentrated in New York. The British fleet was in the harbor waiting and the question was whether the French ships would sail through the Narrows to get at them.

D'Estaing might have been willing to try it, but his officers and the local pilots were not. They were sure that to sail into the British guns was suicide. The French squadron veered off, therefore, and decided to try for the lesser prize of Newport instead.

At Newport, they were about to land, on July 29, when a storm arose. The French ships moved off to be clear of the breakers and found that a British squadron, with freshly arrived reinforcements, was waiting for them. There might have been a battle but the storm grew worse and for a while it looked as though both fleets would be impartially destroyed. When it was over the British ships staggered back to New York while the French ships limped first to Boston, and then to the West Indies for the winter.

Washington could only grind his teeth. Whatever value the French alliance might have, the French fleet, at any rate, had accomplished nothing.

As for Clinton, in his headquarters at New York, it seemed to him that with his grip on the seaports unshaken, he might do well to strike in another direction altogether. So far, the southern coast had been almost untouched by the war. Clinton knew that Loyalist sentiment was particularly strong in Georgia and if he could strike there, he might well establish a valuable base from which he could roll northward.

On November 25, therefore, he sent 3500 men under Lieutenant Colonel Archibald Campbell southward, over an ocean that was still firmly in the grip of British seapower. They were heading for Savannah, Georgia, the southernmost American port. From Florida (in British hands since 1763), a thousand more men under Augustine Prevost marched northward.

The plan worked perfectly. On December 29, 1778, Savannah was taken by the British with very little trouble. An American force of less than a thousand men was simply brushed aside. From Savannah, Campbell pushed northward to Augusta, which was taken on January 29, 1779.

Southern Campaigns 1778-1780
BLUE RIDGE MOUNTAINS
Yadkin River
Salem
Guilford
Hillsboro
Neuse River
New Bern
Pamlico Sound
Cape Hatteras
Cape Lookout
NORTH CAROLINA
Cape Fear River
Elizabethtown
Wilmington
Cape Fear
Charlotte
Kings Mt
Waxhaws
Fishing Creek
Cheraw
Winnsboro
Camden
Ninety-Six
Fort Charlotte
Fort Granby
Kettle Creek
Fort Motte
Savannah River
Augusta
SOUTH CAROLINA
Georgetown
ATLANTIC OCEAN
Briar Creek
Charles Town
Fort Moultrie
Beaufort
Ogeechee River
Purrysburg
Savannah
Fort Sunbury
Altamaha River
GEORGIA

The Americans fought back as best they could, winning some minor battles on the fringes (useful from the standpoint of morale) but neither Augusta nor Savannah could be retaken. The major effort came on September 3, 1779, when D'Estaing brought his French fleet to Savannah from the West Indies. With him he had thirty-five ships and 4000 troops. In Savannah, holding the city, was Prevost with only 3000 troops.

It looked good for the Americans. Some British ships near Savannah were taken and the city was placed under siege. About 1500 American troops under Benjamin Lincoln (born in Hingham, Massachusetts, in 1733), who had done good service at Saratoga, blocked the land approaches and, of course, the French ships closed the city off by sea.

However, it was late in the season and there was every prospect of storms as the autumn wore on. D'Estaing felt his ships to be dangerously exposed and grew more uneasy with each day. On October 9, he felt it necessary to gamble on a direct assault against the British fortified positions — and it was like Bunker Hill in reverse.

The assaulting force was mowed down. D'Estaing was wounded and Casimir Pulaski, charging recklessly at the head of his men, was killed, the first of the important foreign volunteers to die for the American cause. He had fought well at Brandywine and Germantown and had been with the army at Valley Forge.

D'Estaing, thoroughly disheartened, then took his fleet back to France. He had been off the American coast for over a year and had accomplished just about nothing, although, to do him credit, he had tried his best.

By the end of 1779, all of Georgia was in British hands and, after four and a half years of trying, the British could say that they had subdued at least one of their erstwhile colonies.

Balancing the loss of Georgia were certain American successes in the north. Clinton had been cautiously expanding his control of the areas about New York. He raided the Connecticut coast and moved forces up the Hudson River. On May 31, 1779, he took over an uncompleted American fort at Stony Point, thirty-five miles north of New York. He placed 700 men in the fort as a garrison.

The next move was that of General Anthony Wayne (born in Waynesboro, Pennsylvania, on January 1, 1745), who had been with Arnold on the retreat from Quebec, had fought at Brandywine and Germantown, and had suffered through Valley Forge. He had done particularly well at Monmouth where his leadership had played an important part in keeping the battle to a draw after Charles Lee had thrown it away.

Now it was his intention to storm Stony Point with 1500 men. A deserter who slipped away from the army rather than engage in any such foolhardy operation called Wayne a madman for even dreaming of such an action. Wayne not only dreamed it, he did it. On July 16, 1779, at the midnight hour, he launched his wild charge. The overconfident British were sleeping and the entire garrison, together with fifteen cannon and some valuable supplies, was taken at the cost of only a handful of casualties to the Americans. The result of this supposedly mad charge was that Wayne has been known as "Mad Anthony" to historians ever since.

Deeper in the state, John Sullivan, who had fought in Brooklyn and at Trenton, was leading American forces against the Loyalists and Indians who had been carrying through massacres such as those at Wyoming Valley and Cherry Valley. He brought his men northwest from Wilkes-Barre and was joined by another force coming southwest from Albany. A total of 2700 men moved westward to what is now Elmira, New York. There, on August 29, 1779, Butler's Rangers and their Iroquois allies under Joseph Brant were resoundingly defeated.

The American forces then went grimly to work to clean out the Iroquois. The Indian settlements were systematically destroyed, orchards were cut down, grainfields ravaged. The destruction was final and the Iroquois power was destroyed forever.

From overseas came news of additional help, too.

Spain had been fighting Great Britain, on and off, for two centuries, and she was as anxious as France was to weaken her great enemy.

She was more reluctant to do so by helping the Americans than France was, however. Spain, like France, was an absolute monarchy. Unlike France, Spain had no strong body of leftist intellectuals. There was no desire at all in Spain to come to the help of a group of rascals who were prating about liberty and democracy.

And yet if Great Britain were defeated, Spain might be able to seize territory east of the Mississippi River which, added to her present holdings west of the river, might put the entire rich valley in her grip.

Then, too, she had a bitter grievance against Great Britain right at home. Gibraltar, the strong point on the southern coast of Spain, had been taken by Great Britain in 1704 and had been held against all Spanish attempts to regain it.

On April 3, 1779, Spain thought Great Britain was in enough trouble to make a bit of blackmail worthwhile. She asked Great Britain to return Gibraltar and threatened war if this was refused. The British did refuse. Spain came to an agreement with France, therefore, and on June 21, 1779, formally declared war on Great Britain.

Spain was a weak power and, on her own, was no threat to Great Britain. She had a navy, however, and if this were added to the French ships, the chance grew larger that Great Britain might lose control of the Atlantic. If this happened, even temporarily, Great Britain might lose the war in North America.

On September 27, 1779, Congress appointed John Jay (born in New York City on December 12, 1745), as minister to Spain. The son of a prosperous merchant, Jay had been a member of both Continental Congresses. He had been elected to the New York legislature, however, and chose to attend its sessions, so that he missed the chance of signing the Declaration of Independence. On December 7, 1778, he returned to Congress and was elected its presiding officer.

In Spain, Jay's chief task was to persuade that nation to recognize American independence. In this he failed. After all, Spain had American colonies of her own and she did not wish to set any precedent that might then lure her own colonies into attempts at independence. She played, instead, for a compromise peace in which Great Britain would be weakened but the Americans remain in the British grip — an almost impossible bull's-eye to hit.

The entry of Spain into the war encouraged America to suppose that Great Britain might be willing to accept peace terms on the basis of recognizing American independence. Great Britain, however, encouraged by the developments in Georgia, remained intransigeant, and the war went on.

COWARDICE AND TREASON

Despite isolated victories at Stony Point, in the Indian country, and at sea; and despite the Spanish entry into the war; the winter of 1779–1780 looked dark indeed.

Georgia was gone and the French fleet had proved helpless at every stage. Washington's army, in winter quarters in Morristown, New Jersey, where it had been three winters before, was in a bad way again. Supplies were slow in coming, pay was in paper money put out by Congress with which nothing could be bought. Rations had to be cut and by spring parts of the army were on the verge of mutiny.

And worse was to come, for Clinton moved to expand the British victories in the south. Eighty miles northeast of Savannah was Charleston, the metropolis of South Carolina and the most fervent center of radicalism south of Virginia. On June 28, 1776, it had repelled a British force which had been sent to take it and that force had been commanded by Clinton and Cornwallis.

In January, 1780, Clinton and Cornwallis led a fleet from New York to wipe out that stain on their records. They took with them 8500 men, of whom a third were American Loyalists. Prevost marched his British army overland from Savannah to join them. (He had tried to take Charleston without naval support the previous spring but had failed.)

It was politically impossible to abandon Charleston without a fight and Benjamin Lincoln, who had tried valiantly to drive the British out of Georgia and had failed, now headed a force of over 5000 men inside Charleston.

Lincoln's chances were nil, however. By April 11, 1780, 14,000

British surrounded the city by land and sea. On May 12, Lincoln saw he had no choice and surrendered. Some 5400 Americans altogether were taken, including seven generals, four ships, and much in the way of military supplies. It was the most costly American defeat of the war.

Well satisfied, Clinton returned to New York, leaving Cornwallis behind in charge of the southern campaign with a force that was largely Loyalist. Second in command was Sir Banastre Tarleton, who deliberately cultivated a reputation for cruelty and who permitted his soldiers to kill prisoners.

Within a few months after the fall of Charleston, virtually all of South Carolina was in British hands and a second revolted colony had been retaken.

There was guerrilla activity, to be sure, plaguing the British. One guerrilla band was under Francis Marion (born in Berkeley county, South Carolina, in 1732). He managed to get away from Charleston after its fall and, hiding in the swamps, harassed the British endlessly. He was known as the "Swamp Fox." Other guerrilla leaders were Andrew Pickens (born near Paxtang, Pennsylvania, in 1739) and Thomas Sumter (born near Charlottesville, Virginia, in 1734).

Their feats served to help morale but they could not, in themselves, weaken the British hold. Nor did it help much that a Spanish force had taken Mobile on the Gulf coast on March 14, 1780. (In fact, that made matters worse in a way, for any territory the Spaniards took was unlikely to become part of American territory after the war even if Great Britain were defeated.)

To restore collapsing American spirits, a new American army had to be sent south to replace the one lost in Charleston and to balance that defeat with victories.

In April, 1780, Washington sent a detachment southward under Baron de Kalb. Congress, however, against Washington's advice, appointed Gates to command the force and placed him over de Kalb's head. There still clung to him the aura of the victory over Burgoyne at Saratoga.

Gates took over command of the army near Hillsboro in northern North Carolina and decided to march to Camden, South Carolina (120 miles north of Charleston), where Cornwallis had set up a fortified outpost.

The march was a difficult one; it had been so all the way from Washington's headquarters. Supplies were low and the soldiers were largely famished. By the time the army reached Camden, there were less than 3000 men present who were fit for duty and only 1000 of them were veterans from Washington's army.

Cornwallis, who was perhaps the best British general serving during the Revolutionary War, was waiting for Gates with fewer men, but with those few well-trained and in good condition.

On August 16, 1780, the Battle of Camden was fought. Tarleton's brigade charged and, with the forest of bayonets approaching, the Americans broke and fled. De Kalb and his contingent did their best to hold back the British but failed. De Kalb was killed.

As for Gates, he shared in the retreat. Indeed, his horse was reputed to be the fastest in America and he used it to its fullest gallop. He kept on retreating, in absolute panic, all the way to Charlotte, North Carolina, sixty miles north of Camden. Only 700 soldiers made it there with him.

This ended Gates's career, but the loss of a second army in disgraceful rout was a high price to pay for getting rid of an incapable coward.

The fate of the "hero" of Saratoga was, however, better than that of the real hero, for now in this dark year of 1780, Benedict Arnold added the darkest chapter of all.

Few had contributed as much as Arnold to the American cause and had received so little in return. It got him neither promotion nor credit, only wounds. In the summer of 1778, he wasn't fit for active service thanks to his shattered leg, and he was given the easy post of commanding the American forces in Philadelphia. There he lived well, making up for the hardships of his campaigns.

Arnold had never been popular with those officers who possessed less dash and ability than himself, and now his extravagances in Philadelphia earned him further unpopularity. He was accused of violating various military rules and had to ask for a court-martial in order that he might be cleared. The court-martial was finally held in December, 1779, and he was convicted of a couple of minor charges and was sentenced to be reprimanded by Washington.

Washington, who appreciated Arnold's services, had done his best to support him and had kept him from resigning in anger at times in the past. Now he did his best to save Arnold's pride by reprimanding him so gently that it scarcely amounted to a reprimand at all.

Nevertheless, Arnold's pride was wounded past endurance. He had been a widower since 1775 and in the spring of 1779 he had married a beautiful young Philadelphian of Loyalist sympathies. It was easy for her to persuade him he ought to do something about American ingratitude and he began to sound out the British concerning the possibility of selling them information for money.

After his court-martial and conviction, he went further. He asked Washington for the command of West Point, an important fortification on the Hudson River, about forty miles north of New York. Washington, anxious to please the misused general, agreed. In the spring of 1780, Arnold began to negotiate the surrender of the fort to the British in return for twenty thousand pounds.

The British officer who dealt with Arnold was Major John André. André had fought with Howe in the campaign that had captured Philadelphia and, after Howe's retirement, had served as aide to General Clinton in charge of intelligence. He had been at the siege and capture of Charleston and when he got back to New York, in June, 1780, he found Arnold's offer to give up West Point waiting for him.

On September 21, 1780, André went up the Hudson under a flag of truce, met with Arnold and agreed on final terms. Arnold was to get twenty thousand pounds if West Point was successfully delivered, and ten thousand pounds if he tried, failed, and had to flee to the British. The ship that had brought André up the Hudson had been fired on and had had to retire so André stayed overnight and then tried to make his way back to British lines overland.

It seemed scarcely practical to try to do so in the conspicuous scarlet of a British soldier, so he put on civilian clothes. The instant he did so, however, he made himself a spy in terms of military law. With the uniform he would be a prisoner of war if captured; without it, he would be hanged.

As it happened, on his way south, he was stopped and searched by American soldiers. Papers involving West Point were found in his boot and they were promptly sent back upstream to Arnold, who seemed the appropriate authority. Arnold knew that his treason would soon be discovered and at once escaped to British lines, leaving André behind as scapegoat.

Clearly, Arnold was the real criminal and when André was condemned to death by court-martial, Washington offered to hand him over to the British, in return for Arnold. Clinton might have been tempted, but his word had been given to Arnold and his honor required him to refuse – so André was hanged on October 2, 1780.

Benedict Arnold did not hang, but he might better have. Whatever his provocation, his treason was inexcusable. For one thing, he had been supported and appreciated by Washington at least, and his return had been to use Washington's sympathy as a means for setting up the treason. Then, too, he did not do it out of conviction. One might forgive a man for changing sides if he had actually come to believe that justice and honor lay on the side he was now adopting. Arnold did not do this. There was no conviction in his heart as to the rightness of the British cause; he did not come to feel that he had been fighting on the wrong side. He was simply selling himself for money.

It is no wonder, then, that despite all his services to the American cause, he has gone down in history as an unmitigated villain with a name that has to American ears ever since been the very synonym of "traitor."

Nor did he fare well with the British. The British officers might, out of military necessity, be willing to deal with a traitor who would sell his side for money, but they didn't have to socialize with him afterward. In addition, he was considered a moral coward for having allowed André to die for him. Though Arnold fought on the British side for the rest of the war and though he received over 6000 pounds, a grant of land in Canada, and a commission as brigadier general, his career, such as it was, went steadily downhill. He left America a year after his treason and never returned, living out the final twenty years of his life as a bitter and morose man, a failure at everything he attempted.

Yet what Arnold had been before his treason was not entirely forgotten. A century after the Battle of Saratoga, a monument was erected on the site. Four niches were set up and statues of Gates,

Schuyler, and Morgan were placed in three of them. The fourth was left empty, for it would have contained a statue of Arnold had he not committed treason.

And elsewhere on the battlefield, at the site where Arnold fell, wounded, is a monument bearing a carving of a boot – a memorial to the leg wounded in the American cause. The monument speaks of "the most brilliant soldier of the Continental Army" but does not mention his name.

THE AMERICANS HANG ON

The Americans had much to grieve over in 1780. What had followed the triumph of Burgoyne's surrender and the French alliance had been three years of bitter anticlimax. There had been the disappointment at Monmouth, the frustrations of the French fleet, the loss of two southern states, the disgraceful flight of Gates, and the treason of Arnold. Even a new naval move by France (initiated by Lafayette who had visited France in 1779 to urge some strong action) ended in very little.

On May 2, 1780, France sent nearly 7000 troops across the Atlantic on a strong flotilla headed by Jean Baptiste de Rochambeau. They arrived at Newport, Rhode Island, on July 11 and landed there. Almost at once, though, the British fleet arrived and set up a blockade. The French ships remained penned up in Newport for a year.

Rochambeau might have left his ships in Newport and marched his army westward to join Washington. He did not, however, wish to leave his ships, and Washington, to tell the truth, did not want him without those ships.

Ever since the British had evacuated Philadelphia because of the feared arrival of French ships, Washington had felt a healthy respect for sea power. From then on he held land-fighting to a minimum and to add French soldiers to his own would serve no purpose and would only lead, perhaps, to friction between the

French and the Americans. Washington was determined to wait until the French could put a fleet at his disposal as well as men.

And yet there were glimmers of light – one of them in the south where things seemed darkest.

There, with the Battle of Camden over and with both Georgia and South Carolina safely in the British grip, Cornwallis began to move north into North Carolina. Also moving north on a parallel route were about 1400 Loyalists under Major Patrick Ferguson. Against him there came swarming the backwoods settlers, each with his long rifle.

Ferguson decided to make a stand on King's Mountain in western South Carolina, a mile and a half south of the North Carolinian border. On October 7, 1780, 900 Americans swarmed up the height to get at him. Ordinarily, it would have had to be a Bunker Hill, but the Americans didn't go up in line with scarlet uniforms on, as the British had done in the earlier battle. Instead, they went up from rock to rock and from tree to tree.

Whenever an isolated enemy soldier showed himself, he was picked off with deadly rifle accuracy. When Ferguson's forces charged, the Americans faded backward before the bayonets, and then began to pick them off again. Ferguson was killed and half his Loyalist force with him. The rest surrendered. The Americans suffered only 90 casualties.

Like the Battle of Trenton after the retreat across New Jersey, the Battle of King's Mountain retrieved American morale and went far toward neutralizing the disgrace at Camden. It persuaded Cornwallis to put off his northward push till the next year.

On October 14, a week after the battle, Cornwallis went into winter quarters in Winnsboro, South Carolina, forty miles west of Camden. On that same day, General Nathaniel Greene, who had retreated across New Jersey with Washington four years before, was put in command of the southern army.

Less glamorous and noticeable than the victory at King's Mountain were other advances made by the Americans, both economic and political.

Economically, the American cause was at an abysmal low as 1781 opened. American soldiers were being paid in Continental money which was worth just about nothing and even that was behind.

When word came that recruits were being bribed with actual coins to join the army, some of the Pennsylvania troops in Washington's winter camp at Morristown rebelled and demanded hard money for themselves. There were concessions, but many soldiers left in anger anyway. Other rebellions of Pennsylvania and New Jersey troops were only quelled after a few men were shot.

On February 20, 1781, Congress, in despair over the problem of money, appointed Robert Morris their superintendent of finances. (We would call him today the "Secretary of the Treasury.") Morris, born in Liverpool, England, on January 31, 1734, came to Maryland as a boy of fourteen and eventually joined a prosperous business establishment in Philadelphia. He only came reluctantly round to the notion of independence but was one of the signers of the Declaration.

He did his best to keep financial matters on an even keel but it was only after he was given the necessary powers in 1781 that he finally managed to put some order into the American economic position, with the help of loans from France, Spain, and the Netherlands. He also used his personal credit to support Washington's army, and without him Washington might not have been able to fight the crucial battles of 1781.

Another financier of great help to the American cause, in a less official capacity, was Haym Solomon (born in Poland about 1740) who was one of the several thousand Jews who lived in America at the time of the Revolution and who was a whole-hearted partisan on the American side. Altogether he advanced $700,000, a princely sum in those days, to the Continental army. None of it was ever repaid and he died in 1785 virtually penniless.

Politically, the thirteen states, each touchily proud of its independence, managed to achieve a kind of union.

Even before the Declaration of Independence had been signed, the fact of war had dictated some sort of cooperation between the states. They simply could not fight Great Britain as thirteen separate nations making thirteen sets of decisions.

On June 12, 1776, John Dickinson had been assigned to work out the details of such a union and the Continental Congress adopted the scheme he worked out on November 15, 1777, a year and a half later.

The nature of the union, described in a document called "The Articles of Confederation" was feeble indeed. The individual states held most of the power, including the all-important power of taxation, so that Congress could only get the money that the states chose to give it. That was a chief reason for the worthlessness of the Continental currency.

What Congress could do was to handle foreign policy and Indian affairs, regulate coinage, establish a postal system, borrow money, and settle disputes between states. Even in those areas in which it could make decisions, however, there was no apparatus for enforcing them. The Congress could only ask the states to do what was necessary in the way of enforcing them, and the states might, of course, choose not to do so.

There was no executive provided for. Each state sent delegates to the Congress but regardless of the size of the delegation each state had one vote.

For over three years after Congress had accepted the Articles of Confederation they remained unofficial, however, lacking the approval of all thirteen states. The difficulty lay with the question of western lands.

When the colonies had first been established, the royal charters granted them had been very vague as to boundaries (in view of the lack of knowledge concerning the continental interior) and also very generous. In a number of cases, the colonies were granted jurisdiction indefinitely westward. Various states, therefore, claimed land to the west of their area of settlement and, in some cases, the claims of different states conflicted. This was particularly true in the land north of the Ohio River, which was claimed entirely by Virginia and in part by Pennsylvania, Connecticut, Massachusetts, and New York.

On the other hand, some of the states, through the manner in which they had been formed and through their geographic location, had no western claims at all, and had fixed and definite boundaries. These were Rhode Island, New Jersey, Delaware, and Maryland.

The states without claims were small to begin with and seemed destined to become smaller in comparison as the other states gobbled up western territory. One of them, Maryland, decided, therefore, not to sign the Articles of Confederation until such time as the various states gave up their claims to western land. To this resolution, she stubbornly adhered for over three years despite all the pressures of war and despite the fact that the other twelve states, including the small ones, had signed the Articles.

For this resolution on the part of Maryland, all Americans can be grateful. Had the western claims remained, the history of the American states might have become that of the larger ones grabbing land and quarreling endlessly among themselves over boundaries. In the end, there would have been no union at all, but only several independent states as mutually hostile as the various nations of Europe.

One by one, as Maryland insisted, the various states reluctantly gave up their claims to western lands and agreed that those unsettled regions be considered the property of the union of states generally. Connecticut agreed on October 10, 1780; Virginia on January 2, 1781; New York on March 1, 1781.

With New York's cession, Maryland was finally satisfied and on March 1, 1781, she signed the Articles of Confederation. It was only then that they came legally into being. It may be that on July 4, 1776, the individual states became independent, but it was not till March 1, 1781, that a United States of America actually existed by law, and the Continental Congress became the "Congress of the United States."

And while America's financial and political situation was showing improvement, Great Britain's troubles in Europe continued to mount. For over a century, ever since she had defeated the Dutch fleets in the 1660s, Great Britain had controlled the seas. That control had brought her power, an empire, and prosperity. Naturally, this had been envied and resented by other nations.

Now Great Britain was bogged down in a seemingly endless war with her erstwhile colonies, with her people restless and divided among themselves, with France and Spain joining the war against her. Other nations took heart and moved more and more into an anti-British position.

Russia took the lead. She was then under the rule of Catherine II, a capable woman interested in the leftist views of the French intellectuals. When Great Britain tried to apply a blockade against

France and Spain, Russia announced, on February 28, 1780, that she would not abide by it and that Russian ships would protect the rights of Russian merchantmen to sail anywhere they wished. She called for a "League of Armed Neutrality" in which other nations would join her in this action. Almost every neutral European sea power did join her, one by one, through 1780 and 1781.

The League of Armed Neutrality couldn't do much in a showdown. On December 20, 1780, Great Britain declared war on the Netherlands, which was trading extensively with the United States. This trade was slowed to a crawl and though the Netherlands was a member of the League of Armed Neutrality, the other members did nothing.

Nevertheless, Great Britain found herself isolated. The necessity of keeping an eye on all the navies of Europe hampered the British in their naval operations against the Americans and dislike of the war mounted steadily among the British people.

DECISION IN VIRGINIA

As 1781 opened, the British armies still controlled Georgia and South Carolina and were still set to move north. The Battle of King's Mountain had delayed that move but had not stopped it. It was up to General Greene to make that move as difficult as he could.

As soon as Greene took over command, he moved south into South Carolina. He was not strong enough to attack Cornwallis, but he detached 800 men under Morgan (who had distinguished himself at Saratoga) to clear the British out of western South Carolina.

Cornwallis sent Tarleton in pursuit of Morgan, who was quite willing to be caught, provided it was upon ground of his own choosing. This was at Cowpens, in the northernmost part of South Carolina. On January 17, 1781, Morgan carefully placed his men, whose numbers had now grown to a thousand, in three lines, with cavalry hidden behind a hill. All had their instructions.

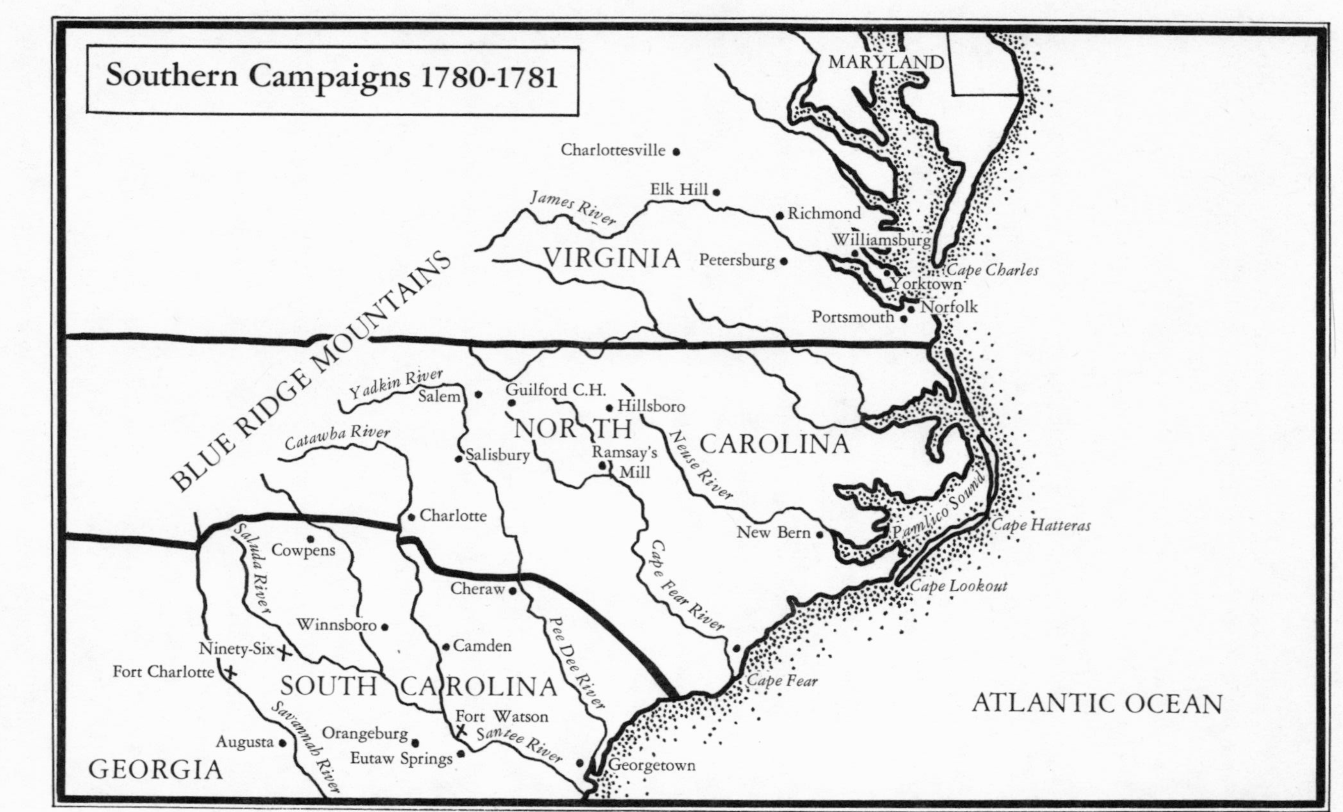
Southern Campaigns 1780-1781
MARYLAND
Charlottesville
Elk Hill
James River
Richmond
Williamsburg
VIRGINIA
Petersburg
Cape Charles
Yorktown
Norfolk
Portsmouth
BLUE RIDGE MOUNTAINS
Yadkin River
Salem
Guilford C.H.
Hillsboro
NORTH
CAROLINA
Neuse River
Catawba River
Salisbury
Ramsay's Mill
Charlotte
New Bern
Pamlico Sound
Cape Hatteras
Cape Lookout
Saluda River
Cowpens
Cheraw
Cape Fear River
Winnsboro
Camden
Pee Dee River
Ninety-Six
Fort Charlotte
SOUTH CAROLINA
Cape Fear
ATLANTIC OCEAN
Fort Watson
Savannah River
Augusta
Orangeburg
Santee River
Eutaw Springs
Georgetown
GEORGIA

Tarleton approached with an equal number of men and promptly attacked. The first line of American riflemen took deadly aim, killed or wounded several dozen of the advancing soldiers, and moved quickly backward. The second line did the same.

The British took their punishment and, feeling that the double retirement meant that the Americans would not withstand their approach, charged forward in wild disorder. The first and second lines had merely retreated to join the third, however, and the combined line stood firm while the American cavalry came charging round the hill.

The British were neatly bagged. They suffered 329 casualties and virtually all who lived surrendered. Morgan's men suffered fewer than seventy-five casualties. It was a second King's Mountain.

Angered, Cornwallis led his main army after the Americans. Quickly, both Morgan and Greene retreated, managing to unite their forces in central North Carolina and then continuing to move north. On the surface it looked as though they were abandoning North Carolina, a third state, to the British, and hastening for refuge to a Virginia which was having its own serious troubles. There, Benedict Arnold, now a British officer, was harrying the countryside. On January 5, twelve days before the Battle of Cowpens, he had plundered and burned Richmond which had been made capital of Virginia only two years before.

Actually, though, Greene had succeeded in leading Cornwallis's forces through a wearying and fruitless pursuit. By the time Cornwallis had reached south-central Virginia, without having caught the Americans, he had to turn back to let his men rest and to gather supplies. He retreated to Hillsboro, North Carolina.

Greene did not intend to allow him any rest. He received reinforcements and turned southward again. Cornwallis was forced to try to stop him and on March 15, 1781, the two armies met at Guilford Courthouse, fifty miles west of Hillsboro.

There, Greene placed his men as Morgan had done at Cowpens. What's more, Cornwallis flung his men at the Americans in a furious frontal assault, exactly as Tarleton had done at Cowpens.

This time, though, things didn't quite go as before. The Americans were not quite the picked force that had followed Morgan. Some of them panicked under the assault. Greene, realizing that the army might be endangered if it remained, pulled his men away. That made it technically a British victory, but those American soldiers who had not panicked had shot well, so that British casualties were heavy and considerably more than Cornwallis could afford.

On March 28, 1781, Cornwallis marched his men to Wilmington, North Carolina, a coastal city through which he could be sure of his supplies as long as the British controlled the sea. There, he waited for reinforcements.

Greene ignored Cornwallis now and marched southward again into South Carolina. He won no startling victories but he managed to restore the state to American control, confining the British to the city of Charleston and its vicinity.

Just as the war in the north had finally netted the British nothing but the seaport of New York, so the war in the south, after nearly three years, left the British with nothing but the seaports of Savannah, Charleston, and Wilmington.

Cornwallis decided on one more throw of the dice. Georgia and the Carolinas had been sufficiently battered to be unable to stand without support from the north. He would therefore attack Virginia, the largest of the rebellious colonies and the base of supplies for the southern American army. If it could be taken, the Americans would have to abandon the entire southern half of the country.

On April 25, 1781, he left Wilmington and hastened northward. On May 20, he joined Benedict Arnold's forces at Petersburg, Virginia, about thirty miles south of Richmond.

In Virginia, he conducted wide-spreading raids. Tarleton led a force to Charlottesville, sixty miles northwest of Richmond, where the Virginia state government was meeting after having fled the capital. There he almost caught Governor Thomas Jefferson and the legislature. The men under Cornwallis now numbered 7500, but the small American forces under Lafayette which were opposing him were growing too, and the Frenchman was handling them very well.

As the summer wore on, Cornwallis felt once again that he had better get to the coast and be sure of his supplies and reinforcements. This time he decided on Yorktown, a coastal city sixty miles southeast of Richmond and near the mouth of Chesapeake Bay. He reached it on August 1, 1781.

With the summer, though, the time had come for Washington to make his move. The French fleet in the West Indies was now under Admiral François de Grasse, and he had actually won some minor victories over the British there. It meant he was free to move on the American coast, if he wished.

In the hope that he might, Washington decided he could use those French soldiers. He met Rochambeau (whose men were still in Newport, Rhode Island) in Connecticut and persuaded him to have his men join the American forces near New York. The junction was effected on July 5.

On August 14, news of the French fleet finally reached Washington. De Grasse had the choice of either moving to block Clinton in New York or Cornwallis in Yorktown, and chose Yorktown because it was nearer to his haven in the West Indies. He sent word that he would be able to stay off the American coast only till mid-October.

At once Washington took his troops to Staten Island as though he were planning an attack on New York. When the British drew in their troops to assume the defense, Washington switched gears and struck suddenly southward, too quickly for the British to try an interception.

On August 30, 1781, De Grasse's fleet arrived off Yorktown and Cornwallis stared aghast at a sea approach in which the ships he saw were those of the enemy. It was the first time in the war that the sea had been anything but a friend and ally to the British; the first time in which a British force in a coastal city was surrounded, for Cornwallis faced De Grasse by sea and Lafayette by land.

British ships arrived almost at once, of course, to challenge De Grasse. On September 5, 1781, however, De Grasse led his ships against the British and held his own nicely, inflicting considerably more damage than he received. When reinforcements for the French arrived, the British ships were forced to draw off and leave Cornwallis in the bag.

De Grasse was all for an immediate assault to take Cornwallis then for he had no illusions about being able to control the sea against the British for long. Lafayette, however, insisted that they wait for Washington to arrive. Washington simply had to be in on the kill and the loyal Lafayette had no desire to try to snatch it for himself.

By the end of September, Washington's main army, with its French contingent under Rochambeau had reached the scene and Yorktown was placed under full siege.

Cornwallis's position was hopeless. By October 17, he saw no alternative to surrender, and offered to surrender to Rochambeau. The Frenchman refused. Cornwallis would have to surrender to the American commander-in-chief. On the 18th, Cornwallis gave in to this, too, and on the 19th, nearly 8000 British troops laid down their arms. Cornwallis's sword was given up to General Lincoln who, a year before, had had to surrender Charleston.

Clinton came with ships and men to relieve Cornwallis, but he was a week too late and, finding the Americans in possession, hastened back to New York.

Washington would have followed and launched the same sort of land-and-sea attack on New York that had succeeded at Yorktown, but De Grasse would have none of it. He had been lucky, so far, in bearding the British, but he would not press that luck an inch further. It was time for him to head back for the West Indies and there he went. (The next spring he was defeated and captured by a British fleet and the year of the French ascendancy at sea was over – but it had been long enough and had come at the right time.)

Clinton was still safe in New York, therefore, but that didn't really matter. The news of the surrender of another British army finally convinced even the most hawkish of the British legislators that the war was a complete failure.

When Lord North received the news of Cornwallis's surrender, he exclaimed, "Oh, God, it's all over," and so it was. On March 20, 1782, having tearfully persuaded George III to agree to consider peace even at the cost of granting American independence, he resigned as Prime Minister. He was succeeded by Lord Rockingham, the same who had been in power at the time of the repeal of the Stamp Act sixteen years before, and it was understood that Rockingham's task was to grant American independence and make the peace.

On April 4, Clinton was relieved as commander-in-chief of the British forces in America and was succeeded by Carleton (who, five and a half years before, had been defending Canada against Montgomery and Arnold). Carleton's task was simply to take care of the British troops pending the peace. He therefore pulled all troops into New York City. Wilmington, Savannah, even Charleston were all evacuated before the end of 1782.

Yet Yorktown did not mean peace for the countryside. Loyalists and Indians continued their raids in the backwoods and they had still to be fought off. Minor battles therefore continued and the last of importance was fought in the west.

George Rogers Clark, who had driven the British out of Ohio Territory three and a half years before, now collected forces and on November 10, 1782, defeated the Shawnee Indians in what is now southern Ohio.

By then, though, peace negotiations were in full swing. Benjamin Franklin, John Jay, and John Adams were in Paris, talking unofficially to representatives of the British government. On September 19, 1782, the talks became official when the British representative was given the appropriate authorization to deal with the Americans. In this authorization, reference was made to the "thirteen United States" which amounted to an official recognition of American independence.

The American negotiators did not have an easy job of it. Although the British were so weary of the war they would have ended it at almost any cost, the Americans quibbled over minor points and risked driving the British out of patience. The British position at sea was getting stronger and there are limits to everything. Then, too, the French and Spanish were by no means anxious to have the new nation *too* strong and they did their best to side quietly with the British against the more extreme American demands.

The Americans, however, stood firm on one point in addition to their independence; and that was that their land was to stretch to the Mississippi and include all the territory south of the Great Lakes that had been British since 1763. France would have been content to see the United States confined to the coastal strip east of the Appalachians, but the United States itself would not hear of this and it won out. The territory was granted in a preliminary peace treaty signed in Paris on November 30, 1782. (To be sure, the Spaniards had taken the Gulf Coast from Great Britain in the last couple of years and insisted on retaining that and on taking Florida, which had been theirs for two and a half centuries prior to 1763. Spain was America's ally, however, and Great Britain was perfectly willing to let the United States take care of that nation on her own.)

The preliminary peace was to become effective when Great Britain reached a settlement with France. This finally came through (despite France's annoyance at the American negotiators for pushing through on their own and gaining terms more favorable than France would have preferred) on January 20, 1783.

On April 19, Congress, which deliberately chose the eighth anniversary of the shooting at Lexington for the purpose, declared the war at an end. Finally, the last formalities were over and the final Treaty of Paris came into force on September 3, 1783.

The war was over and the United States had won its independence.

7

THE ROAD TO NATIONHOOD

AFTER THE WAR

The new nation was enormous by European standards. Its area was 880,000 square miles, or four times that of France. In population, it was still small, but growing quickly. By the end of the war, its population was about 3,000,000, of which 500,000 were slaves. Virginia was still the largest state, with a population of 450,000.

The scars of war were comparatively light. The cities, by and large, had been left untouched and except for the Tory and Indian raids there were no real atrocities. American casualties may have been 19,000, with about 4000 listed as killed in action. The British casualties are not known but are estimated to have been at least twice as high as the American.

The greatest tragedy befell the Loyalists, who had fought for what they considered their country and King. Had the American rebellion been crushed, they would have been heroes; as it was, they were traitors. The best thing they could do was leave a country that was now actively hostile to them. On April 26, 1783,

7000 Loyalists left New York City as what we would today call refugees. Some went to Great Britain, some to Canada. There were many others, for estimates place the total number of Loyalist refugees who left the United States or were driven out at 100,000. Many thousands of others remained, suffering various degrees of ill-treatment until the passions of the war subsided.

The British themselves left also. Through November, the British in New York were pulling back and getting ready to embark. By November 25, 1783, the British were out of New York City, and on December 4 they left Staten Island.

Congress had disbanded the Continental army on November 3 and on December 4, George Washington said farewell to his officers at Fraunces Tavern in New York. He then traveled to where Congress was in session at Annapolis, Maryland, and on December 23, formally resigned his commission. For eight and a half years he had had a backbreaking task and in all that time, through defeat and disaster brought on sometimes by military action, sometimes by unrelenting weather, sometimes by congressional incapacity, he had kept firmly and unwaveringly to the task.

The result was not only victory but the steady admiration for Washington by Americans through all their history, and, indeed, admiration from all the world as well.

Washington's action in retiring rather than trying to use the popularity brought him by a victorious war to gain political power over the nation was much admired both at home and abroad. He was called "the American Cincinnatus" after the legendary Roman general who, in the 5th century B.C. was called from his farm and made dictator so that he could lead the Roman army against a threatening enemy. He led the army to victory, then promptly resigned the dictatorship and returned to the plow.

In April 1783, General Knox, Washington's closest friend, drafted a plan for a "Society of the Cincinnati" to which the retired officers of the Continental army might belong. Two thousand ex-officers joined and chapters were established in every state. Naturally, Washington served as its first president. It had considerable prestige in those early years, and in 1790 a military post on the Ohio River was renamed in its honor and has been the city of Cincinnati (Ohio) ever since.

The Society of the Cincinnati provided for hereditary membership, however, and this created a storm of controversy, since many feared it would harden into an American aristocracy and that it would even support an American monarchy. To oppose it, various democratic societies were established and one of these, which came to be known as Tammany Hall, was a political power in New York City for a century and a half.

By the time the war was over, the United States was a nation in the sense, for instance, that there was a national citizenship. A person living anywhere in its boundaries was an American and not a Virginian or a South Carolinian or a Massachusettsman (although he might consider himself one of those, too). He could travel freely from state to state and could not be considered a foreigner in any of them. Then, too, the United States was represented by single diplomatic agents that spoke for all the states.

Nevertheless, the nationhood was very shallow. Economic power within the nation rested almost entirely with the states, and so did political power. Fortunately, through the fire of revolution, the states had ended up seeing pretty nearly eye to eye in many ways. There were no irreconcilable differences – as yet.

Each of the thirteen states had a written constitution, defining the role and power of each branch of government. This was a departure from the situation in Great Britain which had no written constitution. American radicals had found it hard to argue the doctrine of natural rights without a written constitution to appeal to and they were determined not to be in such a position again. Besides, the states, in the days when they were colonies, possessed charters which had the force of constitutions so they were used to the notion of a written guide to the basic rules of government. (In fact, Connecticut and Rhode Island continued to use their colonial charters as state constitutions, merely removing all references to the King.)

Most of the constitutions showed the effects of American distrust for a strong executive, born of the fight against the King and his royal governors. They generally provided for a strong legislature, which appointed governors of strictly limited power. (The national legislature, Congress, didn't have an executive at all.) Only in Massachusetts and New York were governors elected by popular vote.

In order to keep the legislature from growing *too* strong, there were frequent elections, usually annual, sometimes even semi-annual. Generally, there were two houses to the legislature, owing to the influence of the situation in Great Britain with its House of Lords and House of Commons.

The concern of the Americans with their "rights" in the decade prior to the Revolution, led to a move to place those rights specifically in writing, according to the precedent set by George Mason in Virginia; so that these constitutions generally contained a "Bill of Rights."

One of the major rights so guaranteed was freedom of religion. In state after state, government support for some particular "established" religion came to an end. The Anglican Church which had been established throughout the southern states was disestablished and became the Episcopalian Church. By the end of the war, only Massachusetts and Connecticut had an established church (the Congregational) and Massachusetts, the last state to hold out, didn't disestablish it until 1833.

Additional security for the liberties of the people was the fact that the state constitutions usually contained provisions for their own amendment, so that if changing conditions or changing opinion rendered the constitution, as written, repressive or irrelevant, it could be properly adjusted by some form of vote.

Not only did the new nation eliminate monarchy; it moved toward democracy by eliminating aristocracy either by title or by landholding. The British customs of "entail" and "primogeniture," whereby landholdings could not be sold and must be left, in total, to the oldest son, were abolished. This discouraged the growth of large estates and the inherited wealth and power that came with it.

What's more, there was much land available so that it was not difficult for even a poor man to gain a farm of his own. The estates of the Loyalists were confiscated and so was the property of the Crown. Cheap land was available, too. The states which had agreed to give up their western claims during the Revolutionary War, now, one by one, ceded their actual holdings in the west to the national government. (The last state to do so was Georgia in 1802.) Some land speculators built up fortunes, but the United States

The Original States: Their Claims and Cessions

became, on the whole, a nation of small farmers who owned their land.

The general trend toward "liberty" showed itself in many ways. The penal codes were lightened. Punishments became generally less severe and prisoners were treated more humanely.

The movement against slavery flourished, too. The first abolition society, dedicated to putting an end to slavery, had been founded in Pennsylvania four days before the Battle of Lexington. Everywhere in the northern states, abolition sentiment gained ground. It was clear by the end of the Revolutionary War that in the states north of Maryland, the institution of slavery was on its way out. The east-west boundary between Pennsylvania and Maryland had been surveyed between 1763 and 1767 by two English mathematicians, Jeremiah Mason and Charles Dixon, so it was this "Mason-Dixon line" that was fated to be the boundary between those states in which slavery continued to exist and those where it would be ended. The deadly nature of that division was not, however, to become apparent for another generation.

About the one strongly antidemocratic feature of the state constitutions was that there were property qualifications for participating in the government. Only men worth more than a certain amount in property could hold office. (In South Carolina, the governor had to possess an estate of at least ten thousand pounds). There were also property requirements for voting, though these were generally lower than they had been before the war.

The result was that control of the governments of the states was kept in the hands of the well-to-do, the large landowners, and the prosperous businessmen.

This was sure to cause trouble. The end of the war, when all the excitement of victory was done, brought a depression. Commerce stagnated partly because the European nations, having worked for American independence in order to weaken Great Britain, were not in the least interested in working overtime to strengthen the United States for its own sake. Great Britain, with whom the United States had the largest trade, was vindictive enough to go out of her way to cramp that trade.

Congress had no authority to regulate trade so each of the thirteen states went its own way, making for a kind of anarchy. Foreign powers saw no purpose in trying to make commercial arrangements with Congress. Great Britain scornfully said she would have to sign thirteen treaties with the "Disunited States."

The depression hit the farmers hardest. They were debt-ridden and their land and stock were carted off in payment of those debts to businessmen. Since the legislature was under the control of the well-to-do who were themselves creditors, there was little use in the farmers turning to the state for help.

The situation was worst in Massachusetts, where the commercial interests insisted on payment of debts in metal and refused to allow paper money to be used for the purpose.

With paper money refused, with taxes high (and proportionately greater on the poor), with more and more farmers being thrown off the land, there began to be first grumbling, then meetings, then riots. The most threatening action came when, in August 1786, a destitute farmer, Daniel Shays (born in Hopkinton, Massachusetts, in 1747), who had fought at Bunker Hill and Saratoga, took over the leadership of one group.

Shays's farmers prevented the court from sitting in Springfield, and in general made much noise but did little actual harm. The merchants in the eastern part of the state were, however, very alarmed and found that their notions about rebellion had made a sudden about-face. An army was raised under General Lincoln, and it had no trouble in crushing the poorly organized rebels. By February 1787, "Shays's Rebellion" was all over.

Fortunately, there was no bloodbath. The leaders got out of the state (Shays lived on in New York State for thirty-eight years after the rebellion) and the Massachusetts state government had the good sense to take measures to ease the situation for the farmers with respect to both taxation and debt collecting. Besides, business generally began to improve.

THE FADING CONFEDERATION

In the years immediately after the Revolutionary War it became more and more clear to many people that much of the confusion in the country (and there was unrest in almost every state and riots in several — not merely in Massachusetts) came from the nature of the union under the Articles of Confederation.

It was made up of thirteen governments with power and one central government without power. Congress could not regulate trade, so the individual states set up tariff barriers which choked internal commerce and made prices unnecessarily high everywhere. There was no consistent foreign policy that could be adopted, no unified policy concerning the Indians. There was no way Congress could take action to prevent rebellion within a state or to deal with it once it had begun.

It seemed clear that under the Articles of Confederation the United States could never hope to win respect abroad or security and prosperity at home. What was needed was the reverse situation: a central government with enough power to make it possible for the nation to act as a unit, a central government with power to tax, to regulate, to enforce. Under such conditions, the states would be left with those powers the central government did not need. A situation in which smaller regions join into a larger region, with the larger region possessing most of the power, is "federalism." What was needed was not merely a union but a "federal union."

At least, so more and more began to believe. The strongest argument against such a federal union was that the central government would become oppressive. A state whose interests were not in accord with those of the majority might find itself forced, against its will, into line. Each state had people who feared that possibility.

These fears of future repression had to contend with the fact of present chaos. What was to be done, for instance, with the Potomac River and Chesapeake Bay, the waters of which were shared by Virginia and Maryland? Must the river and bay be forever objects of a tug-of-war between the two states?

This was a matter of concern for James Madison of Virginia (born at Port Conway, Virginia, on March 16, 1751). He had been a member of the convention that had drawn up Virginia's constitution and its bill of rights. He had been particularly active in establishing freedom of religion in the state. He was a member of the Congress in the later years of the war and was particularly disturbed over its lack of power, and attempted (without success) to increase that power. After the war he served in the Virginia legislature but did not cease to advocate a stronger central government.

In 1785, he proposed that Virginia and Maryland meet to take up the problem of the Potomac River. Maryland suggested that perhaps Pennsylvania and Delaware ought to be invited also, and at once Madison seized on that and broadened it. Why not extend an invitation to *all* the states to get together and discuss the commercial affairs of the nation?

Madison managed to interest Washington in the matter and Washington's prestige was enormous. The Virginia legislature issued a call on January 21, 1786, for such a convention.

The call proved rather a fizzle, for when the convention gathered at Annapolis, Maryland, on September 11, 1786, only twelve delegates were present. These were from five states: Virginia, New Jersey, Delaware, Pennsylvania, and New York. Maryland, on whose territory the "Annapolis Convention" was meeting, did not bother to choose delegates; neither did Connecticut, South Carolina, or Georgia. The remaining states chose delegates, but those delegates did not arrive.

John Dickinson, once of Pennsylvania but now of Delaware, who had first drafted the Articles of Confederation, was elected as president of the Convention, but it was clear that there was little else it could do. At least, not at the moment.

Present, however, was James Madison and, even more important, Alexander Hamilton of New York.

Hamilton was born on the island of Nevis in the British West Indies on January 11, 1755. After a difficult and impoverished childhood, he came to New York City in 1772. He studied at King's College (now Columbia) and then threw himself into the radical cause. He fought in the Revolutionary War and won the high regard of Washington, whose aide-de-camp he became, gaining the rank of lieutenant colonel.

After the war, he became a lawyer, interested himself in financial matters, and showed himself to be a prolific and skillful writer in the field of politics. He married into a rich and influential New York family when he espoused the daughter of General Schuyler, and that helped him get into the New York legislature in January 1787, and then an appointment as a delegate to the Annapolis Convention.

Hamilton was heart and soul for a strong central government and he knew from the start that any convention designed to deal with commercial problems only could achieve nothing at all if the Articles of Confederation were left as they were.

He therefore worked to persuade the remaining delegates that there was nothing to do on the spot. Let them adjourn and call for another meeting later on. This the others were willing to do and Hamilton volunteered to draw up the resolution that would make this call.

As written by Hamilton the call was for a convention to meet in Philadelphia (the nation's capital) in May 1787, in order to consider *all* questions in connection with establishing a workable central government. The Annapolis Convention, which had been called to deal with a specific problem of limited character, had no legal right to issue such a call for such a broad purpose, but Hamilton pushed it through anyway. He relied on the mounting dissatisfaction with weak government to make men overlook the illegality and to cause them to appoint delegates for such a purpose once the call was made. He was right.

Though the Annapolis Convention only sat for four days, that was long enough. It managed to push the button for another convention, a much more important one; a convention, in fact, that was to create the United States in the form in which it exists today.

And yet the convention that was to come cannot be given all the credit for making the United States what it now is. Even while those Americans interested in a strong central government, such as Madison and Hamilton, were doing their best to lay the groundwork for what was to be called the "Constitutional Convention," a moribund Congress, under the creaky and all-but-useless Articles of Confederation, prepared to take action on an important matter. And it did so with such wisdom that it set a precedent, never since violated, which made the peaceful growth of the United States possible.

What was involved were the western lands given up by the

thirteen States and now in the hands of Congress. What was Congress to do with them? On April 23, 1784, Jefferson had suggested that the western lands be granted temporary governments distinct from that of the states and that, eventually, when population had grown sufficiently, new states be formed on those lands. He even drew a checkerboard design of states on the western territories and gave them fanciful names. Congress considered the suggestion sympathetically but took no real action.

But then, in 1787, Congress found itself with a chance to get money out of the western lands. A group of land speculators organized the "Ohio Company" and wanted to buy up as much land as possible and then parcel it out to settlers. The Congress was willing to sell (it was one way of getting money without having to go to the niggardly states) but the Ohio Company wanted some security for their money. They wanted something in writing similar to the charters that the British king used to give to colonies.

The Congress therefore decided to set up a legal basis for governing the western lands in order to satisfy the Ohio Company. The section particularly in question was that north of the Ohio River, which made up the northwestern section of the United States as it then existed. What was prepared, then, and passed, on July 13, 1787, was the "Northwest Ordinance," which followed the Jeffersonian notion.

It is a sign of the complete decay of the central government that this absolutely vital action was carried out with only eighteen members of Congress present.

The Northwest Ordinance was drawn up chiefly by two delegates from Massachusetts: Nathan Deane (born in Ipswich, Massachusetts, in 1752) and Rufus King (born in Scarboro, Maine, on March 24, 1755).

The Northwest Ordinance, to begin with, ruled that a governor and certain other officials were to be appointed by Congress to rule over the "Northwest Territory" lying north of the Ohio River and south of the Great Lakes, east of the Mississippi River and west of Pennsylvania. When enough settlers had moved in, a two-house legislature would also be established.

Second, when the population reached a certain level, new states would be formed out of the territory; not fewer than three and not more than five. (In the end, five states were formed: Ohio, Indiana, Illinois, Michigan, and Wisconsin.)

Third, it was decided that the new states would be equal to the old ones in every respect whatsoever, and this was the key point of the Ordinance and fit to be inscribed in letters of gold. Had the thirteen original states seen fit to establish a colonial domination over the western lands, and to form states of subordinate powers which would be puppets in the hands of "senior states" so to speak, the history of the United States would undoubtedly have been one of rebellion and disintegration.

Instead, it was decided that a state was a state regardless of its location, of the length of its history, of the tale of its past deeds. To that principle the United States has ever since adhered. Unsettled portions of its expanding territory have been organized first as "territories" and then as states; and once a state was formed it was a state to the full.

Fourth, the civil liberties won by the populations of the thirteen states as a result of the Revolutionary War were transferred to the territory. These liberties were not the reward only of those who had fought for it, but of everyone who was part of the nation.

In one respect, in fact, the Congress went beyond what had been done by most of the states, for the Ordinance forbade slavery in the Northwest Territory. To be sure, two states (Massachusetts and New Hampshire – the most northerly) had already ended slavery within their borders, but they were states and could do as they wished. Congress, however, here acted to abolish slavery beforehand, arrogating to itself powers that were supposed to belong to the states.

At a later period in American history when the issue of slavery became a much more intense one, this action would undoubtedly not have been permitted. It went through at this time, however, and it, too, set a precedent. It showed that the central government (not merely some individual states) might have the feeling that the "life, liberty, and the pursuit of happiness" proclaimed as natural rights in the Declaration of Independence might be meant for all people and not just for those of European descent.

THE CONSTITUTIONAL CONVENTION

There was no way of telling at the time that the Northwest Ordinance would be so significant. It seemed very likely, instead, to be the meaningless act of an ever more meaningless government, and that the United States of America was on the point of falling apart into an anarchic congeries of independent governments—unless something were done quickly.

But the nation rose to the challenge. Even as the Northwest Ordinance was passed, the work of Madison and Hamilton at the Annapolis Convention was bearing fruit. A new Constitutional Convention was gathering in Philadelphia with its goal the establishment of a more workable government.

Eleven of the thirteen states completed the appointing of delegates to the Convention during the spring of 1787. A twelfth state, New Hampshire, appointed delegates after the Convention had opened on May 25, 1787. The thirteenth, little Rhode Island, remained stubbornly aloof, however. Conscious of her small size, she would have nothing to do with a Convention she felt would end by establishing the federal principle, with the states deprived of their individual rights. It seemed to her that the large and populous states would then be in control and she herself be but a tiny and disregarded patch of land.

A total of fifty-five men from twelve states were eventually involved in the deliberations that went on for nearly four months. These were, for the most part, men of substance and position, conservative in their views. There were well-to-do merchants and lawyers from the northern states and slave-holding plantation owners from the southern states.

George Washington was elected president and since his reputation was almost that of a demigod at the time, this served to give the Convention an atmosphere of importance it might not otherwise have had. Washington, however, did not take part in the hurly-burly of debates but, wisely, saw his own role as that of a steadying influence that was above partisanship. Benjamin Franklin was present as part of the Pennsylvania delegation. He was now eighty-one years old (the oldest delegate by fifteen years) and was performing the last of his myriad services to his country. He had not quite three years of life left.

Alexander Hamilton was there, of course, representing New York, and though his pressure was for a strong central government, he played surprisingly little part in the proceedings. James Madison of Virginia, on the other hand, was probably the hardest-working man in the place. For one thing, he kept a careful journal of the proceedings, which were conducted in secret. It is only through his journal, not published till 1840, that we have any detailed knowledge of what went on at the Convention. Another delegate from Virginia was George Mason, who had contributed to Virginia's liberal state constitution.

There was also Gouverneur Morris of Pennsylvania (born in New York City on January 31, 1752), another advocate of a strong central government. He had worked on New York's state constitution, fighting for religious freedom and the abolition of slavery. He succeeded in the first, failed in the second. He had served in the Continental Congress where he had strongly supported Washington. In 1779, he was defeated for re-election to Congress and left New York to settle in Philadelphia.

During the period of the Articles of Confederation, Morris worked with Robert Morris (no relation) on the finances of the young Republic. It was Gouverneur Morris who first suggested a decimal coinage (ten cents to the dime; ten dimes to the dollar) which was eventually accepted.

At the Constitutional Convention, Morris spoke more frequently than any other delegate, throwing his weight against democracy, since he distrusted the populace and felt it was far safer to leave the running of the government in the hands of those of wealth and good family. It was Gouverneur Morris, more than any other delegate, who was responsible for the actual wording of the Constitution, as it was finally evolved, and it is fair to argue that the clear and simple phraseology of the document helped make it what it became – the most successful written framework of government in world history.

Morris's fellow Pennsylvanian, James Wilson (born in Scotland on September 14, 1742), had emigrated to America in 1765 at the height of the Stamp Act controversy and quickly took the American side. He had been a signer of the Declaration of Independence and while he favored a strong central authority, he was also concerned with individual rights.

Among those who were suspicious of an overly strong central government were Roger Sherman of Connecticut (born in Newton, Massachusetts, on April 19, 1721) and Elbridge Gerry of Massachusetts (born in Marblehead, Massachusetts, on July 17, 1744). Both were signers of the Declaration of Independence.

Almost at once, those in favor of the federal notion began to win victories. It was decided at the outset, for instance, that a new Constitution was to be devised and that the Articles of Confederation would not be used as a basis. It was also decided to conduct debates in secrecy to avoid rousing popular passions (which could be counted to be on the anti-federalist side) that would make compromises impossible – and it was this that made Madison's journal so important. Finally, it was decided that whatever was worked out at the Convention would be voted upon by conventions chosen by popular election rather than by the state legislatures, which would be sure, by their very nature, to be anti-federalist.

On May 29, 1787, four days after the Convention had been called to order, Edmund Randolph of Virginia (born in Williamsburg, Virginia, on August 10, 1753) presented a comprehensive plan for governmental reorganization – the so-called "Virginia plan."

Randolph's plan was bound to carry weight, for his own record was unimpeachable. In 1775, Randolph's father, a royal official, had washed his hands of the rebellious colonies and had left for Great Britain with most of his family. Young Edmund, however, remained behind, choosing his country before his family. He helped draw up the Virginia constitution and in 1786, he was elected governor of the state. As governor of the oldest and largest of the states, his voice had to be listened to.

Randolph proposed a two-house Congress. The lower house was to be elected by popular vote, with the number of delegates from each state in proportion to the population. The upper house (upper because its delegates would serve longer terms) would be selected by the lower house, from candidates put forward by the state legislatures. The executive was to be selected by the two houses together. And all of it together was to be a federal government, dominating the individual states.

There was more to it than that, but the clear point of the Virginia plan was that the lower house was to be dominant, since both upper house and executive were in the last analysis to be lower-house appointed. And since the lower house was to represent the states in proportion to population, the larger states would, in effect, dominate the nation.

The Convention went on to debate the details – whether popular election was safe, whether there should be a single executive or a committee.

The small states, however, chafing over the plan to make the large states supreme, presented a plan of their own. This was the "New Jersey plan" presented on June 15 by William Paterson of New Jersey (born in Ireland in 1745 and brought to New Jersey as a child).

The essential point of the New Jersey plan was that each state was to have one vote in the legislature, no matter how many delegates were present. In this way, no state could have more power than any other, regardless of its size.

The New Jersey plan was unworkable on the face of it. It amounted to keeping the Articles of Confederation and amending it in such a way as to give the Congress a few additional powers. The larger states were certain this would be a ridiculous waste of time and rejected the New Jersey plan out of hand – but that did not persuade the small states to accept the Virginia plan.

The Convention would have fallen apart, and with it the nation, but for the "Connecticut Compromise" worked out by Roger Sherman, who advanced the logical suggestion that features of both plans be incorporated into the legislature. The lower house would be elected by popular vote in proportion to population. The upper house would be elected *not* by popular vote but by appointment by the state legislatures; and in the upper house each state would have an equal vote.*

* Popular election of the delegates to the upper house, or Senate, was not instituted until 1913.

Since both houses would have to concur in legislation, the interests of both the large and small states would be preserved. The large states would have a preponderant voice in the lower house but the small states an equal voice in the upper. The compromise was accepted on July 16.

With it also was accepted another compromise over a dispute between the states in which slavery was common, those south of the Mason-Dixon line, and those in which slavery was increasingly frowned upon, those north of the line.

The question was whether to count the slaves as part of the population in calculating the size of the state delegation in the lower house, and in assessing taxes. The southern states wanted Black slaves counted as people in calculating the size of the state delegation since that would increase their power; and they wanted them *not* counted as people in tax assessment since that would decrease their taxes. They wanted it both ways.

The northern states also wanted it both ways but in reverse. They wanted Black slaves *not* to count as people in calculating the size of the state delegation, but to count as people for tax purposes.

Both sides finally agreed to compromise by counting each slave as three-fifths of a person both in deciding on delegates and on tax assessment.

In the final month of the Convention, further details were worked out. The delegates to the lower house, or House of Representatives, were to have a two-year term; those to the upper house, or Senate, a six-year term that was staggered, so that one third of the Senate was elected every two years. There was to be a single executive, or President, who was to have a four-year term. There was to be a Supreme Court with members appointed for life, and so on.

The method of choosing the President required another compromise. Some advocated popular election in order to insure a strong President independent of Congress. Others, mistrusting the people and suspicious of a strong executive, wanted him appointed by Congress. In the end, it was decided that the people would vote, but only for electors. It was these electors who would then choose the President. In this way, the people's influence would count, but the final vote would rest on the sober judgment of the electors who, it was assumed, would be wiser than the general population.*

Finally, on September 17, the Constitution had been beaten out – the same Constitution, essentially, under which the United States operates today.

Some delegates had dropped out in the course of the proceedings, and three who were present on the day on which the Constitution was adopted by the Convention refused to sign. These were Mason and Randolph of Virginia and Gerry of Massachusetts. The remaining thirty-nine delegates signed, including Roger Sherman, Alexander Hamilton, William Paterson, Benjamin Franklin, Robert Morris, James Wilson, Gouverneur Morris, John Dickinson, James Madison and, of course, George Washington.

THE ADOPTION OF THE CONSTITUTION

The Constitution had no force, however, according to its own provisions, until it was approved of by conventions elected for the purpose in at least nine states.

At once the population began to line up for or against the new document. Those who supported the federal system proposed in the Constitution were called "Federalists." Those opposed were "anti-Federalists."

To some extent, it was a contest between youth and age. The old warhorses who for years had fought against the executive tyranny of Great Britain were not eager to establish a possible executive tyranny at home. Nor were they enamored with the certainty of double taxation since the Federal government would now tax, as well as the home state. What's more, the older leaders of the nation had ended up in control of their individual states as a result of the

* This cumbersome "Electoral College" has existed as a part of the American political system ever since. For many, many years it has been an empty body with each elector voting according to the majority vote in his state. It is still possible for an elector to vote for anyone he chooses, however, and sometimes one does.

Revolution and they did not wish to relinquish power to a central government.

On the other hand, the young men who had come to political consciousness during the Revolution and since, had been spared the long and difficult struggle with Great Britain in the decades before, and knew only the victory. They wanted the strength of a federal government.

The strongest blow struck for the Constitution was a series of seventy-seven articles written for a New York newspaper. These rehearsed the arguments in favor of a strong central government with compelling force. They ran for a period of seven months beginning on October 27, 1787, and were signed with the name "Publius." The actual writers were James Madison, Alexander Hamilton, and John Jay.

Even while the "Publius" essays were running (and they were quickly gathered into book form under the title of *The Federalist*), the Federalists were winning the first battles. Delaware, with a population of under 60,000, was the smallest of the states in that respect and realized that it could scarcely expect any form of central government in which it could have greater power than an equal vote in the upper house. It therefore assembled a special convention which unanimously voted, on December 7, 1787, to accept the Constitution. It was the first state to do so.

Pennsylvania had called together a ratifying convention, too. The Federalists among them, well-organized and working quickly, forced a vote before the anti-Federalists could gather their forces. On December 12, Pennsylvania had adopted the Constitution by a vote of 46 to 23.

New Jersey, another small state, whose "New Jersey plan" had at least secured equal votes in the upper house for the small states, put together a ratifying convention which accepted the Constitution unanimously on December 27. Georgia followed on January 2, 1788, with a unanimous vote, and Connecticut on January 9 by a vote of 128–40.

In the space of five weeks, then, five states had ratified the Constitution. This meant that only four more states had to ratify so that, in a way, the struggle for the Constitution was more than half won.

However, of the five accepting states, four were small in terms of population and would be expected to accept. Only one large state, Pennsylvania, had yet adopted the Constitution and that was largely due to snappy footwork on the part of the Federalists.

By January, though, the anti-Federalists had organized themselves and the time of easy victories for the Constitution was over.

The first real fight came in Massachusetts, where the anti-Federalists had a majority among those chosen for the ratifying convention. The convention met on January 9 and there followed four weeks of political logrolling, in which the Federalists tried to gather votes by promising concessions in connection with the forthcoming central government. They had to promise to support John Hancock for Vice President under the new Constitution, for instance.

In the end, though, nothing could be done. The Constitution simply couldn't be pushed through the Massachusetts convention which was still too imbued with the spirit of the fight against George III. While the Constitution presented a frame of government, it did not sufficiently limit the powers of the government to infringe civil liberties. When the vote finally came on February 6, 1788, Massachusetts did narrowly accept the Constitution, 187 to 168, but only with the recommendation that a list of rights which the Federal government might not alienate be added to the Constitution. It was clear that if this was not done, Massachusetts at least was prepared to make a good deal of trouble.

Maryland followed suit on April 28, by a vote of 63 to 11, also with a recommendation for a "Bill of Rights" to be added to the Constitution. South Carolina ratified on May 23 by a vote of 149 to 73.

By the end of May 1788, then, eight states had ratified the Constitution and Virginia itself was locked in a Homeric struggle pro-and-con. If she, the largest state, ratified the Constitution and made the ninth, that would be it, and rather appropriate, too.

The strongest fighter for the Constitution in Virginia was, of course, Madison. Governor Randolph also supported it. He had refused to sign the Constitution in pique because his plan had not been accepted in the form in which he had advanced it. Second thoughts, however, had convinced him that the Constitution was pretty good anyway and he announced himself converted.

Against the Constitution was George Mason, another non-signer, whose strongly liberal views were offended by the lack of a Bill of Rights in the document, and by its failure to oppose slavery. Patrick Henry and Richard Henry Lee, old stalwarts of the pre-Revolutionary days, also opposed the Constitution strenuously.

While Virginia debated, however, New Hampshire acted. She had hesitated all through the spring but now the urge to forestall Virginia and be the ninth state swung just enough sentiment to carry ratification by 57 to 47 on June 21.

From the legal standpoint, then, the Constitution of the United States became the basic law of the land on June 21, 1788, five years after the end of the Revolutionary War, and nearly twelve years after the Declaration of Independence.

Actually, however, any union which Virginia would not join was doomed, so that the Virginia vote was still crucial. Little by little, Madison was answering all objections with cool logic. Supporting him ably was John Marshall (born in Virginia on September 24, 1755) who had fought in the Continental army through the war and who had been with Washington at Valley Forge.

A last attempt was made by the anti-Federalists to make acceptance of the Constitution *conditional* on the adoption of a Bill of Rights rather than merely recommending that such a bill be adopted. But Washington himself brought all his overwhelming influence down on the side of the Constitution and the attempt at conditional acceptance was defeated. On June 25, four days too late to be the ninth to ratify, Virginia accepted the Constitution by a vote of 89 to 79, as the tenth state.

In New York, where the fight was particularly dirty, Hamilton and Jay finally managed to squeak ratification through on July 26, 1788, by a vote of 30 to 27. New York became the eleventh state to accept the Constitution.

Only two states remained, North Carolina and Rhode Island, and the nation decided not to wait for them but to proceed with the formation of a new government. The Congress, still operating under the Articles of Confederation, set the ball rolling on September 13, 1788, by calling for elections to a new Congress,* operating under the Constitution.

It also arranged for the election of the first President of the United States to serve under the Constitution, fixing his four-year term as beginning on March 4, 1789. The old Congress then simply ran down and died, never meeting again after October 21, 1788, so that for five months the United States remained without a central government at all.

Various states voted for electors, the number to be equal to the sum of senators and representatives of that state. Since each state had two senators and was assigned at least one representative, the minimum number of electors from any state was three (the figure for Delaware, for instance). Virginia, with two senators and ten representatives, had twelve electors, the most for any state.

Only ten states actually chose electors. North Carolina and Rhode Island still hadn't ratified the Constitution and New York did not bother. A total of sixty-nine electors were chosen and these gathered on February 4, 1789. According to the Constitution, each was to vote for two men. The one who got the most votes would become President, the runner-up would be Vice President.

Every single one of the sixty-nine electors listed George Washington as one of the two men he voted for. Washington was thus unanimously elected as first President of the United States. Thirty-four of the electors also voted for John Adams. Since no one else was mentioned as many times, John Adams became the first Vice President of the United States.

Meanwhile, elections to the houses of Congress were proceeding, and on March 4, the Congress was supposed to meet in New York, which was then serving as the national capital. The President and Vice President were to be inaugurated at that time.

It couldn't be done. The land was too large; travel too slow. The United States, for the first and, so far, *last* time in its history, didn't initiate the Congress and the presidency at the legal time.

* This new Congress is referred to as the "First Congress" and Congresses ever since have been numbered from that one, a new Congress coming every two years with the election of all the Representatives and one third of the Senators. At the time this book is being written, the Ninety-third Congress is in session.

It wasn't till April 6, 1789, that enough congressmen had arrived in New York for the First Congress to begin its labors. And by the time the result of the electoral vote had been officially conveyed to Washington and Adams, and they had made their stately journeys from their respective homes to New York, still more time elapsed. It was not until April 21 that John Adams was sworn in as Vice President and not until April 30 that George Washington was inaugurated as President.

Then, finally, the United States of America began to operate as a true nation under the system of government it still possesses nearly two centuries later.

8

ORGANIZING THE NATION

THE NEW GOVERNMENT

The First Congress began to organize the government at once. They established five executive departments under the President. These dealt with Foreign Affairs (with the name of the department soon changed to "State"), Treasury, War, Justice, and Post Office.

One by one, Washington appointed the men who were to head these departments. He appointed Thomas Jefferson, for instance, as the first Secretary of State. Jefferson was not able to take office till March 22, 1790, and John Jay, who dealt with foreign affairs under the Articles of Confederation, served as acting Secretary till then.

Alexander Hamilton was appointed Secretary of the Treasury on September 11, 1789, while Henry Knox, who had been serving as Secretary of War under the Articles of Confederation, remained in that post under the Constitution.

Edmund Randolph of Virginia headed the Department of Justice as the first Attorney General, while Samuel Osgood of Massachusetts (born in Andover in 1748) who had fought at Lexington and Concord and who had served in the Continental Congress, became the first Postmaster General.

Nothing was said in the Constitution concerning advisers to the President but Washington (who, to his own glory and the infinite good of the nation, had no appetite for power) held regular consultations with his department heads and sought their advice. These men, therefore, formed the first Cabinet, and a precedent was set which all Presidents since have followed.

The Supreme Court, called for by the Constitution, was established by Congressional action on September 24, 1789, and Washington appointed John Jay as first Chief Justice. Five associate justices were also appointed. These were James Wilson of Pennsylvania, William Cushing of Massachusetts (born in Scituate in 1732), John Blair of Virginia (born in Williamsburg in 1732), John Rutledge of South Carolina (born in Charleston in 1739), and Robert Harrison of Maryland. All were respectable and capable jurists.

In addition, minor courts were established which were not mentioned by the Constitution, circuit courts and district courts, and all were staffed by experienced judges so that a strong judiciary was established at once to correspond to the strong executive and legislative branches of the government.

All in all, the United States was fortunate in that its government under the Constitution began with a collection of extremely able men in all three branches of the government. It could be argued that never again was the nation to see as consistently high a level of ability in the government – but if so, that might be to the good. If there had to be a "best," it was good that that best came when the fragile infant nation, at its very beginning, most desperately needed wise minds and resolute hands.

Perhaps the most important act of the First Congress was to take up, at once, the matter of the safeguarding of civil liberties, as had been recommended by Massachusetts and four other states in the course of the ratification struggle. The Federalists, who dominated the First Congress, had promised to put through the necessary Constitutional changes and were wise enough to see they had better keep that promise.

On September 25, 1789, Congress, led by James Madison, adopted twelve statements designed to serve as amendments to the Constitution, and to have as much force in fundamental law as the Consititution itself. Ten of these were quickly adopted by one state after another, and on December 15, 1791, this "Bill of Rights" became an integral part of the Constitution.

The First Amendment forbade Congress to infringe on freedom of religion, speech, or the press, or to interfere with the right to assemble or present grievances. The Second forbade Congress to infringe on the right of the people to bear arms.

The Third Amendment forbade the quartering of soldiers in houses without the consent of the owner (one of the pre-Revolutionary grievances against Great Britain), and the Fourth forbade unreasonable searches and seizures (another of the grievances).

The Fifth Amendment forbade placing people on trial twice for the same offense, or forcing a person to be a witness against himself, or imprisonment or confiscation without due process of law.

The Sixth Amendment assured individuals of speedy trials; the Seventh Amendment of trial by jury; the Eighth Amendment guarded him against excessive bail or against cruel and unusual punishments.

The Ninth Amendment carefully explained that just because certain rights were specifically mentioned did not mean that those rights not mentioned were specifically denied.

The Tenth Amendment was a special protector of the states, rather than individuals, for it stated that any rights not specifically granted the Federal government by the Constitution were reserved for the states.

A soon as the Bill of Rights was submitted to the states, North Carolina reconsidered its refusal to ratify the Constitution. It called a convention and, on November 21, 1789, became the twelfth state to ratify the Constitution, by a vote of 184 to 77. It was not till May 29, 1790, that stubborn Rhode Island (helped along by a threat to raise tariff barriers against it) finally joined the rest of the nation and became the thirteenth state to ratify the Constitution, and then only by a vote of 34 to 32.

The nation, under the Constitution, was at last complete and, as it happened, its statistics were presented to the public in the same year. In 1790, the first Census of the United States was carried through and published, and it was arranged to carry through similar censuses every ten years thereafter.

In 1790, the young nation had a population of 3,929,214, fairly evenly divided between the seven states north of the Mason-Dixon line and the six states to the south. It was a rural nation with only 1/30 of its population living in cities. The largest city, Philadelphia, had a population of 42,444. New York was next with 33,131, and Boston third with 18,038.

The number of Black slaves included in the population was just under 700,000, or 18 per cent of the whole. Of these, 300,000 were in the state of Virginia so that its population at the time was 40 per cent Black slaves. The states north of the Mason-Dixon line were not yet in a condition of non-slavery. There were 40,000 Black slaves in the northern states, half of them in New York. Only Massachusetts reported no slaves at all in 1790.

THE NEW FINANCE

The most active and able member of this altogether active and able first administration was Alexander Hamilton, the Secretary of the Treasury. He realized that the United States would not be able to progress far without financial support from the European nations. In order to get money when needed from abroad, the nation had to establish credit; that is, make it plain that money borrowed would be repaid with interest.

The best way to do this was to take care of the debts the nation already had. The United States had piled up a debt of nearly twelve million dollars to European nations (chiefly to France and the Netherlands) in the course of the Revolutionary War, and forty million dollars to various people and organizations within the United States itself.

Hamilton suggested, in a report to Congress on January 14, 1790, that the United States should accept full responsibility for the entire debt, foreign and domestic, and that it issue new bonds as earnest for repayment, these bonds being exchanged for the old certificates issued by the Continental Congress at their full, original value. The new bonds would include interest at six per cent.

Hamilton went on to another point, which was that the United States should also assume the entire indebtedness of the individual states. There were two reasons why he favored this. In the first place, the credit of the United States would not be placed on a sufficiently stable basis, if the central government paid its debts but the individual states did not. Secondly, the central government would be strengthened if the business people of the nation looked to it as an investment rather than to the individual states.

Naturally, money to pay all these debts would have to be found and Hamilton suggested the sale of western lands for the purpose, as well as Federal taxes in the form of new excise taxes and higher tariffs. Such taxes, when imposed by Great Britain, had roused the Revolution but matters were different now. It was an American Congress, not a British Parliament, that would be imposing them for one thing. For another, Hamilton's view was that increasing foreign trade and foreign loans that would follow the establishment of credit would so increase prosperity that the new taxes would be easy to pay.

On the surface, all this sounded well and yet there were objections and pretty reasonable ones, too. The payment of the foreign debt couldn't be argued about, but the payment, in full, of the domestic debt had its unjust side.

Many farmers, veterans, and small businessmen had held certificates of indebtedness from the Continental Congress for material which Congress had bought but for which it had never paid. They had held them as long as they could, but when hard times came, they had sold those certificates for needed cash to those people who had cash to spare. Naturally, the purchase of those certificates was highly speculative because it might turn out that the American government might repudiate them and never pay.

Speculators, therefore, paid much less for the certificates than face value. A man who was hard up and who had a piece of paper that was theoretically worth a hundred dollars would sell it for ten dollars cold cash. That would be money he would at least have right then when he needed it. The speculator stood to lose ten dollars if the government repudiated the debt, or make ninety dollars if it accepted it.

Now Hamilton suggested that the government would pay all the old debts in full and the speculators rejoiced. All the farmers and other people in difficulties who had been forced to sell their certificates were left holding the bag. It was they who had dealt with the government, and had waited for payment, and now it was someone else who would be paid.

It seemed unjust, and many of the leading men in government made their voices heard on the side of the poor. They suggested that payment in full should be made to the first holders of the certificates; that speculators be paid less.

Hamilton was opposed to that. He was in sympathy with the well-to-do merchant class, whom he considered the able and worthwhile members of society. If a poor man lacked sufficient faith in the government to hold on to his certificates, was that not his own fault? And for the government to discriminate between some holders and other holders would be bad business and hurt credit.

The issue split the Federalist Party. Thomas Jefferson and James Madison felt that it was the farmer and not the businessman who was the backbone of the nation and they were anxious to prevent a concentration of wealth and power among the few. Where Hamilton (backed by Washington who admired the younger man greatly) wished to see the United States governed by the "best people," Jefferson and Madison espoused democratic notions and wanted the United States governed by all the people.

Jefferson and Madison also opposed Hamilton's desire for high tariffs. By raising prices on foreign manufactured goods, Hamilton hoped to force the United States to turn to such goods manufactured at home. This would strengthen American industry at the expense of its farmers who would have to pay higher prices for inferior manufactured products. Hamilton felt that this would pay off in the long run, however, when the United States became an industrial nation, but Jefferson and Madison wished to keep the United States a nation of small and independent farmers, feeling that only so could civic virtue be maintained and the corruption of big cities and big governments kept out.

In modern terms, we might say that Hamilton and Washington were conservatives, Jefferson and Madison liberals.

Both developed a following. The followers of Hamilton and Washington who favored a strong central government in control of the finances of the nation still called themselves Federalists. Those who followed Jefferson and Madison, and who now felt that the pendulum was swinging too far in the direction of centralization and who wished for a more democratic republic, eventually came to call themselves "Democratic-Republicans." This was the beginning of the party system in the United States.

The party system quickly took on a sectional tinge, thanks to Hamilton's scheme to have the Federal government take over the debts of the individual states. The trouble was that some states had huge debts which they had made little attempt to pay off, while others had already paid off much of their debts.

Naturally, those states with large debts were delighted to unload them on the Federal government, while those states with small debts felt that they were being penalized for their thrift and stability by being asked to bear a share of the indebtedness of wastrel states.

As it happened, the New England states had the largest debts and had a commercial economy that would be benefited by Hamilton's financial program. The southern states had the smallest debts and would be most hurt by Hamilton's program. It followed, then, that New England became strongly Federalist and the southern states became strongly Democratic-Republican. The middle states remained on the fence.

The southern states managed to raise the necessary votes to defeat, by a narrow margin of 31 to 29, the bill that would provide for the assumption of state debts by the federal government.

Hamilton, a resourceful man, cast about for something he knew the South would want, something that could be given them in exchange for giving in to the assumption of the state debts. That something involved the question of the capital of the United States.

During the Revolutionary War, Philadelphia had been the capital in the sense that it was the place where the Continental Congress met. There the Declaration of Independence had been signed;

there the Constitutional Convention had met. And it was, after all, the largest and most progressive city in the nation.

It was in New York, the second largest city, that Washington had been inaugurated, and it served as capital for a while. Both Philadelphia and New York were, of course, northern cities.

There were disadvantages, however, to making Philadelphia or New York or, indeed, any large city, capital of the United States. In the first place, such cities had large populations that could become unruly when discontented. Thus, in 1783 a mutiny of unpaid soldiers in Philadelphia had forced Congress to decamp hastily and to assemble, temporarily, in Princeton, New Jersey, and, in 1785, in New York. For another, the various cities were under the jurisdiction of one state or another and the Federal government could not be sure that a particular state would properly defend it, especially if that state were discontented with congressional action.

What was needed was to construct a new city, not associated with any state, and one given over primarily to the machinery of government. The chief question, though, was where such a city was to be located.

A sensible place might be along the Potomac River, the boundary between Maryland and Virginia. That was a central location just about midway along the settled coastal strip of the United States. And, since it was south of the Mason-Dixon line, the southern states preferred that location. In particular, Virginia wanted it there and Virginia was the very center of the gathering Democratic-Republican opposition.

In June of 1790, Hamilton met with Madison and offered to get northern support for a capital on the Potomac, in return for southern support of the assumption of state debts by the Federal government. The compromise went through. Enough southern votes were switched to assumption for Hamilton's program to be accepted, and the capital of the United States was fixed on the Potomac River, where it still is today. The capital was to move to Philadelphia till the new site was ready.

A site was laid out in the form of a square, ten miles on each side (the maximum size permitted by the Constitution), straddling the Potomac River, the northeastern two thirds in Maryland, the southwestern third in Virginia. The two states ceded the land to the

Federal government so that there would be no question of any state authority over the Federal capital.

All the development took place in the Maryland section and, in 1847, the Virginia portion was ceded back to that state. The Federal capital is now included entirely on the Maryland side of the Potomac, three sides of a square fronting on the river, with an area of sixty-nine square miles. The area is the "District of Columbia" in honor of Columbus, of course, who discovered America, and also because Columbia had become a poetic synonym for the United States. The city that grew up within it was inevitably named for George Washington.

The planning of the city was assigned to Pierre Charles L'Enfant (born in Paris in 1754), an engineer who had served in the Revolutionary War. He evolved a plan of broad streets radiating out from the part of the city in which the Executive Mansion and the congressional hall were to be placed. (The later was eventually to be called the "Capitol" in imitation of a similar building in ancient Rome.) Between the Executive Mansion and the Capitol was to be a broad avenue.

L'Enfant's plan was too much for the United States to afford and he was dismissed. The capital city then proceeded to grow in haphazard and clumsy fashion. It wasn't till 1901 that L'Enfant's plans were dug out of obscurity and imposed upon the still-growing city.

Hamilton's success in establishing the Federal government as responsible for all state debts at face value led him to a further extension of the Federal power over the economy. He pushed for the establishment of a "Bank of the United States," a bank to serve the Federal government, one that would control and regulate the various state banks and, in particular, control the paper money of the nation.

Jefferson, and those who followed him, opposed such a bank, and argued that the Constitution did not give the Federal government the power to establish such a bank. Hamilton argued that even if the Constitution did not mention such a bank specifically, the whole tenor of the Constitution *implied* such a bank. How could the government collect taxes and regulate trade efficiently without such a bank?

This began the argument between the "strict constructionists" who believed in taking the Constitution very exactly and not going an inch beyond its clearly expressed provisions, and the "loose constructionists" who wished to reason out all sorts of implications from what it said. This argument has been proceeding in the United States ever since with those in power usually loose constructionists and those in opposition strict constructionists.

On the whole, the loose constructionists have won out time after time, and the Federal government has grown steadily stronger with the years and is stronger now than it has ever been.

In 1791, Hamilton, the loose constructionist, won out over Jefferson, the strict constructionist, and the Bank of the United States was voted into existence. It began business operations on December 12, 1791.

The Bank of the United States had a new system of coinage to handle. On the advice of Gouverneur Morris, the British pounds, shillings, and pence were abandoned in favor of the much more sensible decimal coinage we use today. The basic unit, the "dollar," got its name and value from the Spanish peso, which was called a dollar by the Americans.

The Bank acted to control the amount of paper money in circulation and, in doing so, kept the value of the paper money from dropping. This generally favored the commercial classes who were usually creditors since they did not have to accept cheap paper money in payment for their debts. It worked against the rural classes who were generally debtors.

The initial victory by Hamilton and the Federalists during the first years of the Federal government appears, on the whole, to have been a good thing. The United States was placed on a sound financial basis and the principle of a strong Federal government was established. Had either of these developments failed, it is doubtful if the United States could have withstood the vicissitudes ahead.

THE NEW STATES

Another precedent of the greatest importance for the future

existence of the United States was set in 1791. That was the matter of the admission of new states.

To be sure, the Northwest Ordinance had dealt with the future admission of new states on an equal basis with the old, but that was in a restricted territory, the region north of the Ohio River, and it was under the Articles of Confederation. How would it be under the new Constitution?

Under the Constitution, the Federal government was continuing to receive title to western lands outside the boundaries of the thirteen original states. North Carolina gave up all its western titles in 1790 after it had ratified the Constitution, and only Georgia continued to maintain claims to lands out to the Mississippi River. (Georgia finally gave in in 1802.)

The first test, however, did not come in connection with these western lands at all, but rather with the Green Mountain ranges in New England, a territory that lay west of New Hampshire and east of northern New York. The northern part of this territory was French prior to the Treaty of Paris of 1763 and this is still reflected in the name by which the region is known, for it is "Vermont," a distorted form of the French phrase for "Green Mountains."

After 1763, the territory was claimed by both New York and New Hampshire, and that dispute was carried right on through the Revolutionary War and beyond. It was to fight off both New York and New Hampshire that the inhabitants of Vermont organized themselves as the "Green Mountain Boys" under Ethan Allen. The Green Mountain Boys fought at Ticonderoga and at Bennington, as described earlier in the book.

In the course of the Revolutionary War, Vermont declared its independence from the British and organized itself as a state. On July 8, 1777, it adopted a state constitution which was the first to permit complete suffrage for men, without establishing any property requirement at all. It was also the first state constitution to forbid slavery absolutely.

It was a state, however, only in its own eyes. It was not officially recognized by Congress, and New York and New Hampshire still maintained their claims to its territory, although they did nothing about it. In fact, if not in law, Vermont was an independent republic and remained so throughout the period of the Articles of Confederation.

Barring attempts to end this situation by force, which nobody wanted to do, the matter had to be regularized. In 1790, both New York and New Hampshire gave up their claims. In January 1791, Vermont formally adopted the United States Constitution and, on March 4, it was accepted into the Union as the fourteenth state. It had all the rights of the other thirteen states and was in no way penalized for not having been one of the states whose delegates had signed the Declaration of Independence.

The next year, it was the turn of the territory west of Virginia. For many years, Virginia had considered it part of its own territory and had at one time organized it as the county of Kentucky (from the name of the Kentucky River, which was in turn from an Indian word which may have meant "meadowland"). After the Revolutionary War, settlers flooded in and Virginia ceded it to the Federal government. It entered the Union under the name of Kentucky on June 1, 1792, as the fifteenth state. Its state constitution permitted slavery.

After Kentucky's entrance into the Union, Congress decreed that, as of May 1, 1795, the American flag would consist of fifteen stripes and fifteen stars, as a symbol of the acceptance of the new states on a par with the old. The addition of one stripe for each state was seen at once to prove unwieldy, and the flag remained unchanged for a quarter of a century even though five more states had by then been admitted to the Union.

It was not till 1818 that it occurred to Congress to leave the stripes at the original thirteen and to increase only the number of stars. The stars have kept pace with the states ever since, and the present American flag has fifty stars.

The equal powers of the new states were on display at once, for they had the chance to select electors and vote for President in 1792 as George Washington's term of office approached its expiration. On the whole, his presidency had been remarkably successful. The United States was on its feet and the Constitution was working.

Yet the election of 1792 presented the nation with a crisis. Who was to succeed Washington? Could he perhaps succeed himself and be elected for a second term? The Constitution said nothing at all about whether a President might serve one term, two, or as many as he could before dying.

Ideally, in a democracy, as many people take their turns governing as possible. If a precedent is established whereby Presidents can be re-elected, the possibility of a consolidation of power might make it easy for a President to convert himself into a dictator for life, with successive re-elections every four years a mere formality.

Certainly, Jefferson and those who agreed with his views had this in mind and might have been content to see a one-term limit which would allow Washington to step aside, especially since he was more and more pro-Hamilton in his outlook.

And yet the feud between Jefferson and Hamilton, and the hostility between the Democratic-Republicans and the Federalists, had grown so deep that there seemed no chance of agreeing on anyone but Washington or of carrying through an election without him that would not be so bitter as to wound the nation, perhaps fatally.

At all costs, there must be no party fight in 1792, and that meant that Washington must continue as President, since he was the only person on whom all sides could agree. Then, after four more years, the nation might prove strong enough to withstand an election argument.

Washington, who had consistently tried to stay above partisan politics (though his sympathies were with Hamilton) understood the situation and reluctantly agreed to offer himself for the presidency once again.

The electors gathered in Philadelphia on December 5, 1792, and every one of them voted for Washington, who got 132 votes and was, for a second time, unanimously elected President of the United States.

Of the electors, seventy-seven voted for John Adams in addition to Washington. With the second highest number of votes he was Vice President again. Those electors who were Democratic-Republicans, however, voted for George Clinton of New York as their number two candidate.

Clinton (born in Little Britain, New York, on July 26, 1739) had been an outspoken anti-Federalist and, as governor of New York, had fought ratification of the Constitution with all his might. Along with Robert Livingston (who had been on the committee that had drawn up the Declaration of Independence) and Aaron Burr of New York (born in Newark, New Jersey, on February 6, 1756), Clinton had helped organize the Democratic-Republican Party with Jefferson and Madison. Jefferson was not entirely in sympathy with these northerners, but it was important to have the party represented in the north, if it were to have any power at all.

Clinton got only 50 votes (Jefferson had 4 and Burr 1) which shows that the Federalist Party was still in control of the nation. It maintained its control of the Senate, too, for the Third Congress was Federalist by 17 to 13, compared with 16 to 13 for the Second. Control of the House, however, which had been 37 to 33 for the Federalists in the 1790 elections, passed to the Democratic-Republicans in 1792, 57 to 48.

THE INDIANS

Washington's first term was a time of peace abroad for the United States, but there was no peace on the western frontier. Beyond the Alleghenies, there were still the Indians.

Incorporated now within American territory, the Indians were nevertheless not American citizens and there was ingrained hostility against them on the part of frontiersmen. The Indians held land which they populated thinly and left very much as it always had been, while the American frontiersmen wanted land which they could cut up into farms and on which they could found cities where millions of men could live.

The American government professed idealistic principles by which Indians were not to be molested and harassed, and were to be encouraged to become civilized; that is, to become farmers. Their right to their land and their liberty was accepted in the Northwest Ordinance and in an early declaration by the First Congress. Nevertheless, the government was, in this matter, weak and distant, while the frontiersmen were on the spot and were determined.

Little by little, Indian lands were bought from Indians, either with or without a little military persuasion. Treaties were signed with Indians after each acquisition, all nicely sworn to and registered, and regularly broken by Americans in the next push for land.

The Indians, as always, won on very few occasions, but on those few occasions, the matter bulks large in the history books and is often referred to as a massacre. The slow but steady pushing back of the Indians goes largely unmentioned.

For instance, it was felt that the Northwest Territory ought to be fortified at strategic places to strengthen the American position against the British in Canada. To do so meant building fortifications on Indian territory and to this the Indians objected, feeling (probably rightly) that it would be but the entering wedge. The British, from their Canadian posts (to say nothing of some they still held on what was really American territory), encouraged and armed the Indians as a way of keeping the Americans weak in the northwest.

As a result, there began the first of the Indian wars to be fought by the United States as a nation – as opposed to the earlier wars fought by the British and the colonials. The United States was to continue to fight Indian wars for exactly a century and these were to end with the complete subjugation (and, to a large extent, extermination) of Indians on all of American territory.

In October 1790, the Miami Indians, in what is now the state of Indiana, defeated an American army unit and immediately every effort was made to reverse the matter. A defeat, unavenged, would encourage the Indians to get completely out of hand, it was felt.

The next year, therefore, the task of restoring American prestige was entrusted to Arthur St. Clair (born in Scotland in 1736), who was governor of the Northwest Territory. Off he marched with 2000 men, heading northward from what is now Cincinnati, toward the site of the earlier defeat. He was still forty miles short of his goal when, on November 4, 1791, he was caught completely by surprise by a band of Indians, and his force was cut to pieces. He reeled back with nearly half his men killed or wounded.

Washington, who had lived through an Indian surprise on the occasion of Braddock's defeat at the start of the French and Indian

War, had warned St. Clair of such a possibility and was furious. It was absolutely necessary to redeem these defeats and for that he turned to Mad Anthony Wayne, who had stormed Stony Point so effectively thirteen years before.

Wayne trained a new army, and in the spring of 1794 moved them northward through what is now western Ohio in the track of St. Clair's ill-fated advance. Wayne kept his army strong and intact and in northwestern Ohio built Fort Defiance. This was only forty miles southwest of Fort Miami, which, in turn, was ten miles southwest of the southwestern corner of Lake Erie. Fort Miami, though on American territory, was held by the British and it served as supply base for the Indians.

The Indian forces, in whose heartland Wayne now stood, rejected offers of accommodation and retreated toward the British fort, barricading themselves behind a network of fallen trees. On August 20, 1794, Wayne ordered an attack. Recklessly, the American troops sent their horses bounding over the trees and once they got past the barricade, they hurtled on toward the Indians who broke and scattered at once. This "Battle of Fallen Timbers" fought near where the city of Toledo, Ohio, now stands, lasted no more than forty minutes, but it was enough. The Indian spirit was broken for a time.

Wayne followed up his victory by rounding up representatives of the chastened tribes of the Ohio country for a peace conference at his stronghold at Fort Greenville, ninety miles north of Cincinnati. By the Treaty of Greenville, signed on August 3, 1795, large sections of land were ceded by the Indians to the United States, including the sites on which Detroit and Chicago now stand.

9

THE FEDERALIST DOMINATION

SETTLING THE BOUNDARIES

Once the nation was organized, it finally had the leisure to look to its boundaries. The Revolutionary War was over and the British had conceded American independence, but they had not left the North American continent. They remained, in force, in Canada, along the entire northern boundary of the United States. And, in conceding American independence, the British were in no way willing to permit the infant United States to grow strong. A strong United States might yet battle Great Britain for all of North America as France had once done.

Great Britain, therefore, pursued a policy of quiet harassment. She made life difficult for Americans in many ways. For instance, she encouraged and armed the Indians of the Northwest Territory and retained for herself fortified posts on American territory, although by the peace treaty she had agreed to turn them over to the Americans. From these still-held posts, the British profited enormously from a fur trade that the helpless Americans considered rightfully theirs.

The British remained not only in Fort Miami, but in Detroit a few miles to the north, and at Fort Michilimackinac at the junction of Lakes Huron and Michigan. Farther east they held posts in New York state, including the sites at Niagara and Oswego, plus several on the St. Lawrence River and Lake Champlain. (From these last, they encouraged unrest in Vermont in the years before it became a state.)

In all this, Great Britain could find justification in the fact that the United States wasn't living up to its part of the peace treaty either. Under the Articles of Confederation, the separate states refused to pay debts to Great Britain that had been incurred before the war, and Congress couldn't force them to do so. Nor could Congress insure liberal treatment of the Loyalists, to which the United States had pledged itself in the treaty. Loyalist property was confiscated and the Loyalists themselves mistreated and, in many cases, forced into exile.

In the exchange of violations, the balance was entirely against the United States, however. Great Britain arbitrarily restricted American trade and treated American ships and seamen with utter contempt. British ships had no hesitation in stopping American ships on the high seas and searching their crews for men who might be of British origin. These kidnapped seamen would then be forced into British service, an action called "impressment."

British actions, in other words, damaged American prosperity and humiliated American feelings. By the encouragement of the Indians she endangered American lives.

And yet despite this, the 1790s saw an increase in pro-British feelings in the United States. For one thing, the American Revolution was over now and the old Revolutionary war-horses were now safely in control. They wanted no further revolutions and events in Europe had turned Great Britain into the great bastion of conservatism against a revolutionary thunderstorm that was sweeping France.

Furthermore, despite all the harassment and humiliation inflicted by Great Britain on American trade, enough leaked through to keep America prosperous and it was on British good-will, such as it was, that the continuation of the prosperity depended.

It followed, then, that the Federalists, who were supported by the businessmen and commercial interests, were strongly pro-British. Surprisingly, New England, which had been most fanatically anti-British before and during the Revolutionary War, now made a complete about-face and throughout the early decades of American independence became increasingly, almost fanatically, pro-British.

Hamilton took advantage of rising pro-British sentiment to push for negotiations to settle outstanding differences between the United States and Great Britain. It had to be done carefully, of course; the scars of the Revolutionary War had by no means completely healed. For instance, Hamilton himself could not undertake the negotiations (though he would have liked to) for he was too notoriously pro-British and had too many enemies. Instead, he persuaded Washington to send John Jay, Chief Justice of the Supreme Court, to London. Jay was just as pro-British as Hamilton but was less well-known for it.

On April 19, 1794, Jay landed in England and by November 19 he had concluded the "Treaty of London" with the British. In the United States, it was better known as "Jay's Treaty."

By the terms of the treaty, Great Britain made few concessions. The matter of impressment and British help to the Indians wasn't mentioned. All the British granted was a promise that the northern posts would be evacuated and that some of the restrictions on American commerce would be lifted. Considering American weakness, however, and British strength, even these concessions were noteworthy and might not have been granted were it not that Great Britain was becoming involved in war on the European continent and was not willing to get into useless wrangles in North America.

In return the United States agreed to accept arbitration on the state debts; and in the end the Federal government had to turn over two and a half million dollars to Great Britain.

The whole mission was made into a partisan issue from the start. While the treaty was being negotiated, the Democratic-Republicans cried out loudly that the pro-British Federalists were intending a sellout. Once the terms of the treaty were published, they howled that it *was* a sellout. In Virginia, where the indebtedness to Great Britain was great and where it seemed the state might have to undergo sacrifices to pay that debt, indignation was most intense.

Jay was vilified from end to end of the nation and when Hamilton tried to speak in public in favor of the treaty, he was greeted with a shower of stones. ("If you use such striking arguments," he said, dryly, "I will retire.")

But Congress was strongly Federalist. The Fourth Congress, elected in 1794 amid rising American distaste for events in France, saw the Federalist representation in the Senate rise from 17 to 19, against the 13 Democratic-Republicans. As for the House which had had a Democratic-Republican majority in the Third Congress, that was regained by the Federalists in the Fourth, 54 to 52.

Washington's influence also came down hard in favor of the treaty. It was ratified by exactly the two-thirds majority required by the Constitution, and Washington signed it on August 14, 1795.

That was not all, though. Money had to be appropriated to put various parts of the treaty into effect. It was the House of Representatives that had the power to initiate money bills and while the Democratic-Republicans had lost their house majority, they remained strong and seemed utterly determined to block any appropriations.

On April 28, 1796, however, Fisher Ames of Massachusetts (born in Dedham on April 9, 1758) rose to the defense. He was a Federalist who had turned to ultra-conservatism in the wake of Shays's Rebellion. Now in a powerful speech he pointed out that without the treaty, war with England and the destruction of the United States was inevitable. He won over enough votes to carry the appropriations.

On the whole, the treaty turned out to be a lot better than it sounded. For one thing the British *did* abandon the northern posts so the United States was master at last of its own territory. For another, though the treaty did not require them to, the British did, in fact, cease arming the Indians so that the Northwest Territory grew more quiet and its settlement could proceed. The fur trade passed into American hands and the conditions of the rich sea trade with the West Indies were lightened.

What's more, the treaty prevented relations with Great Britain from deteriorating further and perhaps degenerating into open warfare, something the United States could not afford at the time and very likely would not have survived. The treaty only delayed the inevitable, perhaps, but it delayed it seventeen years – and by then the United States was strong enough to survive the crisis.

A somewhat similar situation existed in the southwest where there were still vast Spanish dominions. Although weaker than Great Britain as a world power, the Spanish empire in North America, already nearly three centuries old, was still expanding.

During the Revolutionary War, it had driven the British out of Florida and the Gulf Coast and had regained those areas so that the United States as established by the Treaty of Paris in 1783 was debarred from the Gulf of Mexico. All the northern shore of the Gulf was controlled by Spain. Far away on the Pacific Coast, the Spanish empire was also expanding northward. While the United States was gaining its independence Spanish settlements were being founded in what is now California. San Diego was founded in 1769, San Francisco in 1776, Los Angeles in 1781.

The northward expansion even threatened territory the United States considered its own. By the Treaty of Paris, American territory extended southward to the line that marks the present southern border of Georgia, this line extending westward to the Mississippi River. Spain, however, had operated far to the north of this line during the Revolutionary War. All of Louisiana, the vast territory west of the Mississippi, was hers and at one time in 1781, Spanish forces took a British post at Fort St. Joseph just east of the southern tip of Lake Michigan. Spain had no hesitation, therefore, in claiming as her own those southwestern territories that now make up the states of Alabama and Mississippi. To support these claims, the Spaniards held posts in the southwest and, like the British in the north, encouraged the Indians to resist American settlement of the area.

Worst of all, Spain controlled the lowermost course of the Mississippi River, with a firm hold on both banks, since she owned the great city of New Orleans. Prior to the Revolutionary War, Great Britain had had the privilege of using the Mississippi freely through all territories controlled by Spain. The United States maintained it had inherited this privilege with independence, but Spain felt otherwise. She was no more anxious than Great Britain was to see a powerful United States established on the continent and on June 26, 1784, she closed the Mississippi to American traders. The most important avenue of commerce of the American interior was thus choked off.

Spain, however, since it was weaker than Great Britain, was more willing to negotiate. As early as 1786, it offered to give up its extreme territorial claims, if the Americans would recognize Spanish control of the lower Mississippi. John Jay, who handled foreign affairs under the Articles of Confederation, was willing to accept this in return for trade concessions that would favor the northeast shippers. The southern states, however, were adamant against any concessions to Spain.

Spain then began several years of intrigue in which it attempted to detach the southwestern settlers from the United States by offering them trade concessions. The hope was that an area, theoretically independent, but actually under Spanish control, might be established in the southern Mississippi Valley.

One American who seemed inclined to go along with Spain in this was James Wilkinson of Maryland (born in Calvert county in 1757). He was an amazingly slimy double-dealer of a man with a remarkable ability to get away with it. He had fought in the Revolutionary War and had somehow attained the rank of brigadier general. He had been an intriguer against Washington, then, and had involved himself in financial irregularities. Now, having moved west after the war, he accepted money from Spain.

Where that would have ended, one can't say, but events in Europe interfered. In the 1790s, war was becoming general there and Spain's position deteriorated. The conclusion of Jay's Treaty filled her with the fear that Great Britain and the United States might combine and make common cause against her. She therefore asked for negotiation to settle differences.

The American minister to Great Britain, Thomas Pinckney of South Carolina (born in Charleston on October 23, 1750), was sent to Spain to negotiate a treaty. As a southerner, he was not disposed to concede anything of note.

On October 27, 1795, the Treaty of San Lorenzo (usually known as Pinckney's Treaty) was signed. Between Pinckney's firmness and Spain's nervousness over the Jay Treaty, the United States got all it could reasonably ask. The boundary was fixed at the 31st parallel in accordance with the 1783 treaty with Great Britain, a line that skimmed along within forty miles of the northern shore of the Gulf of Mexico. What's more, the Americans were granted, at least temporarily, the right of free use of the Mississippi River.

By 1795, then, the American boundary was clear along almost every edge. Only the line between Maine and Canada remained in dispute.

THE FRENCH REVOLUTION

Oddly, the nation with which the young United States had the greatest trouble during Washington's second administration was France, her ally in the recent war; an ally without whom independence could not have been established.

There was considerable warm feeling among the American people for France, of course, but there were many who could not afford to allow sheer emotion to sway judgment. After all, however idealistic individual Frenchmen such as Lafayette had been, the French government had helped the United States out of self-interest, and much more out of enmity to Great Britain, than out of friendship to the colonists. Any return the United States might now make would also have to be out of self-interest.

To be sure, the alliance with France continued. In November 1788, Thomas Jefferson, who was minister to France under the Articles of Confederation (and therefore played no part in the Constitutional Convention), negotiated a renewal of the alliance.

The commercial and business interests of the United States, who depended chiefly on trade, that is on Great Britain, finding it to their interest to be pro-British were automatically anti-French. The chiefly rural opposition could more readily maintain the anti-British sympathies of the past and therefore tended to be pro-French.

This situation was reflected in the two American parties from the instant of formation. The Federalists, conservative and business-oriented, were pro-British and anti-French. The Democratic-Republicans, liberal and farmer-oriented, were anti-British and pro-French.

The situation was sharpened and brought to crisis proportions by the fact that France was sinking into chaos and revolution. The government of Louis XVI, unbelievably corrupt and inefficient, was also financially bankrupt (thanks largely to the expenditures involved in its role in the Revolutionary War). Rising discontent among all elements of the population brought France to the brink of violence.

On July 14, 1789, ten weeks after Washington's inauguration as first President of the United States, a Parisian crowd stormed and sacked the Bastille, the most notorious prison in France and for centuries the symbol of the French king's despotic power. Jefferson, still American minister to France but soon to take up his role as Secretary of State, was an eyewitness of the event.

The storming of the Bastille (now celebrated as the French national holiday) opened what is called the French Revolution. The power of the King and aristocracy was steadily limited and radical voices made themselves increasingly heard.

It might seem that the United States would welcome a new revolutionary France that announced some of the democratic ideals that Americans had fought for only a decade earlier. And, indeed, Jefferson and the Democratic-Republicans *did* sympathize. The Federalists, however, who were aristocratic in tendency were altogether out of sympathy with the gathering French Revolution and became more sharply anti-French.

As it turned out, the French Revolution quickly became both more radical and more bloody than the American Revolution had been. There were reasons for this; the French revolutionaries faced a more corrupt and inefficient government, more immediate and threatening foreign enemies, and had no tradition of or experience in representative government. As the French Revolution became more extreme, American sentiment generally shifted toward the Federal side.

The French revolutionaries deposed Louis XVI and declared a republic on September 21, 1792, and then executed Louis on January 21, 1793 (just after Washington's election to his second term). French leftists, called "Jacobins," were then strong and gradually took over control. To the Federalists, the word "Jacobin" carried all the emotional impact of "Communist" to modern American conservatives.

Jefferson and his followers were accused of Jacobin sympathies and at least one sensible reform was rejected because of unreasoning anti-Jacobin feeling. The French revolutionaries devised a decimal system of measurement called the "metric system" which is by far the best and most logical ever invented. The Americans might have adopted it as they had adopted a decimal system of money, and almost did, but the fact that it had been devised by "Jacobins" spoiled it. Never afterward was the metric system accepted, even though it came close on several occasions. The result is that nowadays the whole world is either on the metric system or is adopting it; and *only* the United States clings to its own illogical and useless measurement-mess.

The monarchs who surrounded France were hostile to the revolutionaries from the start, since they felt, quite rightly, that if despotic inefficiency was destroyed in France, their own thrones were in danger. When Louis XVI was executed, they felt their very persons were in danger. Great Britain, although it was not an absolute monarchy, was also hostile, partly out of old enmity and partly out of dislike for French revolutionary tactics.

The French revolutionaries, exasperated at foreign interference, and searching for a way of uniting Frenchmen against a common enemy, declared war on Great Britain, Spain, and Holland on February 1, 1793. That initiated a twenty-two-year war, during which France won enormous victories, gained enormous power, then suffered enormous defeats and lost it all. It also created the situation that made Jay's Treaty and Pinckney's Treaty possible.

Since throughout this war Great Britain strove against French power on the side of conservative stability, Federalists became steadily more pro-British and the Democratic-Republicans, not relishing a *too* strong France, became more lukewarmly pro-French.

The beginning of the war placed the United States in a dilemma. By the terms of the alliance with France, it might seem that the United States ought to come to the aid of her old friend. Certainly, France expected her to. On the other hand, the United States was in no position to go lightly to war.

The parties lined up as expected. Hamilton and the Federalists insisted the treaty with France had been made with Louis XVI and had died with that monarch. Jefferson and the Democratic-Republicans insisted the treaty was made with the French people and had more validity than ever now that the people were in control of the nation.

Washington hesitated, then found a masterly way out. Without accepting or denying the validity of the treaty he merely pointed out that it required the United States to come to the help of France if the latter were attacked. Since it was France who declared war, France was attacking rather than being attacked and the United States was freed of the obligation to come to its help. On April 22, 1793, he therefore issued a proclamation of neutrality in the European conflict. To sweeten this a bit for France, he also took the opportunity to recognize the French Republic.

Before the United States had made its neutrality plain, however, the new French Republic had sent a minister to the United States, who crossed the ocean in the firm belief that he would find an enthusiastic ally. The minister was Edmond Charles Genêt. Since the French revolutionaries had abolished all titles and had decreed that everyone, without exception, be addressed as "Citizen," he is usually referred to in history books as "Citizen Genêt."

Genêt arrived in Charleston, South Carolina, on April 8, and, making the calm assumption that the United States was an ally, he proceeded to commission ships as privateers so that they could prey on British shipping in the French interest. In this he had the cooperation of South Carolina's governor. He also attempted to organize land expeditions against British territory to the north and Spanish territory to the south. No less a person than George Rogers Clark was commissioned to lead an expedition against New Orleans.

In traveling from Charleston to Philadelphia, through Democratic-Republican territory, he was greeted everywhere with wild enthusiasm. The parties he attended and the grandiloquent speeches he heard in adulation of the French Revolution convinced him that the country was with him, and he was perturbed neither by the Neutrality Proclamation (which came two weeks after his arrival), nor by Washington's frigid reception of him on May 18.

Genêt was informed that his activities were violating American neutrality and he promised to behave, but did no such thing. He continued to encourage Americans to commit warlike acts and, indeed, when he was warned again, he threatened to appeal to the American people over Washington's head.

In that, he went too far. The Democratic-Republicans supported France and were against neutrality, but even they were not willing to support a foreign diplomat against their own government. Indeed, his excesses were clearly moving the nation in the direction of Federalism and Jefferson recognized the fact that he was damaging the Democratic-Republican cause. He himself suggested that Genêt be sent away. On August 23, Washington asked France to recall Genêt.

France was willing enough to recall its minister since by that time its government had moved farther to the left, and the leaders of the party to which Genêt belonged were being guillotined. Indeed, Genêt's successor arrived with a warrant of arrest for his predecessor.

Genêt asked for asylum and Washington granted it. Genêt settled in New York, married the daughter of Governor George Clinton, and became an American citizen. He remained an American farmer for forty-one years, surviving to see France ruled by kings again.

The Genêt affair worked to the advantage of the United States in that it put an effective end to the French alliance and gave the United States a chance to maintain its neutrality for nearly twenty years. It also gave the offended Washington the final push toward the Federalists and their pro-British views. Until then, he had insisted on keeping both Hamilton and Jefferson in his cabinet despite their intense feud, but now he was willing to let Jefferson go. Jefferson resigned as Secretary of State on December 31, 1793, and moved openly into the opposition.

HAMILTON AND ADAMS

Not all of Washington's problems in his second administration dealt with foreign policy. There were internal troubles that, for a while, rose to the level where the term "rebellion" was applied to them.

Hamilton, in his effort to make the United States financially stable, had pushed certain excise taxes through Congress in 1791, and one of them was placed on whisky and other distilled liquors. It was a direct tax, very much like the Stamp Act of ill fame a quarter-century earlier, and it met with something of the same reaction.

In western Pennsylvania, opposition was particularly heated. The farmers there had difficulty transporting grain over primitive roads through what was still largely a wilderness. It was usual for them to convert their surplus grain into whisky, which was easier to transport, which could keep indefinitely, and which was in much demand. The tax on whisky cut heavily into their livelihoods and there were fiery meetings in Pittsburgh in 1792 which inveighed against the Whisky Tax in terms very much like those used against the Stamp Act.

A leading spirit among the protestors was Albert Gallatin (born in Geneva, Switzerland, on January 29, 1761) who had come to America in 1780 and, after a short stay in Boston, had settled in the Pennsylvania backwoods. He was a member of a committee that threatened all legal measures would be used to obstruct collection. And so they were. Illegal methods were used also. Tar-and-feathering and other rough treatment greeted the revenue agents.

In 1794, when the laws involving collection of the tax were strengthened, resistance escalated as well and, in July, it seemed as though western Pennsylvania was in outright rebellion. (The actions there have been referred to as the "Whisky Rebellion.")

The governor of Pennsylvania, a Democratic-Republican, would do nothing and Hamilton urged Washington to use direct Federal power. On August 7, 1794, Washington called out 13,000 troops from Virginia, Maryland, Pennsylvania, and New Jersey. Under Hamilton (who always dreamed of military glory) and with Washington himself accompanying (partly to keep a fatherly eye on his protégé) the army marched into the disaffected area and all resistance melted before them. There was no battle. By November, everything was over. Two ringleaders were taken, tried for treason, and convicted, but Washington promptly pardoned them.

The importance of the incident was that the Federal government had demonstrated it could take direct action to suppress rebellion. It did not have to work through the various states. This further strengthening of the Federal government suited Hamilton, although it further exacerbated the opposition of the farming community to the Federalist party.

But as Washington's second administration was drawing to a close, it came to seem less and less to be above the partisan struggles that were rending the country.

Hamilton had, by now, become so controversial a person and so clearly the target of Democratic-Republican rancor that he finally resigned as Secretary of the Treasury on January 31, 1795. He had been the first to fill that office and, in the opinion of many, was the greatest as well. He remained, however, Washington's great friend and adviser and was more than ever the power behind the throne since he could now work more quietly.

An unhappier resignation was that of Edmund Randolph who had been appointed Secretary of State to replace Jefferson. Randolph was as much pro-French as Jefferson had been and evidence was discovered that seemed to indicate Randolph was taking bribes from France. Confronted with the evidence by Washington, Randolph resigned under fire, and retired into private life. He was replaced by Timothy Pickering of Massachusetts (born in Salem on July 17, 1745) who was an ultra-Federalist and a die-hard backer of Hamilton.

All eyes were on the President now. What would he decide with respect to 1796? Would he offer himself for the presidency yet again?

This Washington was determined under no circumstances to do. He was sixty-four years old and anxious to be rid of the load of responsibility under which he had labored almost continuously for twenty years. What's more, his final years in the presidency had seen him increasingly vilified by Democratic-Republican writers and orators in proportion as he shifted to the Federalist side, and he found that hard to take, too.

So he planned to retire and announced it in a kind of Farewell Address to the nation. This was largely prepared by Hamilton, who designed it in such a way as to lend Washington's prestige to

Federalist doctrine. On September 19, 1796, it was published in the newspapers.

In this address, Washington announced that he would not serve a third term and denounced the development of political parties and of the partisan spirit that was increasingly invading American politics. (Alas, his denunciation was of no use.)

He then went on to defend his policy of neutrality, the point over which he had been most frequently criticized. He warned the nation that it should avoid involving itself needlessly in foreign quarrels. His emphasis was that the United States must consult its own interest in dealing with the rest of the world and so therefore "'tis our true policy to steer clear of permanent alliances with any portion of the foreign world."

After all, the United States was a weak nation at the time and while its interests might be served by alliance with one nation at one time, it might be better off with another nation at another time. Washington therefore said "we may safely trust to temporary alliances for extraordinary emergencies."

This wise advice, as it happened, was twisted in after years in order to represent Washington as advising the United States against *all* foreign alliances. This led the nation into a course of isolationism which worked well in the 19th century but which was to serve it very badly in the 20th.

Thus, Washington retired, and for the first time in its history the United States was faced with a contest for the presidency as 1796 drew to its close.

Participating in this contest was a new state carved out of the area west of North Carolina. This area had been claimed by North Carolina as part of itself before the Revolution and, as late as 1783, it was organized as North Carolina's westernmost county, with a capital at Nashville (named for Francis Nash, a North Carolinian general who had died in action in the Revolutionary War).

After the war, when North Carolina put into action its promise to cede its western lands to the central government, the settlers in the area tried to hasten matters by setting up a state they called "Franklin" (after Benjamin Franklin). John Sevier (born in New Market, Virginia, in 1745) acted as its governor but the state went unrecognized and in 1788 trickled away.

As the population grew, however, statehood could not be postponed. On January 11, 1796, a state constitution was adopted, John Sevier was again chosen governor, and on June 1, 1796, the region entered the Union as the sixteenth state, under the name of Tennessee, a name of Indian origin but unknown meaning.

On December 7, 1796, then, 138 electors from sixteen states prepared to vote for president and vice president.

The logical Federalist candidate was Hamilton. To be sure, Hamilton was not native-born, a constitutional requirement for the presidency, but a special clause allowed an exception in the case of those who were citizens at the time of the adoption of the Constitution, even if foreign-born. (This exception was supposed to have been included with Hamilton specifically in mind.)

However, Hamilton had been in the forefront of the battle and while possibly the most brilliant man in America, he was also the best hated. He had been accused of financial irregularities and of affairs with women and some of the dirt was bound to stick. It would just not be practical to try to have him be elected, let alone run the country.

Failing him, there was John Adams. Adams was short, tubby, vain, cold, tactless, and unlikable, but there was no question that he was intelligent, capable, rigidly honest, and deserved well of his country. He had been a leading figure in the fight against the Stamp Act, in the push for independence, in the negotiations for the peace treaty. He had served as the United States' first minister to Great Britain (a difficult position, considering the situation) and had spent eight years at the thankless task of the vice presidency, a position Adams found irritatingly powerless.

But Hamilton disliked Adams, whom he felt to be not Federalist enough and not a sufficiently intense admirer of Hamilton. Hamilton wanted to continue as the power behind the throne and he began a campaign to persuade all the electors who were voting for Adams to vote also for Thomas Pinckney (who had put through Pinckney's Treaty and was therefore popular in areas that would otherwise be Democratic-Republican).

Hamilton's ostensible reason for doing this was to prevent Jefferson from finishing second and thus becoming Vice President. His real reason, it is thought, was the hope that Adams's personal unpopularity might result in having some electors vote for Pinckney, and, at the last moment, decide not to vote for Adams. That would make Pinckney the new President, and that Hamilton would have preferred.

Unfortunately for Hamilton, this boomeranged. Some of his shady intentions were revealed to Adams, and those electors who favored him cast their second votes for Jefferson in some cases in order to spite Hamilton. The result was that of the ballots cast, 71 named Adams, 68 Jefferson, and 59 Pinckney.

Adams became the second President of the United States and Thomas Jefferson the second Vice President.

This election pointed up a serious flaw in the constitutional system of choosing the men to fill the two offices. The makers of the Constitution had envisaged electors choosing men for lofty, idealistic reasons so that the best man would become President and the second best Vice President.

Instead, however, electors voted out of party considerations. This made it very likely, almost inevitable, in fact, that the man with the second highest vote would be of the party opposed to the man with the highest vote, as in this case actually happened.

From the Federalist view, it was fortunate that the vice presidency carried very little power. Then, too, the Federalists did well in Congress, thanks to continuing national dislike for the excesses of the French Revolution. The Fifth Congress, meeting in 1797, showed a gain of one seat in the Senate for the Federalists, who now led the opposition by 20 to 12; and four in the House, where it was 58 to 48.

The worst aspect of the election for the Federalists was that the feud between Hamilton and Adams continued and virtually tore the party in half. Adams, who lacked the deviousness of the successful politician, retained the members of Washington's cabinet in their posts. This included Pickering as Secretary of State even though Pickering was altogether on Hamilton's side and thought nothing of double-crossing his chief. Though Adams knew that certain cabinet members conspired with Hamilton, his cold integrity forced him to keep them on as long as he felt they were doing their jobs well.

CRISIS WITH FRANCE

When Adams was inaugurated on March 4, 1797 (and Washington became the nation's first ex-President), there was a situation facing the nation that was more serious than internal party feuding.

France was furious over Jay's Treaty, which seemed to leave the United States commercially tied to Great Britain, and over what seemed to be American ingratitude for French help fifteen years before.

She therefore began a program of harassing American shipping and in December 1796, when Charles Cotesworth Pinckney of South Carolina (born in Charleston on September 25, 1746, an older brother of Thomas Pinckney and a delegate to the Constitutional Convention) was sent to France as minister, the French government refused to receive him. He was forced to move on to the Netherlands. France, it seemed, had broken off diplomatic relations with the United States on November 15.

This was very close to war and some of the ultra-Federalists were willing to let it come to that. Adams, however, was not ready to risk war without some effort to avert it. He sent two more men to Europe to join Pinckney. One was John Marshall, the Virginia Federalist who was particularly valuable to the party because he was a to-the-death opponent of Thomas Jefferson. The other was Gerry of Massachusetts, an ardent Democratic-Republican. (This established a precedent that in foreign affairs the opposition party must not be totally ignored.) All three men were instructed to smooth things over with France. The French government agreed to negotiate with them and they arrived in Paris on October 4, 1797.

At the time, the "reign of terror" which had marked the most radical period of the French Revolution was over and France was being run by a mild but very corrupt "Directory" of five men. Their Minister of Foreign Affairs was the brilliant Charles Maurice de Talleyrand-Périgord, who had, among his failings, an inordinate liking for money and a perfect readiness to take bribes.

Talleyrand's three agents met the American delegates and quickly made it plain that what was needed was money. If the Americans wanted peace, they would have to pay for it.

The American delegates had no authority to offer money, but when they tried to negotiate rationally, it always came down to a bribe. Finally one of the French agents said so bluntly and demanded an answer.

The exasperated Pinckney gave him one. It was "No, no, not a sixpence." (The legend arose later that he had said, "Millions for defense, but not one cent for tribute," but that is the kind of phrase that public relations men invent after the fact.)

That ended matters. Pinckney and Marshall went home. Gerry, the Democratic-Republican, remained a while, hoping against hope that France would decide to be reasonable. Then he left also.

France's stupid action (no other word will do) was a windfall for the Federalists. Adams ordered the details of the matter published (substituting X, Y, and Z for the names of Talleyrand's three men, so that it has been called the "XYZ Affair" ever since) and the United States rang with wild indignation.

For the first and only time in his life, Adams was, briefly, a popular idol. The song "Hail, Columbia" was written at this time by Joseph Hopkinson of Pennsylvania (born in 1770). It eulogized Washington by name and Adams as "the chief, who now commands." It was sung everywhere to maniacal applause and the Democratic-Republicans were struck dumb. Even Jefferson had nothing to say.

On the wave of patriotism that resulted, the Federalists reached the very peak of their power. In the mid-term elections for the Sixth Congress the Federalists gained six more seats in the House of Representatives, leading the Democratic-Republicans 64 to 42. Even though they lost a seat in the Senate, their majority there remained a comfortable 19 to 13.

The ultra-Federalists, sensing the mood of the nation, clamored exultantly for war. The government leader in this demand was Timothy Pickering, the Secretary of State.

Adams resisted going too far, however. If there was to be war, France would have to declare it. American policy would confine itself to preparations for war and to defense if attacked, but there would be no formal declaration.

First steps were taken and millions were indeed spent on defense. In 1797 the first notable warships of the American navy were built. The *United States* was launched in Philadelphia, the *Constellation* in Baltimore, and the *Constitution* in Boston. A Navy Department independent of the Army was established on April 30, 1798, and a marine corps was also established. The army was increased in strength and Washington was called out of retirement, once again, to be its head.

It was Hamilton who really wanted to head the army but this Adams would under no circumstances allow. Washington would not take over, however, unless Hamilton was made second in command and Adams had to go along with that – which meant that the Hamilton-Adams feud grew even more bitter.

There followed an undeclared naval war between the two nations, in which for a year or so French and American ships battled when they met on the high seas. Each side captured about 100 of the other's ships, and the most notable battle was one on February 9, 1799, when the *Constellation* captured the French frigate *L'Insurgente*. On the whole, the Americans had the better of it.

In 1799, the French Director was overthrown by an astonishingly capable thirty-year-old general, Napoleon Bonaparte. He now ruled the nation as "Consul" and he had enormous plans in which a piddling war with the United States played no part. Therefore, when Adams made a move toward renewed negotiations (to the horror of the ultra-Federalists) Bonaparte accepted eagerly.

On September 30, 1800, the Treaty of Mortfontaine (usually known as the "Convention of 1800") was signed. France agreed to accept an American minister and to treat him with dignity. What's more, the alliance of 1788 was formally ended and the United States entered the new century completely disentangled from all foreign alliances.

Adams handled the whole matter remarkably well; indeed, without a flaw; but in doing so, he split the Federalist party. The ultra-Federalists became so openly rebellious that Adams had to fire Pickering as Secretary of State in 1800 and appoint John Marshall to his place.

Adams was not as wise in internal affairs. The wave of resentment against France hardened into a harsh Federalist move against foreigners and dissenters. Immigrants were flocking to the United States and were bringing their European attitudes with them. Many of them, particularly those of French origin, lent their support to the Democratic-Republican cause.

Conservative Americans then (as almost constantly since) were suspicious of "foreign agitators" and the ultra-Federalists saw the chance of making their domination of the country permanent and converting it into an aristocratic republic rather like a kingless Great Britain.

In the summer of 1798, riding the height of the anti-French feeling, a series of laws was pushed through the Federalist-dominated Congress. One of these, passed on June 18, increased the residence requirement for naturalization from five years (where it had been set in 1795) to fourteen years. Another gave the President the right to order aliens out of the country if he regarded them as dangerous or suspected them of an inclination to treason. What these two laws amounted to was a blanket permission for the President to kick out, at will, any alien during a period of fourteen years after his arrival. Any "foreign agitators" would have to keep quiet.

But what about those who were already citizens or who had been born in the United States – and were nevertheless troublemakers? On July 14, 1798, a law was passed against native sedition. Strong penalties were imposed against anyone, alien or citizen, who conspired to oppose execution of laws or to harass any federal officer trying to carry out the law or to gather in crowds for the purpose of creating a disturbance. What's more, penalties were also imposed for "any false, scandalous or malicious writing," aimed at harming the reputation of the President, Congress, or the Federal government generally.

There was something to be said for these "Alien and Sedition Acts" as they were called. The Federal government was still young and untried, and there was real danger that it might be shaken to pieces if there were no restraint on the part of the political partisans. Nor was there restraint. It was a period of scurrilous eloquence and easily stirred violence.

Though it was clear the acts violated the freedom of speech and press guaranteed by the First Amendment to the Constitution, they might have stirred less resentment if they had been enforced in a nonpartisan manner. The Federalists, however, misjudging the temper of the country, proceeded to make of the laws a political weapon. Hundreds of aliens were evicted, but all were of Democratic-Republican sympathies. Seventy individuals were imprisoned under the Sedition Act, all of them Democratic-Republican.

The Democratic-Republicans, under leaders such as Jefferson and Madison, whose prestige placed them above reproach, reacted violently and found it quite easy to compare the situation with what it had been under George III. The result was that although the Federalists seemed more powerful than ever in executing these laws, they lost ground with the people.

The Democratic-Republican opposition went so far that the state legislatures of both Kentucky and Virginia passed resolutions, toward the end of 1798, that denounced the Alien and Sedition Acts in terms that resembled the view of James Otis and Patrick Henry thirty years before.

The Kentucky Resolutions (drafted by Jefferson) and the Virginia Resolutions (drafted by Madison) both claimed that the Alien and Sedition Acts were unconstitutional and that the Federal government, in enforcing them, was engaging in illegal activity.

Both sets of resolutions, particularly those approved in Kentucky, took the stand that when the Federal government engaged in illegal and unconstitutional actions, it was up to the state governments to step in and, presumably, forbid the execution of those laws within its borders.

Neither Kentucky nor Virginia actually attempted to do this and both states stressed their complete loyalty to the Union, but this theory that the states were sovereign and had the right to sit in judgment over the actions of the Federal government, remained a firm belief of many. This notion of "states' rights" was to rise again and again in the nation's history.

The doctrine of states' rights, with each state the final master over its own territory, would certainly destroy the Union if it were really applied rather than merely proclaimed – and the time was to come when it nearly did.

But, for a moment, the gathering passions were stilled by the news that George Washington had died.

On December 12, 1799, he developed laryngitis after unwisely exposing himself on horseback to the effects of a cold, snowy day. Left to himself, kept warm and rested, he would undoubtedly have recovered. The doctors got at him, though, and, following the medical practice of the day, bled him heavily four times and succeeded in killing him. He died on December 14.

Henry Lee of Virginia (born in Prince William county on January 21, 1756) who had been a cavalry leader during the Revolutionary War and was known as "Light-Horse Harry" in consequence, and who now served as Congressman after an earlier stint as governor of his state, wrote a eulogy on Washington. It was read into the Congressional Record on December 19 and in it occurs a passage stating that Washington had been "first in war, first in peace, and first in the hearts of his countrymen." The phrase has been associated with Washington ever since. He is also commonly known as "Father of his country," a phrase first applied to him by Henry Knox in 1787.

10

THE STRUGGLE FOR PEACE

THE PRESIDENTIAL TIE

The pause over Washington's death did not last long and, with 1800, the nation was ready for the battle. The Federalists had as their strongest card the manner in which they had faced down France. As though to symbolize the new prestige gained by the Federal government, in the same summer in which France backed down, the seat of the government was transferred to the new town of Washington, D. C. John Adams became the first President to occupy the Executive Mansion in that city. Congress convened there for the first time on November 17, 1800.

The successful undeclared naval war with France had, however, brought its difficulties. The efforts to build ships and enlarge the army had, inevitably, brought higher taxes. In addition, trade with France had declined while the British, under pressure from their own wartime needs, were continuing to harass American shipping. The Democratic-Republicans, making capital of all these undesirable side effects, also used the Alien and Sedition Acts and the cry of "tyranny" as levers against the Federalists.

The Democratic-Republicans had no problem in choosing their leaders for 1800. Thomas Jefferson who had founded the party and led it from its birth was its natural candidate for president in 1796 and now again in 1800. For Vice President, they ran Aaron Burr of New York, a leader of the northern branch of the party.

Aaron Burr had served in the Revolutionary War, had been at Quebec with Benedict Arnold, and had fought at the Battle of Monmouth. After the war, he gained success as a lawyer, became one of the most important political leaders in New York, and at every point he found himself facing Alexander Hamilton. In 1791, he defeated Hamilton's father-in-law in a contest for the senatorial seat from New York and thereafter the feud continued with no holds barred.

The Federalists had a great deal more trouble. One might have thought that they would automatically run John Adams for re-election, but Adams's peaceful settlement with France had bitterly offended the ultra-Federalists. Hamilton did his best to work undercover for the dumping of Adams. Somehow Aaron Burr came across the evidence for what Hamilton was doing and promptly (and gleefully) made it public. Hamilton was badly embarrassed and Adams was renominated. For Vice President, the Federalists chose Charles C. Pinckney, popular because of his part in the XYZ affair.

On December 3, 1800, 138 electors gathered to vote and Hamilton did his best to persuade at least one of the Federalist electors not to vote for Adams in order to make Pinckney President. It was worse than useless; it was Pinckney who suffered a lost vote (given to John Jay) so that the day ended with 65 votes for Adams and only 64 for Pinckney.

That didn't matter at all, however. The majority of the electors, 73 of them, were Democratic-Republicans and they voted solidly for Jefferson and Burr, 73 for each, and the result was a tie for the presidency, the only tie in American history. (It is surprising the Democratic-Republicans hadn't forseen this.)

It wasn't truly a tie, of course, since every elector had clearly the intention of voting for Jefferson for President and Burr for Vice

President. The Constitution, however, did not allow either post to be specified. In case no candidate got a majority, the election had to be decided "immediately" in the House of Representatives, with each state having one vote.

The Democratic-Republicans found themselves in an absolutely horrifying position. They had clearly won the election, but it was Jefferson they wanted, not Burr. Nor did Burr back out and say he would not accept the presidency. He allowed himself to remain in the battle (for which Jefferson was not to forgive him).

If it had been the newly elected House that was to decide, there would have been no problem. The Democratic-Republicans had, for the first time, won control over Congress, for the Seventh Congress, which would soon meet, had a Democratic-Republican lead of 18 to 14 in the Senate and 69 to 36 in the House. It was, however, the old House of the Sixth Congress, strongly Federalist, that had to vote, and the Federalists (or at least some of them) were quite capable of voting for Burr simply to annoy the opposition.

For a week, there was a deadlock in the House, as the Federalists took up the role of spoilers. It was broken by Hamilton who found himself in the unenviable position of having to choose between two enemies. He hated both men but he knew Jefferson was a statesman, however mistaken his policies from Hamilton's standpoint, while Burr was an unprincipled conniver. Hamilton exerted his influence to switch some of the Federalist votes to Jefferson and on February 17, 1801, on the thirty-sixth ballot, the tie was broken and Jefferson was elected by ten states to four.

The event made it clear that the constitutional system for electing the President would not work under the party system and that every election from then on would be ruined by constant bickering within each party to adjust the votes so as to make one candidate President and the other Vice President.

As it happened, the Constitution could be amended. What was required was a two-thirds approval by each house of Congress and approval by three fourths of the states. It was a hard hurdle, to prevent light-hearted tampering with the Constitution, but not an impossible one. The Bill of Rights had been accepted as the first ten amendments, and on January 8, 1798, an eleventh amendment had been adopted in which the Federal government was forbidden to involve itself in the suit against any state by a citizen of another state or another nation.

Now another amendment was prepared in which painstaking directions were given for presidential voting and in which each elector was directed to vote for President and Vice President separately. This was ratified and became part of the Constitution as the Twelfth Amendment on September 25, 1804. It was done in time for the next election and nothing like the Jefferson-Burr embarrassment ever happened again. (There was not to be another amendment to the Constitution for over sixty years.)

The Federalists went out of office with the poorest grace imaginable. Laws establishing additional courts and legal officers were quickly passed by the almost dead Federalist Sixth Congress, just five days before the end of Adams's term. Taking advantage of this "Judiciary Act," Adams spent his last day in office appointing good Federalists to all the various offices. The result was that although the Democratic-Republicans controlled the executive and legislative branches of the government from 1801, the judiciary remained Federalist. As a result, Jefferson was to find himself in a losing feud with the judiciary through most of his administration.

Adams also had a chance to appoint a Chief Justice of the Supreme Court after he had lost the election. Oliver Ellsworth of Connecticut (born in Windsor in 1745), the second Chief Justice, had resigned for reasons of health. As third Chief Justice, Adams appointed John Marshall on January 20, 1801.

In doing so, Adams must have been aware that Jefferson and Marshall were nearly as bitter enemies as Hamilton and Burr. But Adams did better than he could have known. John Marshall, a firm Federalist, remained Chief Justice for thirty-four years and kept the doctrine of a strong Federal government alive by the decisions he reached — decisions which gave the Supreme Court the power it has today.

On March 4, 1801, Jefferson was inaugurated President over a nation of 5,300,000 (so said the census of 1800) in a ceremony marked by the utmost simplicity.

With this inauguration, an end was placed to Federalist domination and to all attempts to convert the United States into an aristocratic republic. Jefferson saw to it that all the repressive acts of the Adams administration were repealed and he did his best to establish the philosophy of government by all the people. Indeed, the history of the United States as a democratic republic dates from Jefferson and some historians therefore speak of the "Revolution of 1800." (Nevertheless, Jefferson was wise enough to refrain from any attempt to reverse Hamilton's financial policies or to try to weaken the Federal government. He had opposed those policies but he saw that they worked.)

A new cabinet was sworn in, of course, and the leading figures there were James Madison as Secretary of State and Albert Gallatin as Secretary of the Treasury. This was the same Gallatin who had played a part in the Whisky Rebellion and it is not surprising that under the new administration the excise tax on whisky was soon removed.

Jefferson was a confirmed pacifist. His dearest wish was to have only peace, to abolish the army and navy as far as possible, and to carry on a government in the most economical method he could. Unfortunately he could not establish peace all by himself. Europe was in the early stages of a series of wars between Napoleon Bonaparte of France and all the rest of Europe, led by the British. It was a vast hurricane of war in which the United States was tossed about almost helplessly but which Jefferson was determined to ride out.

Oddly enough, the immediate danger of war coming hard upon Jefferson's inauguration involved something else altogether, far less important yet far more immediately irritating.

The southwestern Mediterranean shore was occupied, at the time, by a series of Moslem powers, called the "Barbary States." From west to east these were Morocco, Algeria, Tunis, and Tripoli and they made serious nuisances of themselves. Their ships preyed on commerce passing through the Mediterranean and the European powers paid what amounted to "protection money" to keep their ships safe. Great Britain or France could easily have cleaned out these nests of pirates if they wanted to. However, the war would have cost more than it was worth and besides the two powers were busy fighting each other. They let it go.

Once the United States was independent, American ships could no longer count on safety under the British flag. They had to pay protection money on their own. What's more, the Barbary States, realizing that the United States was more distant and was far weaker than Great Britain and France, demanded greater bribes than they expected of the great powers.

Under Washington and Adams, the American government fumed, but paid between twenty and thirty thousand dollars a year to each of the Barbary States. It was nothing less than tribute despite the fact that the American people were, at this time, busily shouting in another connection that they would pay millions for defense but not one cent for tribute.

The worst of it was that the Barbary States saw no reason to keep their treaties. They charged what the traffic would bear and on May 14, 1801, ten weeks after Jefferson's inauguration (and perhaps because they counted on Jefferson's anxiety to keep the peace), the ruler of Tripoli repudiated the treaty and declared war on the United States.

Reluctantly, Jefferson authorized action against Tripoli and began to strengthen the navy. He moved slowly and mildly, hoping always that it wouldn't come to serious fighting, but by 1803 he had to send a squadron of American ships to the Mediterranean under Commodore Edward Preble (born in Portland, Maine, in 1761).

On October 31, 1803, the Tripolitans scored a coup. An American ship, the *Philadelphia,* had gone aground in the harbor and the Tripolitans, having captured and imprisoned the crew, were doing their best to make use of the ship on their own behalf.

To prevent the humiliation of having the Tripolitans fight with the help of an American ship, Preble, on February 16, 1804, sent a detachment under the command of Lieutenant Stephen Decatur (born in Sinnepuxent, Maryland, on January 5, 1779) into Tripoli harbor. Under Decatur's skillful leadership, the men boarded the ship, set it on fire, and got back without casualties. The American squadron then placed Tripoli under close blockade and began to bombard it.

Meanwhile, an American adventurer, William Eaton (born in Woodstock, Connecticut, on February 23, 1764) with ten U.S. Marines and with some Arabs whom he recruited in Egypt, marched west from the Nile and attacked the Tripolitan town of

Derna, about 500 miles east of Tripoli. On April 27, 1805, with the help of bombardment from American ships offshore, he took it.

Tripoli had had enough. On June 4, 1805, a treaty was signed in which the American government was freed of the obligation of paying tribute, though she still agreed to pay ransom for captured American seamen. The American naval squadron was then withdrawn and it was up to the ruler of Tripoli to honor the treaty, which, of course, he only did when he chose to. The other three Barbary States continued as before.

It wasn't much of a war or of a victory, but American ships had taken action when the European powers hadn't, and had carried it through well, considering the distance of the United States and the reluctance of the administration. It was the first offensive war engaged in by the United States against anyone but Indians. It was the nation's first overseas adventure.

Nor did the marines forget their first glamorous feat. The Marine Hymn begins: "From the halls of Montezuma to the shores of Tripoli."

THE NATION IS DOUBLED

The Tripolitan War could scarcely be viewed as anything more than a minor annoyance when compared with the vaulting ambition of the French consul, Napoleon Bonaparte.

Bonaparte had world-girdling dreams that were not always practical. Among other things, he dreamed of renewing the French empire in North America which had been lost forty years before. Thus, having settled the penny-ante war with the United States with the Convention of 1800, he turned on Spain the day after.

On October 1, 1800, Bonaparte forced feeble Spain to agree to the secret Treaty of San Ildefonso, by the terms of which Spain ceded to France the territory still known as Louisiana (see *The Shaping of North America*). This meant, roughly, all the territory watered by the western tributaries of the Mississippi River, a territory about the size of the United States as it then was. It put France back on the North American continent in force; or at least it eventually would since Bonaparte, for the time being, made no move to implement the transfer.

Before Bonaparte could make something of Louisiana, he needed peace in Europe. On June 14, 1800, he had won one of his great victories at the Battle of Marengo over Austria, and the European powers were forced to accept the situation sullenly. Even Great Britain grew tired of the war and finally accepted the so-called "Treaty of Amiens" on March 27, 1802, so that Bonaparte finally found himself entirely at peace — and victorious, too.

The other thing he needed was a secure base in the rich West Indies. There, through trade, he might build up a sound financial structure by means of which he could develop the raw wilderness of Louisiana and establish a new France.

France had owned the western part of the island of Santo Domingo (the part now making up the nation of Haiti) from the 17th century and in 1697 gained it all from Spain. By then its population consisted largely of Black slaves. In the wake of the French Revolution, these slaves were freed, but mere freedom from slavery wasn't enough. The Blacks wanted independence and were ready to fight for it.

Bonaparte, who felt he needed the island, sent an army to Santo Domingo. The Blacks fought heroically but could not withstand the well-equipped and well-trained French.

So for a while, in 1802, Bonaparte must have thought he had gambled and won. He had peace in Europe, an island base in the Caribbean, and vast Louisiana in the American interior.

And then everything fell apart. The victorious French army in Santo Domingo fell prey to an enemy it could not fight — yellow fever. French soldiers died in battalions and it quickly appeared that virtually none of them would return to France and that Bonaparte did not have his island after all. Furthermore, the Peace of Amiens turned out to be shaky indeed. The British, unrelievedly hostile, regretted the peace the instant it had been made and were only seeking an excuse to return to the wars.

Without an island and without peace, Louisiana was useless to Bonaparte after all. Once war was renewed, the British, who had a secure base in Canada, would take Louisiana. If Bonaparte could not have Louisiana, he wanted more than anything else that Great Britain at least not have it. What was the alternative? And at this point, he must have thought of the United States.

The United States had learned about the secret treaty that transferred Louisiana to France in May 1801, shortly after Jefferson's inauguration. By and large, the nation was horrified. To have a relatively feeble Spain in control of the mouth of the Mississippi River was bad enough; to have a powerful and victorious France in its place was intolerable.

Jefferson, pro-French and anti-British as he was, could not help feeling that if the Louisiana transfer actually went through, the United States would have to form an alliance with Great Britain against France. But meanwhile, nothing was done to make the transfer actual and Jefferson hesitated.

As 1802 wore on and as Bonaparte realized more and more clearly that he could not hold Louisiana, he decided to give Jefferson a push. Spain had been allowing trade on the Misssisippi River ever since Pinckney's Treaty of 1795. Now, as a result of undercover French insistence, Spain violated the treaty and closed the Mississippi to American commerce on October 16, 1802.

This meant either war or negotiation, for the United States could not tolerate a closed Mississippi. Jefferson, the apostle of peace, decided on negotiation. Perhaps the United States could *buy* the mouth of the Mississippi; something that would be safer and, in the long run, less expensive (if less "glorious") than fighting for it.

The American minister to France at the time was Livingston, who had been with Jefferson on the committee to draft the Declaration of Independence a quarter-century before. Jefferson sent his fellow-Virginian, James Monroe (born in Westmoreland county on April 28, 1758), to France with instructions to Livingston to offer two million dollars for New Orleans and for the mouth of the Mississippi River generally, and to be prepared to go to ten million.

No doubt, Livingston and Monroe expected to have considerable trouble negotiating the purchase of the Mississippi mouth. Opposite them was none other than the astute master diplomat Talleyrand, who was foreign minister under Napoleon, as he had been under the Directory – and would be after Napoleon, too.

What the Americans didn't realize was that Bonaparte was irritated by their moderation. Just the mouth of the Mississippi? Talleyrand put that to one side and, smiling blandly, asked what the Americans would give for *all* of Louisiana.

The American negotiators must have been struck dumb for a moment. They had absolutely no authority to negotiate for the purchase of all of Louisiana. Nevertheless, when the vertigo had passed, they realized that authority or not, they dared not turn down the absolutely magnificent opportunity presented them. They actually haggled for a while and then finally agreed to a price of fifteen million dollars for a territory of about 828,000 square miles, a price which came to three cents an acre. The acquisition of Louisiana would double the area of the United States at a stroke and it represented a territory that would eventually be divided up into all or part of thirteen states.

The agreement was signed on April 30, 1803, and just in time, too, for war between Great Britain and France broke out again within two weeks. Had the territory still been French once war had begun, Great Britain might have been tempted to occupy it. As it was, Great Britain, preferring to let the United States have it than to risk war in the wilderness with France and Spain, actually facilitated the transfer. British bankers lent the United States money with which to pay Napoleon. (Indeed, the stars in their courses seemed to be fighting for the United States in 1803.)

Of course, the "Louisiana Purchase" created a problem for Jefferson. As a strict constructionist, he did not believe the Federal government had the constitutional power to purchase territory in this fashion. The Federalists, however, as loose constructionists believed the Federal government *did* have such power.

On this occasion, as might be expected, principle took a beating. Jefferson decided that, constitutional considerations notwithstanding, he could not pass up the chance, and he accepted Louisiana. The Federalists, deciding they hated Jefferson more than they loved their own views, promptly opposed the purchase. But it went through the Democratic-Republican Congress despite their opposition and on December 20, 1803, the Louisiana territory was legally turned over by France to the United States.

Jefferson, perhaps the most scientifically minded of any of our

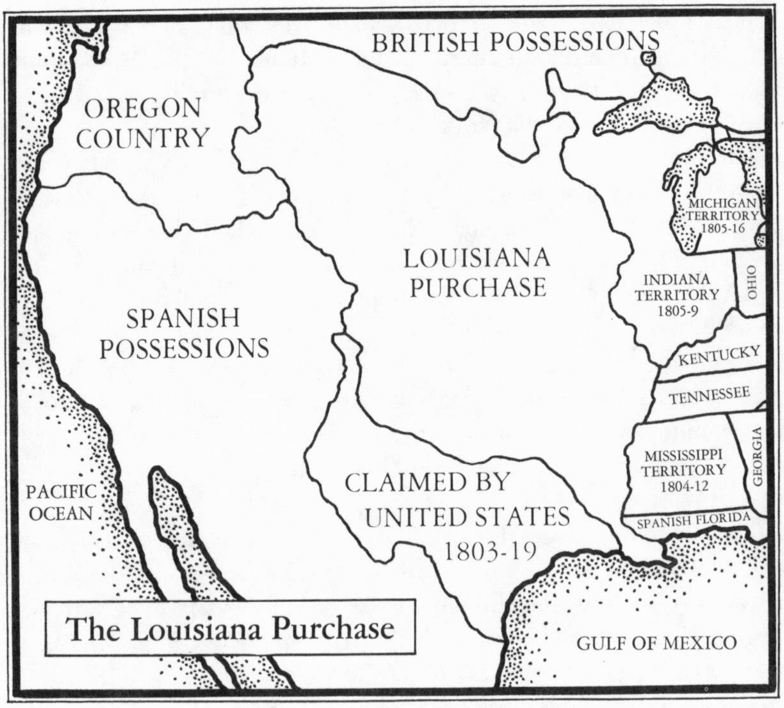

The Louisiana Purchase

Presidents, arranged at once for the exploration of the new territory. In fact, he had been planning something of the sort even before there had been any thought of purchasing the territory. For the purpose, he had been grooming Meriwether Lewis of Virginia (born near Charlottesville on August 18, 1774) who had much experience with the wilderness. Jefferson had made Lewis his private secretary in 1801 and had encouraged him to educate himself in those subjects necessary to exploration.

Lewis apparently did not want the sole responsibility of the expedition and suggested that a fellow-Virginian, William Clark (born in Caroline county on August 1, 1770) join him as co-leader. Clark was a younger brother of George Rogers Clark and had fought at the Battle of Fallen Timbers.

Some forty men were selected to accompany them; all young. Clark, who was thirty-three when the expedition started, was the oldest. The party went to St. Louis (founded by the French in 1764 before the men on the spot learned the territory had been lost to Spain the year before) and there they remained during the winter. Then, on May 14, 1804, they moved westward from the Mississippi River into the virtually unknown territory that was now part of the United States. In three boats they made their way up the Missouri River.

In what is now western Montana, they found that the Missouri broke up into three streams, which they named the Jefferson River, the Madison River, and the Gallatin River after the three leading men of the administration. The Jefferson River was the westernmost and they followed that back to its source.

Strictly speaking that marked the end of Louisiana, but beyond that was an unexplored region called the "Oregon Territory" which had no fixed ownership. It represented, indeed, the last portion of the shores of the American continents that had not yet been staked out. To the north were the Russians in Alaska, to the south the Spaniards in California, but neither had made effective any of the vague claims they advanced to the territory.

Others had claims, too. Captain Cook, the British explorer, had sailed along the coast in 1778. American ships had also been in the waters. The American navigator, Robert Gray (born in Tiverton, Rhode Island, in 1755), was the first to carry the American flag around the world, completing a circumnavigation in 1790 and a second one in 1793. In the course of his second circumnavigation in his ship, the *Columbia,* he sailed into a river on the Oregon coast and named it the Columbia River for his ship.

Now Lewis and Clark went on into the Oregon Territory. They crossed the Continental Divide, beyond which the rivers flow not into the Atlantic, but into the Pacific Ocean. They came to the headwaters of the Columbia River and followed it down to the ocean, which they reached on November 15, 1805. It was on the basis of the explorations by Gray and by Lewis and Clark that the United States was to lay claim to the Oregon Territory forty years later.

Lewis and Clark began their return voyage on March 23, 1806, and were back in St. Louis on September 23. They had made the first overland trip across the North American continent to the Pacific Ocean and back.

In accordance with Jefferson's instructions, Lewis and Clark kept extensive diaries, mapping and describing the territory and producing virtually an encyclopedia of knowledge of a territory which at that time was almost unknown except to the Indians who lived there.

Another explorer of the Louisiana Territory was Zebulon Montgomery Pike (born in Lamberton, New Jersey, on January 5, 1779, the first person mentioned by name in this book who was born after the United States had declared its independence). With instructions to search out the headwaters of the Mississippi River, Pike headed northward from St. Louis on August 9, 1805. He traveled into what is now Minnesota and there, in February 1806, he found British traders. He told them, quite firmly, that they were operating in American territory and would be held accountable by American law for their actions.

In July 1806, Pike was sent off again, this time to explore the southwestern portions of the Louisiana Territory. He made his way into Colorado where, on November 15, he sighted the mountain now known as Pike's Peak. Pike tried to climb it but lack of warm clothing forced him to turn back.

He continued westward, ignoring Spanish warnings that he was infringing on their territory, and was finally taken by them in what is now New Mexico. His papers were confiscated and he was not released till July 1, 1807.

JUDGES AND TRAITORS

Jefferson's administration went on swimmingly at home. Gallatin, Secretary of the Treasury, imposed a stringent economy on government expenditures including the military budget. Despite the Tripolitan War and the Louisiana Purchase, taxes were cut and the national debt was reduced from $83 to $57 million.

Land acts were passed which enabled the government to sell land cheaply to settlers and to give them financial aid as well.

Settlers flocked westward and Cleveland (founded in 1796) was growing rapidly. The state of Ohio was carved out of the easternmost portion of the old Northwest Territory and it entered the Union on March 1, 1803, as the seventeenth state.

But Jefferson, despite the successes of his administration, was continually frustrated by the Federalist hold on the judiciary, something Adams had made certain in the last days of his term. Jefferson's administration tackled this problem from every angle.

For one thing, Madison, in his post as Secretary of State, refused to deliver the commission to new justices of the peace whom Adams had appointed for the District of Columbia. One of them, William Marbury, sued, and the case of "Marbury vs. Madison" came up before the Supreme Court which was now headed by Jefferson's arch-enemy, the Federalist John Marshall.

Marshall's court dismissed the case on February 24, 1803, but in doing so managed to declare that the Congress could not pass, nor the President enforce, a law that was in violation of the Constitution of the United States. What's more, Marshall denied that either the President or Congress could judge the constitutionality of a law but that this was a matter entirely up to the Supreme Court. To point the matter, Marshall's Supreme Court found one of the sections of the Judiciary Act to be unconstitutional.

This was the first time the Supreme Court declared a Federal law unconstitutional and it was not to do so again for over half a century but the precedent was established.

Another step was taken in 1810, when questions arose over measures taken by the Georgia legislature to counter some very shady land dealings by former members of that legislature. The matter came up to the Supreme Court in a case known as "Fletcher vs. Peck" and John Marshall handed down a decision which, in part, declared a Georgia state law to be unconstitutional and therefore void. He thus extended the power of the Supreme Court over the states as well as over the Federal government. With that the Supreme Court took on its present shape.

Since judges were named for life and since few resigned, Jefferson saw no way of ending the Federalist hold except by impeachment. Any officeholder (including the President) could be impeached (that is, accused) of actions that made him unfit for office.

He could then be tried by the Senate and, if convicted, removed from office in strict accordance with the Constitution.

Jefferson therefore directed impeachment proceedings against a New Hampshire judge who was extremely Federalist and whose actions in court were so bizarre as to indicate him to be insane. The judge was tried, convicted on March 12, 1804, and removed from office.

With this as a precedent, Jefferson moved against a much more important target — Samuel Chase of Maryland (born in Somerset county on April 17, 1741). Chase was a signer of the Declaration of Independence and had been an associate justice of the Supreme Court since appointed by Washington in 1796. He was a Federalist who, when he presided over court cases, did so in a highly partisan manner, but not psychotically. He was impeached and tried before the Senate in February 1805. Despite the full pressure of the administration, he was acquitted on March 1, and Jefferson gave up the offensive. He settled down to enduring the judiciary since he could do nothing else.

What victories the Federalists could win by means of the courts were woefully insufficient for the ultra-Federalists of New England, now under the leadership of Timothy Pickering, who had once been Secretary of State under Washington and under Adams. He had become a senator from Massachusetts, one of only nine Federalist senators left in Congress after the midterm elections of 1802 (less than half of the twenty there had been six years earlier).

Pickering was a native of Salem in Essex county and because some other leaders of ultra-Federalism also came from that county, that portion of the party was eventually called the "Essex Junto." ("Junto," a distortion of a Spanish word meaning "council," has come to be used for a faction or clique.)

Pickering and his cohorts saw in Jefferson's farmer-centered administration the destruction of New England's commercial prosperity. The Louisiana Purchase was the last straw, for each new western state added to the Democratic-Republican majority, and out of the Louisiana Territory many farming, noncommercial states would be made.

Pickering saw no way out but the formation of a separate nation. The commercial states would bring to an end their earlier acceptance of the Constitution and resume their sovereignty. They would "secede" from the Union, in other words. Pickering saw the new nation as including the five New England states, plus New York and New Jersey. The Essex Junto was even willing to accept British help in bringing about this "Northern Confederacy." (One wonders what Sam Adams – a staunch Democratic-Republican – would have said, but even as the Junto was making its plans, Sam Adams, aged 81, died on October 2, 1803.)

Hamilton was approached in the matter. Would he swing New York into line?

Hamilton turned down any such possibility in the strongest terms. He had hailed the Louisiana Purchase when other Federalists had condemned it and he would not break up the Union just because it wasn't going his way. But then, anything that Hamilton was against, Burr was for, and Burr was an unscrupulous man who would stick at nothing. The Essex Junto approached Burr.

Burr was not going to run for Vice President in 1804 since, after having let himself be used by the Federalists in the tie vote of 1800, he had been virtually drummed out of the party by the angered Jefferson. Burr therefore decided to run for governor of New York, and was willing to make another deal with the Federalists. Let them support him and he would swing New York into the Northern Confederacy.

In the spring of 1804, the election for the governorship of New York was held and Burr was defeated. It seemed to Burr that the reason for his defeat was not far to seek. Hamilton had electioneered hard against him so that Federalist support did not swing to him as it might have.

It was the last straw for Burr. Hamilton had kept him from being President, and now from being governor.

In June, Burr found an occasion for offense in something Hamilton had said about him, and challenged his enemy to a duel. There was nothing to compel Hamilton to accept the challenge. He disapproved of dueling and only three years before his oldest son had died in a duel. He knew Burr to be a bitter man and a good shot. Yet Hamilton lacked the courage to seem a coward and lose his status as a "gentleman."

He accepted the challenge, and on July 11, 1804, the duel was fought in Weehawken on the New Jersey shore of the Hudson River. Burr (who was still Vice President of the United States) took careful aim and shot Hamilton just below the chest. A little more than a day later, Hamilton was dead at the age of forty-nine.

But so were all plans for a Northern Confederacy. Burr in his blindness had utterly ruined his political career, made Hamilton into a martyr and hero, and had sunk the Essex Junto into sour impotence.

The result was glaringly obvious when it came time for the 1804 presidential election. For the first time candidates were selected by congressional caucuses – that is, by meetings of the congressmen who were members of a given political party. Jefferson was re-nominated by the Democratic-Republicans, of course. In place of Aaron Burr, they selected George Clinton, the long-time governor of New York, for the vice presidency.

As for the Federalists, they nominated Charles Pinckney (the vice presidential candidate of 1800) for the presidency, and Rufus King of New York, one of the designers of the Northwest Ordinance, for the vice presidency. He had been a member of the Constitutional Convention and was recently minister to Great Britain.

The chief campaign issue was the Louisiana Purchase and the Federalists could not have done worse than to oppose it. The acquisition of a vast territory sat so well with American pride that almost all the electors chosen were Democratic-Republican.

The result was a Democratic-Republican landslide on December 5, 1804. In this first election in which electors voted for a President and Vice President separately, Jefferson and Clinton got 162 electoral votes to 14 for Pinckney and King. Only Connecticut and Delaware went Federalist.

The Ninth Congress, chosen in this same election, was more Democratic-Republican than ever. The Democratic-Republican lead was now 27 to 7 in the Senate and 116 to 25 in the House. The Federalists had dwindled to pygmy exasperation.

As for Aaron Burr, he had nowhere to go but into the shadow-land of conspiracy. Execrated for the murder of Hamilton and with warrants out for his arrest both in New York and New Jersey, his political career was ended. He moved westward and met his friend, General James Wilkinson.

Wilkinson, who had been receiving money from Spain all through the 1790s, had, with the usual incredible luck he never deserved, been made governor of all but the southern tip of the Louisiana Territory in 1805. A dozen years before he had intrigued to split off the Gulf regions with the help of Spain. Now his plans had grown more grandiose. He dreamed of an empire that would not only include the southwestern section of the United States, but Spanish territories as well, with himself as ruler and with New Orleans as capital. Why not? Bonaparte, who had begun as an impoverished Corsican army officer, had made himself dictator of France, the most powerful man in Europe, and on December 2, 1804 (three days before Jefferson's re-election) actually French Emperor, as Napoleon I. What an example for others!

Burr, who had already indicated his willingness to break up the United States, fell in with Wilkinson's vague plot. Burr had a winning personality and the smooth plausibility of a con man. He met many people out west whom he dazzled with his schemes, and in 1806 he began recruiting men for an invasion of the Spanish dominions. He was but waiting for his allies in New Orleans to declare Louisiana independent.

How far it would all have gone, how well it would all have worked, we will never know. James Wilkinson, having decided the plot would not work after all, or having decided that Burr was stealing all the glory, or both, decided to extricate himself at Burr's expense. Never hesitating at betrayal, Wilkinson wrote a letter to Jefferson, in which he revealed the conspiracy, placed all the blame on Burr, and held himself up as a patriot. When Burr heard of this, he fled toward Spanish Florida while Wilkinson once again came up smelling of roses.

Jefferson, who needed no encouragement to squash Burr, at once had him tracked down. Burr was arrested in what is now Alabama on February 19, 1807. He was put on trial for treason on March 30, in Richmond, Virginia.

The presiding judge over the U.S. Circuit Court before which Burr was tried was none other than John Marshall. Marshall had no love for conspiracy, treason, or Aaron Burr, but his hatred of Jefferson took precedence. Burr became the object of a duel between the President and the Chief Justice, the former moving heaven and earth to convict, the latter to acquit.

The Chief Justice won by temporarily adopting a strict constructionist attitude. He insisted on adhering to the strict definition of treason, which, the Constitution said, consisted of "levying war against the United States or adhering to their enemies."

Burr had not actually levied war or adhered to enemies. He had been stopped before he had done so, and it was impossible to prove that he had actually intended doing so. Consequently, after a month-long trial, Burr was acquitted on September 1, 1807, and Marshall had the grim satisfaction of thwarting his enemy, the President.

Burr left for Europe where he remained for some time, and although he lived on for nearly thirty years, dying at the age of eighty in New York, it was a life of penury and obscurity. He was well-punished after all.

CAUGHT BETWEEN THE GIANTS

But while Jefferson was battling judges and traitors, the real danger was beyond the borders.

The war between Great Britain and Napoleon was in some ways a godsend to American commerce. The United States was the strongest maritime neutral and its ships carried goods in wartime quantities and at wartime profits. For a while, this wartime prosperity gave the United States more ships and more commerce on a per capita basis than any nation in the world and trade boomed even with far-off China.

But it was a dangerous and shaky prosperity, though, for a great part of it had to be carried on in defiance of the British, who controlled the seas.

France, unable to use its own shipping in the face of British enmity, depended on American shipping as a way of getting what it wanted from the world outside Europe. American ships carrying goods from French or Spanish colonies to France or its then-ally Spain, could be confiscated by the British as carrying "contraband," that is, materials useful to the war-making capacity of Napoleon.

What American ships did was to take the cargoes from the colonies to the United States, since the British did not forbid the neutral United States to import material. Once that was done, and some formalities observed, the cargo became American. The ship then went on to France or Spain. It was now a neutral American ship carrying an American cargo and was therefore immune to British seizure. It was all a transparent fiction, but in 1800, Great Britain had accepted this principle of "broken voyage."

As the war in Europe grew more desperate, however, there was less and less desire on either side to be too meticulous about the rights of neutrals. In 1805, Great Britain smashed the French navy at the Battle of Trafalgar, and its control of the sea became absolute. France, however, won the Battle of Austerlitz over Russia and Austria, and Napoleon was more powerful than ever.

Only Great Britain stood in the way of Napoleon's drive toward virtual world dominion; and only Great Britain's navy protected it from a Napoleonic invasion. Great Britain lacked the army to challenge France on land; France lacked the navy to challenge Great Britain at sea. Both used economic weapons. Great Britain blockaded France and Napoleon tried to prevent the European powers from trading with Great Britain.

American shipping was caught and crushed between the two giants. The British, beginning in 1805, would no longer allow the fiction of the broken voyage. British warships and French privateers both began to seize American vessels, and American commercial prosperity ended.

Because Great Britain controlled the sea she was capable of doing more damage to American shipping than France could do, so that anger rose higher against the former. In addition, there was the issue of impressment, concerning which rage mounted.

Great Britain needed seamen, for her ships were her defense and without them she would be destroyed. The British class structure was such, however, that its leaders knew no way of treating seamen but as dogs. Such was the miserable treatment of sailors on board ship, the miserable food they were given, the frequency with which they were flogged for minor infractions, that no sane man would volunteer for service. The way the British got sailors, then, was to round up able-bodied men of low social status, and put them on board ships by force, if necessary. Such "press-gangs," who produced the sailors Great Britain needed, were part of the British way of life.

Naturally, once a Britisher found himself on board ship, he would not have been sane if he did not do anything he could to desert. Despite the harshest measures and the strictest watch, many did. The desertion worked best when the sailors could reach the United States, where there was no language barrier, where they could easily obtain forged citizenship papers, and where they could work for higher wages and with better treatment. All told, the British may have lost as many as 2500 men a year to American ships.

Great Britain could not afford this loss. Never grasping the notion that the loss could be prevented by better treatment, she used force. She did not recognize the right of British subjects to become American citizens and felt compelled, by the exigencies of war, to stop American ships on the high seas, and search for deserters. In so doing, the British did locate many deserters – and they also carried off many American citizens, even some native-born Americans.

Such actions were so humiliating to Americans that it roused mounting hatred of Great Britain. The Federalist party, which had once benefited from American indignation against France, now continued to shrink before the anti-British storm. In the midterm election for the Tenth Congress, Federalist representation dwindled to 6 in the Senate and 24 in the House, a loss of one seat each.

Jefferson, still a man of peace, tried to negotiate with Great Britain, but the British, who considered their war with Napoleon paramount, would not make any substantial concessions.

To be sure, the situation was growing steadily more critical for the British. In 1807, Napoleon, having won further battles, controlled all of Europe west of Russia and was on the point of making an alliance with Russia, too. The French Emperor mobilized the entire European continent into an economic war on Great Britain and the British, in their fury and desperation, were striking out ever more harshly in their only arena of supremacy, the sea.

On June 22, 1807, the American warship *Chesapeake* left Norfolk for African ports. She expected no trouble and her decks were so cluttered with odds and ends that it was difficult for her crew to reach the guns.

Not far outside American waters, she was stopped by a stronger British warship, the *Leopard,* which demanded that the *Chesapeake* submit to search since four British deserters were reported aboard. The *Chesapeake* refused and the *Leopard* opened fire. The *Chesapeake,* unable to use her guns properly and outgunned even if she had been able to, surrendered after half an hour, suffering three killed and eighteen wounded. A British boarding party searched the ship and carried off four men they claimed were deserters.

The United States exploded in fury and a war fever swept the nation. If Jefferson had declared war, he would have had popular support, but he knew that the United States was not prepared for conflict. His own policy of economy had reduced the American navy virtually to nonexistence and British ships would have free range of the exposed American coastline.

He could only bend to the storm. At the moment, the two European giants, Great Britain and France, were each practicing open war on any ships trading with the enemy, and Jefferson, seeing the United States caught between the giants, let each have the victory.

On December 22, 1807 he put through an "Embargo Act." By the terms of this act, American ships were to refrain from any foreign trade at all. The rather desperate notion behind it was that Great Britain and France, suffering from the lack of American trade, would make concessions.

It didn't work that way at all. Under the British blockade, France's overseas trade was so small that the loss of American ships was a minor matter to her. As for the British, France went to war against its old ally, Spain, in 1808 and that meant that the ports and ships of Spanish America were open to Great Britain. That more than made up for the loss of the United States and, indeed, British merchant ships actually benefited from the disappearance of American shipping.

The damage the Embargo did was to the commercial areas of the United States itself. The commerce of New England and New York was destroyed and the region sank into a deep depression.

11

THE PLUNGE INTO WAR

THE BEGINNING OF CHANGE

Jefferson's second administration was ending in disaster. Between the nation's helplessness against Great Britain, the disgraceful Burr affair, and the utter failure of the Embargo, it had been as dark as the first administration had been light.

Nevertheless, Jefferson could have had a third term if he had wanted it. He had, however, had enough. After forty years in public life and eight years as President, he was as anxious to retire as Washington had been. He therefore made it abundantly clear that he would not run for a third term. This, together with Washington's refusal to do so, set the precedent of a two-term maximum that was to remain for 132 years, even though the Constitution did not require it.

The Republicans turned to Madison, architect of the Constitution, Jefferson's faithful right-hand man and fellow-Virginian, and Secretary of State through all eight years of Jefferson's presidency.

George Clinton was nominated once again for the vice presidency. The Federalists clung to Pinckney and King.

The result was another Democratic-Republican victory, but by a reduced margin. Madison received 122 electoral votes to 47 for Pinckney on December 7, 1808, and was elected fourth President of the United States. The Federalists gained in the Eleventh Congress. Though their representation in the Senate remained unchanged, they doubled their numbers in the House of Representatives, which, however, remained Democratic-Republican, 94 to 48.

The Federalists returned in full force to New England, though, and some northern Democratic-Republicans, while not turning Federalist, nevertheless refused to support another Virginian for the presidency and held out for Clinton (who actually received six electoral votes for the presidency).

It was clear that it was the Embargo that was restoring Federalist fortunes and that it could only continue to do so. On March 1, 1809, therefore, three days before he left office, Jefferson lifted the Embargo in order that Madison might start his administration without that albatross about his neck. The prohibition of trade with Great Britain and France remained, but American ships could go anywhere else they liked.

Madison continued to try to improve the situation on the sea by means of negotiation and at first matters seemed hopeful. The British minister to the United States, David M. Erskine, tried to reach a settlement and, in his enthusiasm, granted more than his instructions permitted. Madison joyously lifted restrictions on trade with Great Britain but then the British government sourly repudiated Erskine's settlement and Madison, disappointed and embarrassed, had to reimpose restrictions.

These restrictions, however, continued to do much harm and little good so on May 1, 1810, Congress took a hand. A law was passed which permitted trade with Great Britain and France, but promised that if either of those nations would lift all restrictions on American shipping, trade with the other would be embargoed.

It was a rather foolish gesture, since Great Britain could not give in, whereas if France did, her restrictions being of little account, it would scarcely matter.

France did lift the restrictions or, at least, she pretended she did.

While assuring the United States there were no restrictions, she continued to restrict in practice. Madison, eager to net some gain from the diplomatic writhings of the powerless United States, accepted Napoleon's gesture and quickly embargoed commerce with Great Britain again on March 2, 1811.

To the American public, it seemed that France was being conciliatory and Great Britain intransigeant, and anti-British feeling continued to rise. The British government, on the other hand, which had had first-hand experience with Napoleonic duplicity, could not believe that the United States had been taken in. The British felt that the Democratic-Republican President was simply indulging his pro-French prejudice and refused to be stampeded into lifting their own restrictions on American shipping.

That was too bad, for the British were in a position to be lenient. Napoleon had foolishly involved himself in an unwinnable war in Spain in 1808 and all Europe was growing increasingly restive under his harsh control. Nevertheless, Great Britain had her pride and still felt a smoldering resentment against her former colonies and would not give in.

So events began to move relentlessly toward war.

Yet if the United States seemed helpless in comparison to Great Britain and France, the fact remained that it was growing rapidly. In 1810, the national census showed the nation's population to be 7,239,881, about two and a half times what it was when independence had been won in 1783.

Nor was it only numbers that counted. The nature of the American economy was beginning a slow change in the direction Hamilton had hoped for, and nothing Jefferson or the Democratic-Republicans could do could stop it.

In 1789, an Englishman named Samuel Slater (born in 1768) arrived in the United States. He had worked in those English factories which were beginning to use the steam engine to power devices that spun threads and wove cloth, replacing the slower hand labor. It was this which marked the beginning of the "Industrial Revolution." Slater had the designs of such machinery in his head, and in 1790 he established a powered factory in Pawtucket, Rhode Island. In this way, the Industrial Revolution came to the United States.

Oliver Evans (born near Newport, Delaware, in 1755) was building high-pressure steam engines before 1802, and with these, factory after factory could be powered. Francis Cabot Lowell (born in Newburyport, Massachusetts, in 1743, and after whom Lowell, Massachusetts, is named) built elaborate spinning and weaving mills.

What began then was, in a century and a half, to make the United States the most industrially advanced nation the world had ever seen and was slowly but steadily to wipe out the nation of small farmers that Jefferson had idealized.

One consequence of American inventiveness, however, was to prove nearly fatal to America.

Ever since the Revolutionary War, the institution of slavery had been growing more unpopular, and the move for making it illegal was gaining ground. Even in the South, where most of the slaves were to be found, there were few apologists. The use of slaves was not very profitable and was an embarrassment, considering the high ideals of democracy professed by the Democratic-Republicans of the South. And indeed such men as Washington and Jefferson, though they owned slaves, detested the institution.

One of the important crops of the South was cotton, which was increasingly in demand as the powered factories of Great Britain began to turn out cheap cotton cloth in quantity. The difficult step was that of plucking the cotton fibers from the seed. This was dreadfully tedious work which Black slaves were forced to do, but which could be done only slowly.

Mrs. Nathaniel Greene, the widow of the Revolutionary War general (who had died in 1786), was living in Savannah, Georgia. One day in 1793, she was entertaining some southern planters who spoke feelingly about this difficulty. Present on the occasion was Mrs. Greene's young protégé, Eli Whitney (born in Westboro, Massachusetts, on December 8, 1765), an ingenious gadgeteer. In a few weeks, he had built a simple spiked cylinder which, when it rotated, entangled the fibers and pulled them off the seeds mechanically.

This "cotton gin" (short for "engine"), which Whitney patented on March 14, 1794, increased the amount of cotton that could be picked off the seeds fifty-fold. At once, it became possible to grow far more cotton since all the slaves could be used in the field and practically none would have to be wasted picking at lint. The cotton plantations spread, slavery became more profitable and all opposition to it gradually died away in the South. Indeed, southerners began to feel that without slavery their economy would be destroyed. So the stage was set for the great American tragedy of civil war seventy years later.

(Whitney made no money out of the cotton gin. It was so simple that anyone could build it and Whitney saw the uselessness of trying to sue for infringement of his patent. He went to Connecticut and there, in 1798, turned to the manufacture of firearms. He did this with precision and was the first to manufacture parts so nearly identical as to make any part fit any gun. This was even more important in the long run than the cotton gin was.)

The growing enterprise and inventiveness of Americans also helped neutralize the weakness inherent in the nation's vast extent of territory. Madison was President over a nation with an area of 1,700,000 square miles, far larger than any European nation except for Russia. Under the conditions of the time, transportation and communication over its undeveloped distances were so difficult as to make it reasonable for adventurers such as Wilkinson to dream of detaching outlying portions.

But development was proceeding apace. The "turnpike" (that is, toll road) had been developed in Great Britain, and on April 9, 1791, it was introduced to the United States when a sixty-two-mile turnpike was opened between Philadelphia and Lancaster. By 1810 there were three hundred turnpike corporations in the northeast, and canals (roads for ships, really) were also being built. Men were increasingly able to move about quickly and easily and the vast American area was becoming less of a liability each decade.

The new era of steam power was also applied to transportation. As early as 1787, John Fitch (born in Windsor, Connecticut, on January 21, 1743) had built, and was running, a steamship on the Delaware River. Bad breaks drove him into bankruptcy, but in 1807 Robert Fulton (born in Lancaster county, Pennsylvania, in 1765) had better luck on the Hudson River. The steamship, also, worked to improve internal commerce.

So far, then, from feeling its vast territory to be a weakness, the United States looked toward still further expansion. There was the question of Florida and the Gulf Coast, for instance.

In acquiring Louisiana from France, there was considerable uncertainty as to Florida. In 1810, what we now call Florida was "East Florida" while the section of the Gulf Coast from the present northwestern boundary of Florida, westward to the Mississippi River, was called "West Florida." The question was whether either or both of these regions was included in the Louisiana Purchase.

Spain vigorously denied that any of it was but Jefferson as vigorously insisted that West Florida, at least, was included, since only by its inclusion could the mouth of the Mississippi River be in American hands on both banks.

On October 27, 1810, after American adventurers from the South had invaded the territory, Madison proclaimed that West Florida was part of the United States. The western section of that region, the part that now makes up that portion of the state of Louisiana which lies east of the Mississippi River, was actually occupied.

The position further east was clung to by Spain, which held on to its fort at Mobile, but even so the American grip on the lower Mississippi River was made total.

RESORT TO ARMS

The Indians of the Ohio Territory were keenly watching the increasing tensions between the United States and Great Britain. Since the Battle of Fallen Timbers, the influx of white settlers had proceeded steadily and it was clear that the movement would not stop until all the land was taken and all the Indians were gone.

But if there was to be war, then the Indians might be able to count on British help. With that in mind a new leader, Tecumseh (born near where Springfield, Ohio, now stands, about 1768), set about preparing a united Indian front against the United States.

In this he had the help of his brother, a charismatic religious leader called "the Prophet." The two of them, serving as political and spiritual leaders, respectively, were producing considerable results.

The center of their power was in Indiana Territory where "the Prophet's Town" was located. Governor of the Territory since 1800 was William Henry Harrison (born in Charles county, Virginia, on February 9, 1773), whose father, Benjamin Harrison, had been one of the signers of the Declaration of Independence.

Harrison took action to scotch the Indian dreams before the union of tribes could be brought about. By very dubious means, he managed to have a great deal of Indian territory signed over to the United States, partly in order to limit the territory open to Tecumseh and partly to goad the Indians into premature battle.

With the same view in mind, Harrison waited till Tecumseh had gone off to the south to gather Indian support there, and then led a force of eleven hundred men from Vincennes, his capital, northward up the Wabash River. On November 7, 1811, they arrived at the Tippecanoe River near which the Prophet's Town was located. He camped there and, sure enough, with Tecumseh absent, the Prophet alone could not resist those who clamored for an attack on the American army.

The Indians charged and in the first fierce moments of the Battle of Tippecanoe the Americans fell back and were nearly surrounded. Fighting back hard, however, they drove off the Indians after two hours. They had suffered two hundred casualties but they destroyed the Prophet's Town before leaving.

The Battle of Tippecanoe broke the back of Tecumseh's plan and forced him into outright dependence on the British. Since war had not yet come, it meant he would have to wait.

As always, news of a victory over the Indians was greeted with wild enthusiasm. The narrowness of the victory was smudged over and Harrison was made the hero of the day. Since it was widely felt that the British were backing the Indians, the battle led to a further rise in anti-British sentiment.

The intensifying war mood had already been reflected in the midterm election of 1810 which chose the Twelfth Congress. In this Congress, the Democratic-Republicans strengthened their hold on the Senate and won back half the 1808 losses in the House of Representatives.

What was more important was that the congressional election saw a massive loss of the old names that had more or less dominated the government in the twenty years since the Constitution had been adopted. New young leaders had been voted in to whom the Revolutionary War was a thing of the past that they could not remember. They had grown up as independent Americans and were filled with dreams of power.

Those from the north were aching to attack and take over Canada, maintaining that while it existed in British hands, it would always be an arsenal from which the Indians would be armed and urged on to warfare. Those from the south were as enthusastic about taking over Florida. All dreamed of showing Great Britain she could not trample on American honor.

These new men were sarcastically called the "War Hawks" by John Randolph (born in Prince George county, Virginia, on June 2, 1773), one of the survivors from the previous age. He was a die-hard Democratic-Republican who had broken with Jefferson when the latter seemed not Democratic-Republican enough.

The leading member of the War Hawks was Henry Clay of Kentucky, the first man, prominent in American politics, to be associated with a state outside the original thirteen. He had been born in Hanover county, Virginia, however, on April 12, 1777. Such was the strength of war sentiment now that Clay was elected Speaker of the House of Representatives.

The War Hawks were not always wise in their anti-British fervor, however. There was the case of the Bank of the United States, whose twenty-year charter was up for renewal in 1811. On the whole, it had done its work well, but it was viewed as a symbol of Federalism and as a tool of the commercial power. Besides, some two thirds of its stock was held by the British and to an increasingly anti-British public, this made it seem that the Bank was a tool of the enemy.

The Twelfth Congress, therefore, refused to renew its charter. In the Senate, the vote was a tie, and Vice President Clinton exercised one of the few vice presidential privileges, that of voting to break a senatorial tie. He voted against the Bank. The ending of the Bank worsened the financial situation of the United States considerably and made it less capable of fighting a war, which was not, of course, what the War Hawks had in view.

And another dramatic act of war took place at sea. The British warship *Guerrière* (a French word meaning "warrior") was hovering off New York City, impressing seamen. On May 16, 1811, the American warship *President* was sent out to put an end to this.

The *President* spied a British warship it took to be the *Guerrière* and gave chase. Actually, the ship was the *Little Belt,* only half the size of the *Guerrière* and no match for the *President* at all. The *President* caught up with the other off Cape Charles at the opening of Chesapeake Bay and there was an engagement. The far outgunned *Little Belt* was disabled, suffering nine killed and twenty-three wounded. The *President* was untouched.

To the Americans, this seemed but revenge for the affair of the *Chesapeake.* To the British, however, it seemed to be the case of a cowardly Yankee deliberately picking on a ship much smaller than itself. The British public began thirsting for war, too.

The governments of the two nations were on the whole reluctant to resort to arms, however popular that might be. The long war with Napoleon was beginning to tell on the British. In 1811 there was a severe depression in Great Britain and American trade could have been most useful even at the price of some leakage into France. As for the United States, Madison was beginning hasty preparations, enlarging the army and polishing the navy. He knew that there was a long way to go before the United States could really be ready for war.

The result was that Madison pressed for negotiations and the British were coming very reluctantly to the conclusion that they ought to yield somewhat. The British Prime Minister, Spencer Perceval, prepared to repeal all restrictions on American trade and give in to all American demands except for the touchy matter of impressment.

And then Fate took a hand. On May 11, 1812, a mentally unbalanced person assassinated Perceval who thus became the only British Prime Minister of modern times to be assassinated. For a period of time, the British government was plunged in confusion

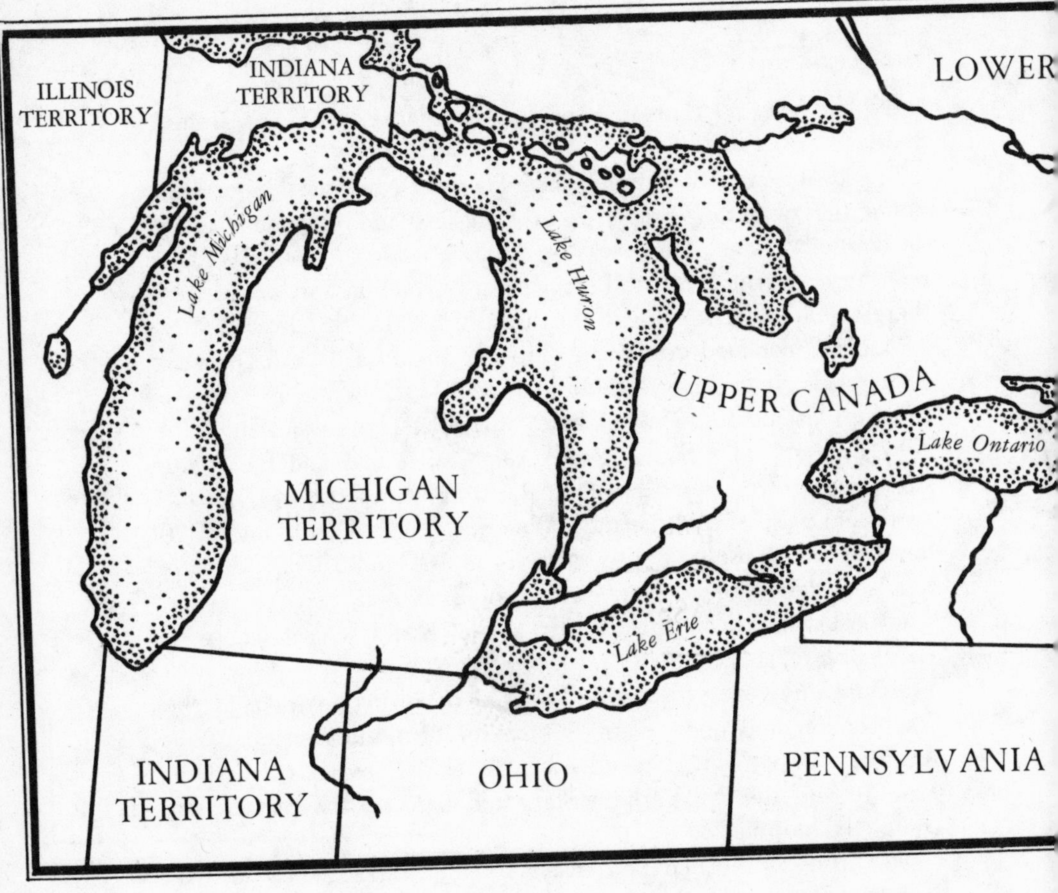

the war, as it opened. The frontier with Canada would seem to be the logical war front and in Canada, Great Britain had only 7000 troops (including but 4000 British regulars) to cover a frontier over a thousand miles long. The Canadian population of half a million was still strongly French in culture and might not be counted on in the British service. Furthermore, the British, as in the Revolutionary War, would have to reinforce its troops by sending them three thousand miles across the stormy Atlantic. Great Britain's situation was worse than in the Revolutionary War, moreover, in that the nation was worn out with the war it had been fighting against France for twenty years, and had its best troops tied up in Spain. Even its greatest weapon, its hold on the sea, was not to be as useful against the United States as it had been against France for the Americans had built a small navy that was well-designed and

and there was no time to consider the quarrel with the United States.

The delay came at a time when Madison could no longer hold down the mounting pressures in Congress and elsewhere for a declaration of war. There was no Atlantic cable in those days and no way of learning about Perceval's assassination for weeks, and therefore no understanding of the disarray in Great Britain.

Madison confined American ships to their harbors to prevent their seizure if war came, then on June 1, 1812, sent a message to Congress asking for war. Debate was hot. The coastal states of New England, as well as New York, New Jersey, and Delaware, strongly anti-French and pro-British, voted against the war, but the south and west carried the day. War was declared by a vote of 79 to 49 in the House of Representatives and 19 to 13 in the Senate. Madison signed the declaration on June 18 and, for the second (and last) time in its history, the United States was at war with Great Britain.

Meanwhile, Great Britain had settled down in the wake of the assassination and once again the matter of trade restrictions on American shipping was taken up. All restrictions were lifted on June 16 and the last parliamentary red tape on the matter was completed on June 23.

So the news traveled both ways simultaneously across the Atlantic, and both sides learned that they were at war over an issue that had already been settled. Yet it is hard to undo a war once the foolish cry of "national honor" has been raised. The United States offered to declare an armistice if the British, in addition to what they had already agreed to, would also give up the right of impressment. This the British would not do and so it remained a matter of war despite everything.

DISASTER AND TRIUMPH

The United States seemed to have a considerable advantage in

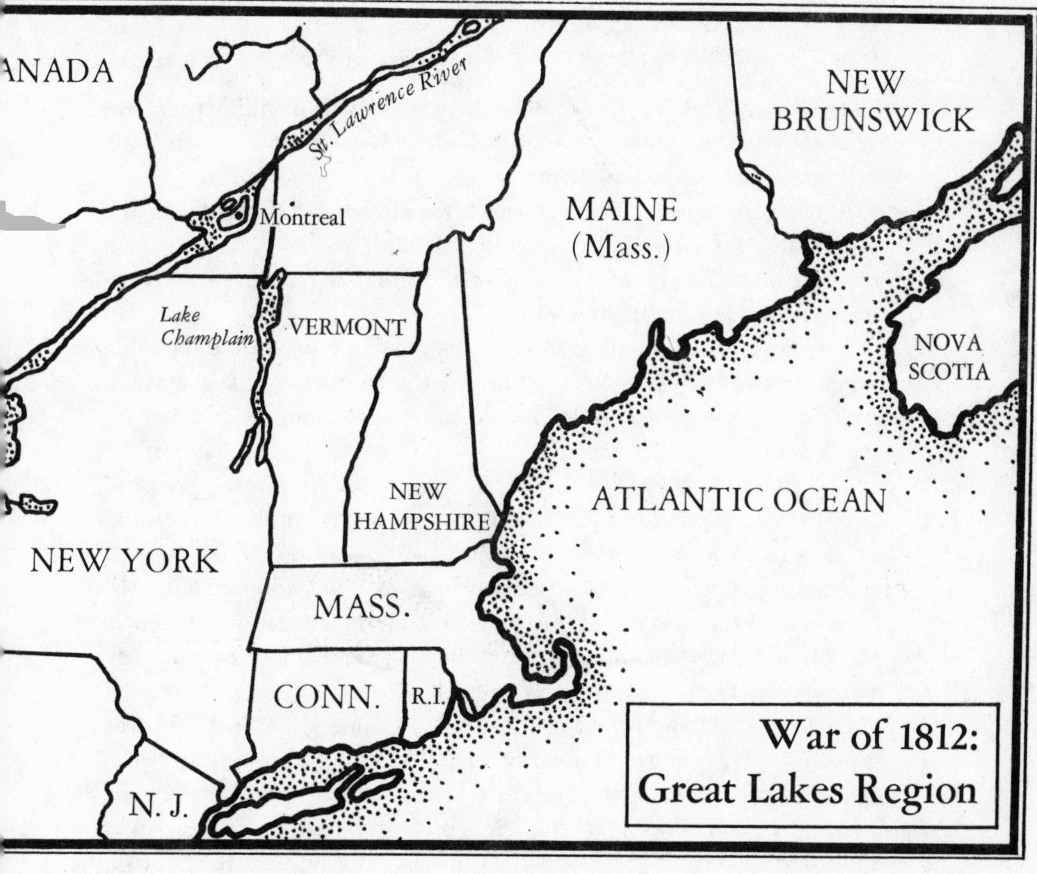

manned by skilled sailors – something the British did not know but were soon to find out.

The United States, however, did not have it all its own way. Though its population was fifteen times that of Canada and it was fighting at home, the richest part of the country, the commercial northeast, was so utterly against the war that they were almost ready to break away from the Union. Neither their manpower nor their money was contributed to the support of the war. Indeed, New England traded with Canada and Great Britain throughout the war and openly contributed to the enemy war effort.

Worst of all was the fact that the United States began the war with a group of generals who were old and utterly incompetent, and with an army that was small and virtually untrained.

Despite this, the United States dreamed of Napoleonic victories.

(The example of Napoleon Bonaparte, who was a military genius, fired all other generals of the time, though few had even a tenth the brilliance that made Napoleon a success.)

A triple-pronged offensive was planned against Canada at the very start of the war. From Lake Champlain, there was to be a drive toward Montreal and Quebec; from Niagara a push westward; from Detroit a push eastward.

However grand it all looked on the map, it was an impossible scheme. The British controlled the sea and the Great Lakes, and the American army was a collection of untrained men under aged incompetents.

The push from Lake Champlain, which was the most important part of the offensive, never even got off the ground. It required soldiers from New England, and the governors of the New England states simply would not contribute men to what they called "Mr. Madison's War." Without the push against Montreal and Quebec, the other two prongs of the offensive were meaningless, but they went on anyay.

General William Hull (born in Derby, Connecticut, in 1753) was governor of Michigan Territory. He had fought in the Revolutionary War but had no military talent whatever. He took up his position in Detroit on July 15, 1812, and prepared (or at least was supposed to prepare) to invade Canada. But it was the British, under a very capable leader, Major General Isaac Brock, who took the offensive.

On July 17, the British took Fort Michilimackinac in northern Michigan with no trouble at all, and the Indians of the northwest, convinced that the British were going to win the war, flocked to them and rose against the United States. Tecumseh was given the rank of brigadier general by the British and he set about harassing the American forces.

Hull, with 2200 men, trying to organize his invasion, crossed the strait into Canada but was quickly in despair. He returned to Detroit and sank into paralyzed inactivity. On August 15, the British took Fort Dearborn, which had been built in 1803 on the site of present-day Chicago, and their Indian auxiliaries massacred many of the American defenders.

General Brock, having secured the northwest, marshaled his

forces (not many), brought them to Detroit, and dressed untrained soldiers in the uniform of British regulars to make his numbers seem more impressive. He demanded that Hull surrender, hinting that there would be an Indian massacre if fighting was allowed to start.

Hull, who had his own daughter and grandchildren in Detroit among the 5000 civilians who had now gathered in the area for protection, was terrified at the possibility of such a massacre. He therefore surrendered without a blow and the British occupied Detroit on August 16.

American attempts to invade Canada across the Niagara River were handled equally fecklessly. This part of the push was under the command of Henry Dearborn (born in Hampton, New Hampshire, on February 23, 1751), who had fought in the Revolutionary War and had served as Secretary of War for eight years under Jefferson. Fort Dearborn was named for him.

Dearborn was as incompetent as Hull and his ill-trained troops showed no liking for combat. Many of them refused to fight even when those among them who crossed into Canada were being defeated in front of their eyes by a small force hurried to the scene by Brock. About all that could be counted as an American gain was that Brock was killed in combat on October 12, and the British were not to have another commander of his caliber during the rest of the war.

The news of the surrender of Detroit horrified Americans. William Hull was court-martialed and condemned to execution (though he was eventually reprieved in view of his services in the Revolutionary War), but that didn't restore the situation.

American morale would have sunk dangerously low, if there had not been astonishing successes just where Great Britain might have been assumed the strongest — at sea.

The American ships, built at the time of the naval war with France, were strong and seaworthy and were handled by men as skilled, at least, as any in the British navy. They were so heavily timbered that they could withstand cannon shot that would destroy any other ships in the world.

The most famous of these was the *Constitution,* for which the metalwork had been made by Paul Revere himself. It was supposed to carry forty-four guns, but really had fifty-four, and could outshoot any ship of its size in the world. Commanding the ship was Isaac Hull (born in Derby, Connecticut, on March 9, 1773). He was the younger brother of the useless William Hull and as competent as the older man was not. Isaac Hull had fought in the naval war with France and had bombarded Derna in support of Eaton during the Tripolitan War.

On July 18, 1812, the *Constitution* had skillfully evaded a squadron of four British ships and on August 19 it encountered the *Guerrière* alone. The *Guerrière* had been impressing seamen and had been missed by the *President* the year before. Now, facing an encounter one to one, the *Constitution* advanced to the fight. On paper the *Guerrière* was roughly equal to the American ship, but in actual fact it was outgunned and outmanned. In two and a half hours, all told, the *Guerrière* was riddled into a worthless hulk that had to be sunk, with seventy-nine casualties to fourteen on the American side.

It was the Bunker Hill of the War of 1812 and was the most important single sea fight in American history. It came three days after the humiliating surrender of Detroit and the Americans needed some good news desperately. In the second place, the defeat of a British ship in single combat was unprecedented and was as humiliating for Great Britain as the loss of Detroit had been for the United States.

What's more, the victory of the *Constitution* over the *Guerrière* was only one of a series. On August 13, six days before, the American ship *Essex* had taken the British *Alert*. On October 18, the American ship *Wasp* captured the British *Frolic*, 600 miles off the Virginia coast, suffering ten casualties to ninety for the British.

On the other side of the Atlantic, off the island of Madeira, the American ship *United States* under Stephen Decatur took the British *Macedonian* on October 25, and brought her back to New London, Connecticut, for the disaffected New Englanders to see – and to cheer, despite themselves.

On December 29, the *Constitution,* under William Bainbridge (born in Princeton, New Jersey, in 1774), replacing Isaac Hull who had been relieved of command at his own request, destroyed the

British *Java* off the coast of Brazil with 33 casualties for the Americans against 150 for the British. It was this battle that the *Constitution* received its nickname of "Old Ironsides" when cannonballs bounced off its walls harmlessly, a name that it has kept ever since (for the ship still exists and is kept as a priceless national treasure).

Nor did the new year bring relief for the harassed British navy. On February 24, 1813, the American ship *Hornet* under James Lawrence (born in Burlington, New Jersey, on October 1, 1781), who had been with Decatur at the destruction of the *Philadelphia*, sank the British ship *Peacock* off British Guiana.

However much the British might remind themselves that they were fighting the Americans with only the little finger of their left hand, and that the bulk of their energy was consumed in the fight against Napoleon, the first half-year of the war was hard for them to bear. The whole world could see that, ship for ship, the Americans were superior to the British and the powers of the world could not help finding something laughable in the fighting cock of the ocean backing off, bloody-nosed, from the Yankee bantam.

Despite the months of war, the disaster on land and the triumph at sea, the election of 1812 went through on schedule. Eighteen states were now voting, for on April 30, 1812, the southernmost section of the Louisiana Purchase, well-populated from French and Spanish days, entered the Union as Louisiana. It was the first state to be carved out of territory west of the Mississippi River.

The election of 1812 was the first wartime election in the nation's history and it set a precedent. In all the time since the ratification of the Constitution, the quadrennial presidential elections and the biennial congressional elections have never been suspended for any reason no matter what the crisis. Nor has there ever been any formal limitation of the right of an opposition to do what it could to unseat incumbents, whatever troubles might be afflicting the nation.

The Democratic-Republicans nominated Madison again, of course. They would also have renominated George Clinton, but he had died on April 20, 1812, the first Vice President to die in office. The Democratic-Republicans, aware that they were weakest in the northeast, sought a New Englander they could add to the ticket.

(This sort of "balanced ticket" has been a general feature in American politics.)

They picked Elbridge Gerry of Massachusetts, the most pronounced Democratic-Republican of the region. He had just completed a term as governor of Massachusetts and had added his name to the nation's political vocabulary. While governor, he had rearranged the boundaries of the state legislative districts in such a way as to concentrate Federalist populations into as few districts as possible and give Democratic-Republican victories in as many as possible. Some of the districts had odd shapes, of course, and one was described as looking like a salamander.

"Salamander!" growled a newspaper editor, on February 11, 1812, "say rather a Gerrymander." The term "gerrymander" has been used ever since to describe the manipulation of political boundaries to secure partisan advantage.

The Federalists, in an effort to increase their strength, decided to nominate someone who was not from New England and was not particularly identified with Federalist doctrine. Antiwar Democratic-Republicans of the commercial areas had nominated DeWitt Clinton (born in Little Britain, New York, on March 2, 1769) for President, to run against Madison. He was the mayor of New York City and a nephew of the just-dead Vice President. The Federalists decided to support him.

For Vice President, they chose Charles Jared Ingersoll (born 1749), a moderate Federalist from Pennsylvania. Ingersoll was totally unimportant and he was the first nonentity, but not the last, to be run for President or Vice President by a major political party.

The electors voted on December 2, 1812 and Madison won by a majority similar to that in 1808. (No American President has ever been defeated in wartime.) The 1812 victory was sectional, however. Madison won the entire south and west, but above the Mason-Dixon line he won only Pennsylvania and Vermont. The Federalists gained in both the Senate and the House. Indeed, their representation in the House stood at sixty-eight in the Thirteenth Congress, nearly double what it had been in the Twelfth. Nevertheless, the Democratic-Republicans retained firm control of both houses of Congress.

ON THE GREAT LAKES

The glamour of American victories at sea in 1812 did not lessen the backbreaking load on the incompetently led American armies. Worse yet, Great Britain was feeling the load upon its shoulders lightening in 1813.

Just as the War of 1812 opened, Napoleon had gone marching off to Russia. Many Americans felt that Napoleon was carrying American fortunes with him and, indeed, if Napoleon had won the quick victory he dreamed of and had smashed the only continental power that still dared oppose him, Great Britain would very likely have been forced to make peace with the United States on American terms.

But that was not what happened. Napoleon won fruitless victories in Russia, was forced to march out again through the snow, and left his entire army behind him. With that, Napoleon's star was permanently dimmed. He was no more the supergeneral and the European nations he had subdued began to rise against him. Great Britain was still deeply involved, but the aura of crisis had begun to lift and she could spare more time for the annoying Americans.

On December 26, 1812, the British declared a blockade of Chesapeake and Delaware Bays and in the spring of 1813, they extended it to all American ports *except* those in New England. (There was no need to hamper New England trade since that was going very largely to the benefit of the British. Besides, by giving the region special treatment, Great Britain hoped to encourage New England to secede from the Union.)

On the whole, the British blockade grew steadily tighter throughout 1813 and 1814. Goods grew scarce in the United States, prices rose, men were thrown out of work. The individual feats of American ships continued (at a declining rate) and American privateers captured over 1000 British merchantmen during the war, but this did little to abate the general overall superiority (by numbers if not by quality) of the British fleet and the fact that the American coast was, and remained, blockaded.

There were even naval defeats to add to the gloom.

The *Chesapeake,* which had been the victim of the attack by the *Leopard* in the years before the war, was now under the command of James Lawrence, who had taken the *Peacock* early in 1813. On June 1, 1813, the *Chesapeake* encountered the *Shannon* just thirty miles outside Boston harbor. The two ships were equally matched in guns, but the unlucky *Chesapeake* was manned with a green crew that had not yet been trained into shape.

Lawrence could not bring himself to flee before the enemy, and accepted battle. It was hopeless. The *Chesapeake* was raked with gunfire and in fifteen minutes suffered 146 casualties to the British 83. Lawrence himself was mortally wounded and as he was carried below, he gasped out orders to speed up the fire and keep on fighting. "Don't give up the ship!" he said.

The ship *was* given up and the British carried it off to Halifax, but Lawrence's professional attitude, which put his dying thought on his ship and not on himself, gave his death a kind of glamour and has made him and his cry a legend to the American navy ever since.

And what of the northwest? After the surrender of Detroit, there was almost an American vacuum in the region. The area north and west of the state of Ohio was virtually abandoned and if the British did not occupy it in force, the reason was their own weakness in numbers and not anything the Americans could do.

In desperation, the Americans turned to the only Army officer who had in any way gained renown in recent years – William Henry Harrison, the hero of the dubious victory at Tippecanoe. Harrison was given ten thousand men and told to retake Detroit.

Harrison advanced northward from the Ohio River in the winter of 1812–1813, toward the general area where the Battle of Fallen Timbers had been fought nearly twenty years before. He established himself south of Lake Erie and sent columns toward Detroit. One of them, working its way forward through horrible weather, reached Frenchtown, about forty miles south of Detroit. No one bothered to set up a night patrol so the force was surprised by the British under Colonel Thomas Proctor and wiped out. Those Americans who weren't killed were captured.

Proctor and his Indian allies under Tecumseh then moved southward against Harrison's fortifications. Harrison stood his ground during the spring and summer of 1813 but there was no chance whatever of his resuming offensive operations as long as the British controlled the Great Lakes. The British could ship men and supplies to Detroit and the west easily from the centers of Canadian power further east. American supplies and reinforcements, however, had to come painfully overland through what was still largely a wilderness.

Attempts were made by the Americans to puncture the lake front farther east. On April 22, 1813, some 1600 American troops under the explorer, Zebulon Pike, embarked at Sackets Harbor on the easternmost edge of Lake Ontario and sailed 150 miles westward to land at York (on the site of which there now stands Toronto).

The expedition was under the overall direction of Dearborn, who had been ordered to move toward Montreal. He thought, however, that if he could take over the naval craft at York, Lake Ontario would be under American control and a move to Montreal would then be more effective.

York was indeed taken and a couple of ships destroyed (with Pike killed in the course of the operation) but the Americans did not manage to take control of the lake. Instead, American soldiers got out of control and gratuitously burned government buildings in York, thus setting the precedent for other cases of purposeless destruction.

The raiding party then returned eastward. A second attempt was led by Colonel Winfield Scott (born near Petersburg, Virginia, on June 13, 1786), who was proving himself that rarity of the War of 1812, a competent American officer. He led a raid across the Niagara River on May 27, 1813, to Fort George on the southern shore of Lake Ontario. The British evacuated the fort and moved westward. The Americans followed and at Stony Creek, seventy-five miles west, the British stopped. On June 6, at the Battle of Stony Creek, Scott was wounded and put out of action, and the Americans fell back before smaller numbers of British. The offensive could proceed no farther.

Dearborn was relieved of his command on July 6 and, incredibly enough, was replaced by James Wilkinson who had never in his life showed competence in anything, not even in the treasons he had forever been undertaking. At the moment, alas, he was basking in some glory for, on April 13, he had taken Mobile from the Spaniard's feeble grip and placed all that remained of West Florida in American hands. (It was the only territorial gain made by the United States in the War of 1812, and, ironically, it came at the hands of the same Wilkinson who had so long striven to take territory away from the nation.)

Wilkinson was ordered to take Montreal and a two-pronged attack was planned. Wilkinson was to move down the St. Lawrence River and another force under Wade Hampton (born in Halifax county, Virginia, about 1752) was to move north from Lake Champlain. Each general was incompetent, and each hated the other. No better recipe for the failure of a two-pronged attack could possibly be invented.

Wilkinson moved down the St. Lawrence to Chrysler's Farm, ninety miles southwest of Montreal. There a part of his army was defeated by a British force considerably fewer in numbers. Wilkinson promptly quit for the winter.

Hampton moved northwestward in gingerly fashion, was beaten by a small British force, and quickly returned to his starting point.

As though that weren't bad enough, the American troops retreating from the Canadian side of the Niagara River in December, saw fit to burn some villages as they moved out. There was no purpose to it, just general mischief. The result could have been foreseen. On December 29, 1813, the British burned Buffalo in retaliation.

As far as land fighting was concerned, then, 1813 was nothing to cheer about. For the Americans it had been a series of fiascos, and in Europe Napoleon was suffering further gigantic defeats, this time in Germany. The time was coming closer when Great Britain might turn her full attention to the United States.

In fact, the United States might have had to accept a losing peace in 1814 but for one man, Commodore Oliver Hazard Perry (born at South Kingston, Rhode Island, on August 23, 1785), who had already seen service in the Mediterranean. He was only twenty-eight years old at the time, and is the first person to figure prominently in this book who had been born after the Treaty of Paris had established American independence.

He was assigned the task of wresting control of Lake Erie from the British so that the United States could supply the northwest. He arrived at Erie, Pennsylvania, on March 27, 1813. He had no fleet. He was waiting for the equipment required for the building of six small ships, equipment that was arriving painfully overland from Philadelphia.

With that, and by using green timber, the ships were built under Perry's breakneck driving force. When Scott conducted his raid across the Niagara River, Perry was able to bring in some additional ships from Buffalo, the one useful result of the fighting in the Lake Ontario region.

In the end, Perry had a fleet of ten ships and by August 2 they moved off into the lake, searching for British ships. Perry's flagship was the *Lawrence,* named for the captain of the *Chesapeake,* who had died two months before. The cry "Don't Give Up The Ship" was inscribed on the *Lawrence*'s battle-flag.

It was not till September 10 that battle was forced. Perry found himself facing six enemy ships at Put-in Bay in one of the islands in western Lake Erie, not far north of where Hull's forces remained under siege. The two fleets were fairly evenly matched in number of guns, but the American guns worked more rapidly.

The squadrons banged away at each other for three hours. The British concentrated on the *Lawrence* which was soon riddled, with 80 per cent of its men killed or disabled. Perry could not oversee the battle from its deck so he got into an open boat and was taken to another ship, the *Niagara,* under a hail of small-arms fire. The successful transfer roused the spirits of the Americans and the fight continued with heightened fury. Casualties were about equal on both sides but it was the British squadron that was battered into surrender. All the British ships gave up and Perry sent a message to Harrison that turned out to be one of the most famous announcements of victory in military history. He said, "We have met the enemy and they are ours."

The American victory at the Battle of Lake Erie was the Saratoga of the War of 1812. It meant that now it was the Americans who could be easily supplied and reinforced and not the British. The British under Proctor were forced to evacuate Detroit on September 18, just eight days after the battle.

Harrison now moved to the offensive. He shifted 4500 men

northward across Lake Erie and landed them on Canadian territory. The British retreated before them and the Americans pursued until they came to a point on the Thames River about sixty miles east of Detroit.

Proctor would have retreated further but Tecumseh, who had opposed the evacuation of Detroit and was furious at the retreat, insisted on a battle. Proctor gave in and on October 5, 1813, the Battle of the Thames was fought.

It was the one American land victory of the year, due particularly to the dash of the Kentucky cavalry under Colonel Richard M. Johnson (born near Louisville in 1780). There were fewer than 50 casualties on either side, but nearly 500 British were taken prisoners and most important of all, Tecumseh himself was killed. (Johnson claimed that he himself had done the killing.)

The Battle of the Thames ended the war in the northwest, though the British held on to far northern Fort Michilimackinac, and the disgrace of Hull's surrender of Detroit was more or less avenged.

12

SAFELY THROUGH

BATTLE IN THE NORTH

The year 1814 opened with an American land victory, of a sort, in the south. By mid-1813, news of British successes in the north had lured the Creek Indians into opening hostilities against the Americans. The Creek War that followed took the form that almost all Indian wars did. It opened with a surprise Indian attack and victory. On August 30, 1813, just a couple of weeks before the Battle of Lake Erie, the Creeks attacked Fort Mims, about thirty-five miles north of Mobile, killing most of the people in the fort.

In response, the flamboyant Andrew Jackson of Tennessee (born on the boundary line between the Carolinas on March 15, 1767), with one arm temporarily useless from a dueling wound, led a company of militia southward in November. In the space of half a year, Jackson's forces pushed their way southward (against stiff Creek resistance) until a climactic battle was fought at Horseshoe Bend in what is now eastern Alabama, on March 27, 1814. The

Creeks were forced to surrender and the Indian power was broken in the southwest.

A victory over Indians, however, was insufficient to make 1814 look anything but dark. On April 11, 1814, two weeks after the Battle of Horseshoe Bend, Napoleon was finally defeated, forced to abdicate, and was eventually exiled to Elba. Great Britain was complete victor in the European war and its prestige had reached a new peak. It had army veterans who had fought long years in Spain and who were the most formidable land force the nation had had at its disposal in many years.

Great Britain was ready, therefore, to make war on the United States in earnest. It tightened its blockade and now included even New England, which had, after all, never actually broken away from the United States.

The British prepared an offensive that was intended to crush the United States once and for all. Three more or less simultaneous actions were planned, one in the north at Lake Champlain, one in the center at Chesapeake Bay, and one in the south at New Orleans.

Considering the American record so far in the war (on land, at least) it might have seemed the United States could scarcely avoid being smashed. However, two years of fighting, while Great Britain was chiefly occupied elsewhere, had done some good. A body of trained soldiers had slowly been built up and many of the dead-wood officers had broken and had been shoved aside. Wilkinson, for instance, was finally retired in disgrace and his role in American history was at last over. Those generals who had displayed some talent were now in charge.

The Americans were of course aware that they might look forward to a strengthening of the British forces in the north where the major land fighting had been proceeding for two years. They attempted to strike before those British reinforcements could arrive.

Once again the Americans crossed the Niagara River into Canadian territory. The American force was only 3500 in numbers but they were well-trained professionals now and they were under the lead of the competent Major General Jacob Jennings Brown (born in Bucks county, Pennsylvania, in 1775).

On July 3, 1814, the Americans took Fort Erie, just across the river from Buffalo, and marched northward along the river toward

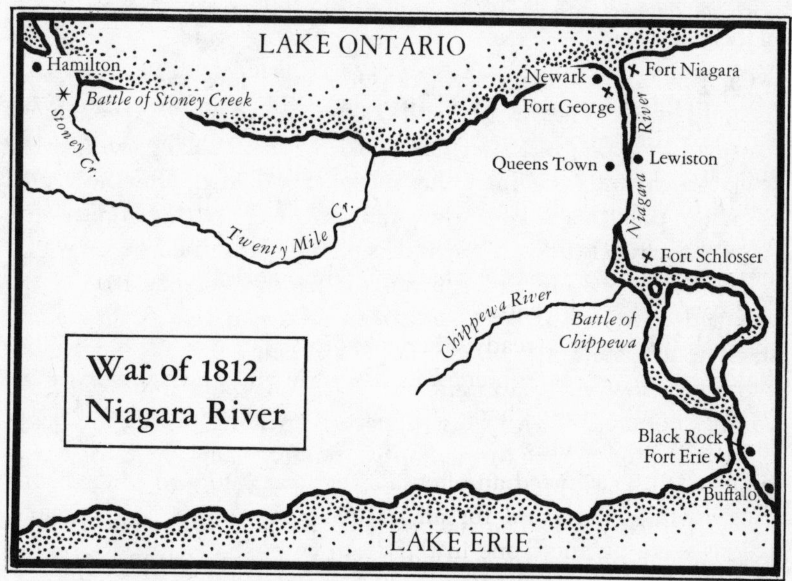

Lake Ontario. The British prepared a defensive line on the northern banks of the Chippewa River, sixteen miles north of Fort Erie and about halfway between the two lakes.

The advance forces of the Americans were beaten back by the British and for a moment there was confusion, for some of the American soldiers were celebrating Independence Day. A brigade under Scott managed to get into action, however, and were so skillfully handled that the British were maneuvered into a concave American line which could greet them with fire on both flanks. The British, suffering 500 casualties to 300 for the Americans, broke and fled.

This was the first time that equal numbers of British and Americans had met in open battle with no advantage of position on either side — and the Americans had won. The Battle of Chippewa, in a way, marks the birth of the American army as a *professional* fighting force.

Brown probed further northward. The British gathered reinforcements, however, and about three miles north of the field where the Battle of Chippewa had been fought, they prepared defensive positions at Lundy's Lane, a small village just on the Canadian side of Niagara Falls.

On July 25, battle was joined. Once again, it was a matter of banging away. The British with 3000 men to 2600 for the Americans had the edge but after five hours of hard hacking, with every man thrown into the fray, the battle ended in a draw with 900 casualties on either side. Brown and Scott were both wounded and so were the two leading commanders on the British side.

The Battle of Lundy's Lane was the hardest-fought battle of the war and once again the American soldiers had shown they could stand up to the best the British could hand out.

Brown, however, had failed to get American ships on Lake Ontario to come down to his support. Unwilling to risk the possibility of having to face further British reinforcement, he retreated to Fort Erie and left the British in possesion of the field.

The British now advanced in their turn and laid siege to Fort Erie, through the entire month of August. The Americans defended themselves skillfully and, in sorties, did considerable damage to the besieging forces, who were finally forced to withdraw on September 21. Brown then planned another advance but again failed to secure naval cooperation and, on November 21, 1814, abandoned Fort Erie and crossed back to the American side of the Niagara River.

Brown's campaign, though far more skillfully conducted than any of the earlier forays of the war, had nevertheless ended in frustration. For two and a half years, the Americans had been probing at Canada and they had not yet gained a single acre of its territory. Nor were they ever to. Never again, after Brown's recrossing of the river, were the enemy feet of any foreign enemy to stand on Canadian soil.

While the American effort was concentrated on the Niagara front, the British were planning their main effort farther east at Lake Champlain. There the Governor General of Canada, Sir George Prevost, was in command of 11,000 British veterans of the Napoleonic wars. In addition, there were 800 men on board the sixteen British ships on Lake Champlain's waters. It was the best and largest army that Great Britain had sent to North America in this war. The American forces in the area had, on the other hand, been diminished because half of them had been sent to the Niagara front. Only 3300 men remained to face the British.

It did not appear that there was anything that could prevent Prevost's army from doing what Burgoyne had failed to do thirty-seven years before – marching down Lake Champlain and the Hudson River to New York City, splitting off disaffected New England and perhaps joining up with the British army which was attacking the heart of America farther south. If this could be carried through, the United States would have to surrender and accept whatever terms a victorious Great Britain would see fit to offer.

And had it been a better commander in charge of the British drive, this might have happened. It was Prevost, however, and he was a fearful man. He did not wish to march too far southward unless he were sure that his supply lines across the length of the lake were secure. They could not be secure in his eyes unless a small American flotilla of fourteen ships could be removed from Lake Champlain.

Consequently, when he crossed into New York State on August 31, 1814, he only marched about twenty-five miles to Plattsburg, halfway down the western shore of the lake. There, on September 6, he paused and waited for the news that the American ships had been disposed of.

The American ships were commanded by Thomas McDonough (born in Delaware on December 31, 1783), who had been with Decatur at the burning of the *Philadelphia.* He had two fewer ships than the enemy and six fewer guns. However, his short-range guns were more powerful than those of the British ships so his task was somehow to maneuver the enemy into close quarters.

He therefore deliberately placed his ships along a narrow channel. The British ships, if they were to move southward to support Prevost, would have to pass within 300 yards of the American ships. It was that, or not move at all, and Prevost, caught in the trap of fear, insisted they move.

The British ships came down on September 11, 1814, and for two hours the two squadrons bombarded each other furiously. McDonough handled his ships masterfully, bringing his own flagship around so that it could better place its broadsides in the enemy flagship. In the end, both sides suffered over a hundred casualties, but McDonough's ships were still alive while the British ships were battered into helplessness.

As a result of the Battle of Lake Champlain, the Americans had gained complete control of the lake and Prevost, in despair, gave up the offensive and, abandoning his supplies, returned to Canada. He was recalled in disgrace by the British government, while McDonough got a gold medal from Congress and estates were voted for him by the legislatures of both New York and Vermont.

So though the Americans failed honorably on the Niagara front, the British failed rather more disgracefully on the Lake Champlain front, and the war in the north finally came to an end with each side on its own side of the boundary.

BATTLE IN THE CENTER

The central prong of the British triple offensive got off to a better start.

In August, 1814, while the Americans on the Niagara front had retired after the Battle of Lundy's Lane and while Prevost was preparing to march southward in force, ships of the British blockading squadron, with 4000 British veterans aboard, entered Chesapeake Bay. They moved up the Patuxent River and, on August 19, landed at Benedict, Maryland, twenty-five miles southeast of Washington, D.C.

One of their aims was to seize certain gunboats which were under Commodore Joshua Barney (born in Maryland in 1759), who had been one of the most successful privateers of the Revolutionary War. The only way Barney could keep the gunboats out of British hands was to destroy them, and this he did.

With the gunboats gone, the British turned to their next objective, a march on Washington. Under General Robert Ross, the British force moved northward along the Patuxent. Presumably,

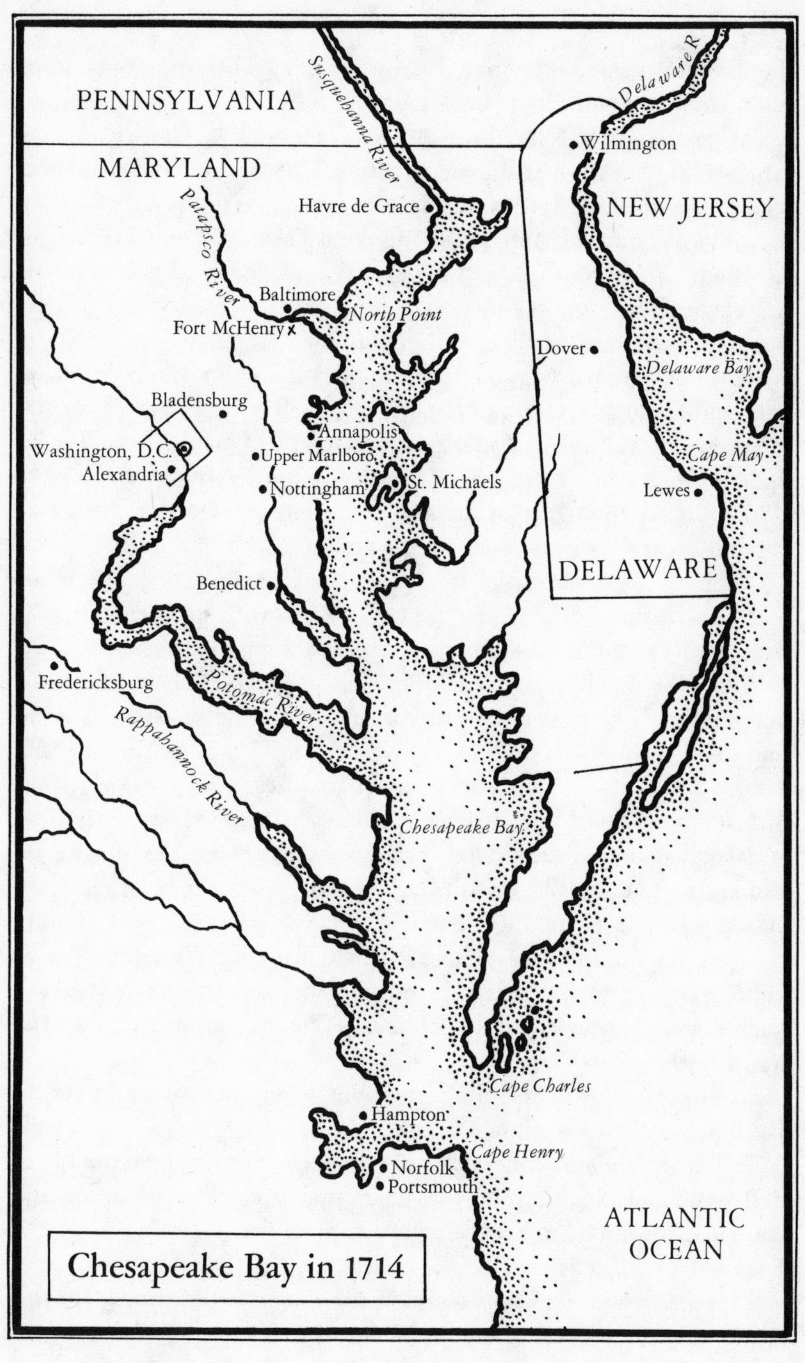

Chesapeake Bay in 1714

they expected resistance, but there was none. The Americans were completely and entirely unprepared.

The Secretary of War, John Armstrong (born in Carlisle, Pennsylvania, in 1758), was an incompetent and that is not surprising when you consider he was a close friend of Wilkinson. It never occurred to him that America's long coastline might be attacked by an enemy that controlled the sea. What's more, the individual American states, while eager to defend themselves, felt no obligation to defend the District of Columbia.

Some 7000 troops were scraped up, of whom only a few hundred were professional soldiers, and of whom the best were the 400 sailors whom Barney had marched overland to Washington after he had destroyed his gunboats. These were under the command of William H. Winder, one of the remaining incompetents of the army, kept on because he was cousin of the governor of Maryland.

When, on August 24, the British reached Bladensburg, five miles north of Washington, Winder hastened there with his forces. President Madison and most of his cabinet came along to observe.

What they saw was an American disgrace. The Americans outnumbered the British two to one and had a better position. The untrained American soldiers, however, could not withstand the enemy fire. After suffering a few casualties, they broke within fifteen minutes, and fled, leaving Washington open to the enemy.

Barney's 400 sailors added a touch of glory to the defeat by stubbornly holding the British back for half an hour, but they were outnumbered ten to one. Barney, wounded in the fight, finally ordered them to give way. Ross's British army marched into Washington, D.C., and for the first and only time in the history of the United States after the Revolutionary War, its capital was in the hands of the enemy.

President Madison and the rest of the government were forced to flee most precipitously into Virginia.

The British commander had been specifically ordered to effect destruction of the seat of the government in retaliation for the American burning of York and other places in Canada. This the British did with relish.

They set fire to the Capitol and to the Executive Mansion, as well as to most of the other public buildings. There was no looting, however, and no destruction of private buildings. The next day, the 25th, a bad thunderstorm doused the smoldering fires and the British left the city, having accomplished their purpose. Madison and other members of the government crept back on the 27th and Secretary Armstrong was forced to resign by popular demand.

(It was only by a narrow margin that Congress voted to rebuild Washington, rather than to establish a new capital elsewhere. The Executive Mansion was painted white to hide some of the effects of the fire and it has been known as the "White House" ever since.)

The British, meanwhile, had moved on to a more important task, an attack on Baltimore.

Baltimore was an important port and had it been attacked directly and at once it might have been taken. The British had, however, turned aside to wreak a petty revenge on Washington, and the delay had given the Americans time – which was what they needed more than anything else.

General Samuel Smith (born in Carlisle, Pennsylvania, in 1752), who was a senator from Maryland, set the citizens of Baltimore to work and supervised the building of a formidable set of defense works about the city. While the British wasted their time setting fires in Washington, Smith gathered 13,000 men and placed a thousand men in Fort McHenry, which controlled Baltimore harbor.

The British fleet moved up the Chesapeake and on September 12, eighteen days after the burning of the Executive Mansion, and the day after the Battle of Lake Champlain had ended the British thrust in the north, they arrived at North Point, ten miles southeast of Baltimore.

British troops disembarked and marched toward Baltimore. At Godly Woods, five miles east of Baltimore, they met a contingent of Americans sent forward by Smith. This was no Bladensburg. The British found themselves being badly battered and Ross, the conqueror of Washington, was killed.

The Americans, after inflicting 300 casualties to their own 200, finally withdrew but the British could see that they would not be able to storm Baltimore by land. The city would have to be softened up first by bombardment from the sea.

On the night of September 13, therefore, the British ships drew up as closely as they could to the guns of Fort McHenry and began a night-long bombardment. On board one of the ships was an American lawyer, Francis Scott Key (born in Frederick county, Maryland, August 1, 1779), who was trying to negotiate the release of an aged physician, a friend of his who had been captured in Washington.

He had to remain on board during the bombardment and spent an anxious night wondering if Fort McHenry would be forced to surrender. When the dawn was breaking, the old physician, just as anxious, kept asking, "Is the flag still there?"

Inspired, Key wrote a four-stanza poem expressing their feelings. The first two stanzas are as follows:

Oh, say, can you see, by the dawn's early light,
What so proudly we hailed at the twilight's last gleaming?
Whose broad stripes and bright stars, through the perilous fight,
O'er the ramparts we watched, were so gallantly streaming!
And the rockets' red glare, the bombs bursting in air,
Gave proof through the night that our flag was still there:
O say, does that star-spangled banner yet wave
O'er the land of the free and the home of the brave?

On the shore, dimly seen through the mists of the deep,
Where the foe's haughty host in dread silence reposes,
What is that which the breeze, o'er the towering steep,
As it fitfully blows, now conceals, now discloses?
Now it catches the gleam of the morning's first beam,
In full glory reflected now shines on the stream:
'Tis the star-spangled banner! O long may it wave
O'er the land of the free and the home of the brave.

Key called the poem "The Defense of Fort McHenry." It was published on September 20, a week after the bombardment, and achieved instant popularity. It was noted that the words could be made to fit an old drinking-song called "To Anacreon in Heaven" and the poem, sung in this fashion, and eventually called "The Star-Spangled Banner," was one day to become the national anthem of the United States.

As the poem indicates, the bombardment of Fort McHenry was a failure for the British. The whole project was given up. The British soldiers re-boarded their ships and left Baltimore on September 17.

A month later, the fleet left Chesapeake Bay for the West Indies. The attack in the center, though it had made more of a splash at the start, was as great a failure as the attack in the north.

Meanwhile, peace negotiations were proceeding. The more Napoleon's star declined after his defeat in Russia, the more anxious President Madison and Secretary of State James Monroe had become to work out some sort of peace before the full British fury could be turned on the United States. The American peace mission, which was attempting negotiations in Europe, included Gallatin (who had remained Secretary of the Treasury under Madison) and John Quincy Adams (born in Quincy, Massachusetts, on July 11, 1767, and the eldest son of ex-President John Adams).

For well over a year the American negotiators struggled for something they could live with. At first they had insisted that any peace must include the abandonment by the British of the right of impressment, but when Napoleon abdicated and the American cause seemed to be growing desperate, that point of view was given up. On instructions from home, they agreed to accept a peace treaty that did not mention the matter of impressment.

The British, however, were not easy to placate. In their view the Americans had stabbed them in the back when they were fighting the world menace of Napoleon. The British were determined, therefore, not to let the despised Yankees off the hook too easily. They demanded territorial concessions of all sorts, which the Americans could not grant. The news of the burning of Washington made the British attitude haughtier still, but soon thereafter came the news of failures at Lake Champlain and Baltimore and there was a sudden deflation of British pride.

The British government turned to the Duke of Wellington, who was their greatest general and who had done much to help defeat Napoleon, and asked him if he would take over the war in North America. Wellington said he would do so, if ordered, but that without control of the lakes it would do no good. He advised a peace without territorial changes.

That did it. On December 24, 1814, a peace treaty was signed at Ghent, in what is now Belgium. The Treaty of Ghent did nothing more than restore matters as they had been. There was no mention of impressment, no straightening out of problems of trade, no changes in territory. However, with the Napoleonic wars over, it was reasonable to expect that the British attitude would now relax and so it was enough that there would now be peace. The United States, after two and a half years of more defeat than victory, was in no mood to ask for more.

BATTLE IN THE SOUTH

There was one serious catch, though. The Treaty of Ghent did not become legally binding until it was ratified by both governments and it would take some six weeks for the news to reach Washington, D.C. If, somehow, the people on the battle scene knew the treaty was signed then active hostilities would cease, pending ratification, but there was no Atlantic cable in 1814. The fighting went on.

The third prong of Great Britain's triple offensive, the one against New Orleans, was slated to start in the fall of 1814 and it proceeded.

What's more, Andrew Jackson was in progress, too. Jackson was easily the most colorful personality of the period in American history. As a teenage boy, he had been taken prisoner by the British during the Revolutionary War and was struck across the face with the flat of a saber for refusing to polish an officer's boots. Since Jackson rarely forgot an injury, he remained anti-British the rest of his life.

After the Revolutionary War, he lived in North Carolina, became a lawyer, and soon moved to Tennessee. He was part of the convention that drafted a constitution for the new state, then on its behalf, served a time in each of the houses of Congress. He returned to Nashville where he sat on the bench as a judge and found himself briefly attracted by Aaron Burr's smooth schemes. As soon as Jackson realized that Burr was planning treason, he withdrew his support.

When the war of 1812 broke out, Jackson, who headed the

Tennessee militia, virtually foamed at the mouth with eagerness to get at the British. When he finally was assigned a task, however, it was to serve against the Creek Indians.

The successful conclusion of that campaign, plus the treaty by which the Creek Indians gave up most of what is now the state of Alabama to the United States, made Jackson a hero to the west. Eagerly, he advanced southward to tackle the British.

It was certain in 1814 that the British would attack in the south and aim ultimately at New Orleans. Jackson, however, felt that the best strategy was for the British to seize a base on the Gulf Coast, Mobile, perhaps, or better yet, Pensacola in Spanish Florida, and from that move to strike at the Mississippi north of New Orleans in order to take that rich port by suffocation.

With that in mind, and against instructions (he rarely paid

attention to instructions), he established a base of his own at Mobile and, striking eastward, invaded Florida and placed an occupying force in Pensacola on November 7, 1814. His reasoning was that Spain was allied to Great Britain in the war against Napoleon, and the ally of your enemy is also your enemy.

The British offensive got under way on November 26, when a fleet carrying 7500 veteran British soldiers left the West Indies and headed into the Gulf of Mexico. Leading those troops was General Edward Pakenham, whose sister was married to the Duke of Wellington.

It took a while for Jackson to realize that the British were heading directly for New Orleans and were not going to attempt to establish a base on the Gulf Coast first. When that became clear, Jackson raced westward to Baton Rouge, eighty miles northwest of New Orleans, to await developments.

On December 13, the British fleet entered Lake Borgne, an inlet of the Gulf of Mexico, the western edge of which was only twelve miles east of New Orleans. At once, Jackson sped his troops to that city, placed it under martial law, launched rapid attacks that kept the British off balance, and built up a defense line southeast of the city.

While the two sides maneuvered for position, the Treaty of Ghent was signed. There was no way anyone could tell this, however.

On January 8, 1815, ten days after the treaty was signed, Pakenham launched his attack. He sent 5300 men against the breastworks behind which were 4500 men from Kentucky and Tennessee, each one with a long rifle and each one an expert marksman. For the British it was suicide; they were merely animated bull's-eyes.

The American riflemen fired at their pleasure and in half an hour they had killed or wounded 2000 British soldiers at the cost of 21 casualties for themselves. Three generals, including Pakenham himself, were among those killed.

The British drew back and, after a stunned waiting period, re-embarked on January 27 and were on their way to try their luck at Mobile after all when the news of the peace treaty came.

Although the Battle of New Orleans would never have been

fought if Americans had known the Treaty of Ghent was signed it was, in some ways, the most influential battle of the war.

For one thing, the news of the lopsided victory reached the American public before the news of peace did, and it gave the United States the feeling of having won the war. If the duel between the *Constitution* and the *Guerrière* had been the Bunker Hill of the War of 1812, and the Battle of Lake Erie had been the Saratoga, the Battle of New Orleans was the Yorktown.

After that, the news of a compromise peace that solved none of the points for which the war was fought neither disheartened nor humiliated the nation. The news of the treaty arrived in New York on February 11, 1815, and peace was formally proclaimed by President Madison on February 17. By that time, with the Battle of New Orleans under their belts, Americans could look the British in the eye and defy them to maintain that the War of 1812 had been an American defeat.

As another fillip to American pride, there was the matter of the Barbary States. The ruler of Algeria had seized the occasion of the War of 1812 to declare war on the United States, seize American ships, and imprison American nationals. As soon as peace came, Stephen Decatur was sent with ten ships to the Mediterranean. By June 30, 1815, he had forced Algeria to capitulate and all troubles with the Barbary States were over.

As a matter of fact, the news of the Battle of New Orleans had an even more salutary effect upon the British. On the whole, the British public, which learned of the peace virtually as soon as it was signed, was very dissatisfied. The glory of having defeated Napoleon and the fact that the British had burned Washington, D.C., made them feel that nothing less than absolute victory over the United States was acceptable. A compromise peace they felt to be a base surrender. If nothing more had developed, it is possible that British resentment might have made the peace unstable.

The news of the Battle of New Orleans had a calming effect on British public opinion. Bloodthirsty demands for crushing the Americans suddenly seemed pointless. On top of that, shortly after the news of the British defeat arrived, there came the tidings that Napoleon had left Elba and had landed in France. Suddenly, the war against Napoleon flared up again and the British had far more serious matters to think of than the Yankees across the sea.

Napoleon's new effort didn't last long and, on June 18, 1815, he was crushed once and for all by the Duke of Wellington at the Battle of Waterloo. That was enough glory for the British and they needed no more at the expense of the United States.

As a result, while there were to be many periods of friction and anger between the two nations, they settled down at last to a mutual toleration, and even friendship. The wounds of the half-century period covered in this book were forgotten and there was never again to be war between Great Britain and the United States.

Indeed, the Battle of Waterloo ushered in a period of almost exactly a century in which there were only local wars, usually brief and not bloody, in Europe. In that time, Great Britain remained in unchallenged control of the seas, and behind the barrier of the British navy, the United States could, for a century, grow and develop without much fear of external interference.

Insofar as this was the result of a British toleration born of the calming effect of the Battle of New Orleans, that battle was one of the most useful ever fought by the United States and, if events of the 20th century are considered, by Great Britain as well.

THE AFTERMATH OF PEACE

By 1815, it can fairly be said that the United States had proved itself to have had a successful birth and to have survived its critical infancy. It was never again to be in danger from a foreign power and so certainly did this seem to be the result of the safe passage through the War of 1812 that that war is sometimes called "The Second War of Independence." For that reason a book entitled "The Birth of the United States" finds this a convenient place to stop.

For a while after 1815, it must have seemed that internally there had been similar success, for, almost miraculously, party dissension began to disappear and almost all Americans became Democratic-Republicans.

The Federalists had dug their own grave. Their bitterness against the war was great enough to make their actions seem treasonable. They refused to fight in the war and they made no secret of their desire to increase their own power at the expense of a central government they felt to be in the grip of the south and west.

All through 1814, when Great Britain seemed ready for the kill, delegates from the five New England states were being chosen or elected, and on December 15, 1814, they gathered in Hartford. The national atmosphere was grim since most people were sure the British would soon take New Orleans and no word had yet arrived that the British were easing their territorial demands.

The "Hartford Convention" sat for three weeks, till January 5, 1815. The leading figures in the convention were George Cabot (born in Salem, Massachusetts, in 1752) and Harrison-Gray Otis (born in Boston, in 1765, and a nephew of James Otis).

The convention adopted a set of resolutions calling for the considerable weakening of the Federal government – a single term for Presidents, limitations on military conscriptions and embargoes, restricted rights for naturalized citizens, and so on. The most important demand was that each state use Federal taxes collected within its boundaries for its own defense.

Naturally, with each state responsible for its own defense, any united action in wartime would be impossible and the nation would fall apart at the smallest touch from outside. The Federal government could not possibly consider such a thing unless it were already smashed into humiliating defeat and had no power left.

But this was what the men of the Hartford Convention expected would happen and they appointed Otis to head a delegation to go to Washington and place their demands before President Madison.

The Hartford Convention had, like the Constitutional Convention, decided to keep its deliberations secret. Considering that it was wartime, however, and that New England was notoriously disaffected, this was an unwise move. The Democratic-Republicans proclaimed loudly that the Hartford Convention was plotting treason and the nation, on the whole, believed this. Why else should they have been so secretive?

And although the resolutions were not, indeed, a matter of

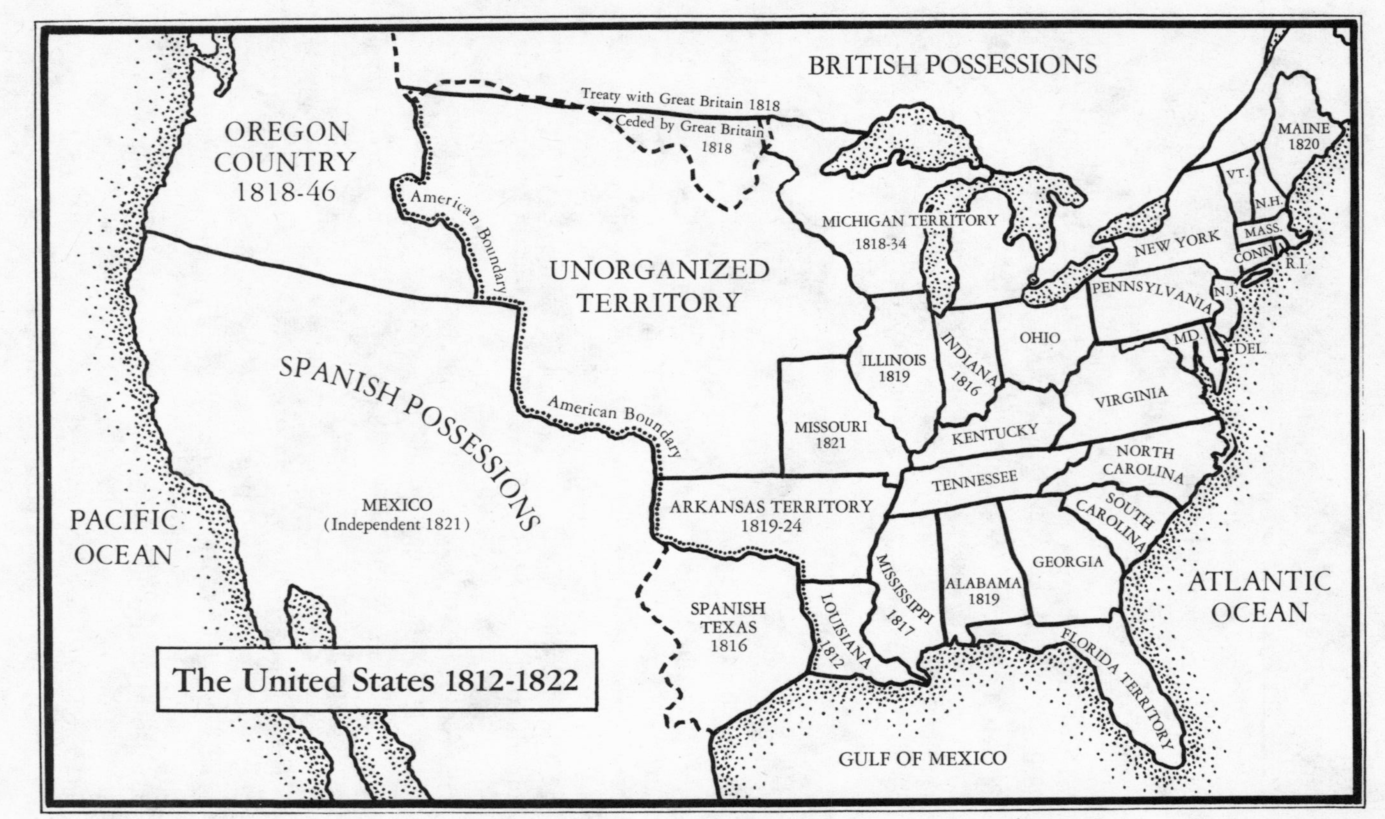

The United States 1812-1822

outright treason, it is easy to believe that the Otis delegation intended to threaten secession if President Madison did not give in to their views.

The Otis delegation cared nothing for accusations of treason, but when they reached Baltimore the news arrived of the enormous victory at New Orleans. Suddenly, it seemed to them that Madison would perhaps refuse to listen to reason. Then came the news of a peace that left the United States entirely intact and one that, in combination with the Battle of New Orleans, could be considered victorious. Now it seemed that Madison would not even talk to them.

They hung about futilely in Washington for a while and then, unable to do anything, left. They, along with the Hartford Convention, and all the Federalists everywhere, inspired what was far worse than fear and anger – ridicule and contempt.

The Federalist Party withered under the laughter resulting from the most grotesquely mistimed political gesture in American history and within a few years had disappeared altogether. There followed what is sometimes called "The Era of Good Feeling" because it seemed that all Americans were now agreed on fundamentals and would move forward united.

Stephen Decatur, on his return from the Mediterranean, was a hero of the hour. When he was toasted at a party in Norfolk in 1816, he responded with one of his own that seemed to breathe this sense of a united self-assurance among a people confident in their own destiny: "Our country! In her intercourse with foreign nations, may she always be in the right; but our country, right or wrong."

From the time of the signing of the Declaration of Independence to the sounding of Decatur's grandiloquent toast, exactly forty years had passed. Five signers of the Declaration were still alive: John Adams, Thomas Jefferson, Charles Carroll of Carrollton, William Floyd (born in Brookhaven, New York, in 1734), and William Ellery (born in Newport, Rhode Island in 1727).

With foreign danger gone, with internal peace seemingly assured, what could go wrong?

And yet something did. Within four years of Decatur's toast, a loud debate arose over the admission of new states, a debate that marked the beginning of a quarrel that for another forty years was to grow more heated, more bitter, more hate-filled, until the nation upon which so bright a sun seemed to be shining did what no foreign enemy could possibly have done.

It nearly destroyed itself.

But how that came about, and how the United States survived, must be the subject for another book.

A TABLE OF DATES

1760 October 26 George III becomes King of Great Britain

1761 February 24 James Otis denounces the Writs of Assistance

1762 Jean Jacques Rousseau publishes *The Social Contract*

1763 Charles Mason and Jeremiah Dixon begin survey of the "Mason-Dixon Line"

February 10 The Treaty of Paris ends the French and Indian War

April George Grenville becomes British Prime Minister

May 7 Pontiac's War begins with the blockade of Detroit

August 2 British defeat Indians at the Battle of Bushy Run

October 7 Royal Proclamation forbids settlements beyond the Allegheny ridge

December 1 Patrick Henry argues for home rule in the Parson's Cause

1764 St. Louis founded by the French

March Grenville announces plan for a Stamp Act in the colonies

April 5 Sugar Act passed, raising tariffs

April 19 Currency Act forbids colonists to issue paper money

November 17 Active fighting ends in Pontiac's War

1765 March 22 Stamp Act becomes law

May 15 Quartering Act orders colonists to house soldiers

May 29 Patrick Henry denounces Stamp Act

June 8 Massachusetts takes initiative in calling Stamp Act Congress

October 7 Stamp Act Congress opens sessions in New York

November 1 Stamp Act goes into effect

1766 January 17 London merchants petition for repeal of Stamp Act

February 13 Benjamin Franklin testifies against Stamp Act before Parliament

March 18 Stamp Act repealed
July 24 Treaty of Oswego ends Pontiac's War

1767 May 8 Charles Townshend's "champagne speech"
June 15 New York Assembly is suspended
June 29 Townshend duties are imposed on colonists
September 4 Townshend dies
November 20 Townshend duties go into effect
December 2 John Dickinson begins publication of *Letters of a Farmer*

1768 February 11 Circular letter prepared by Samuel Adams sent to other colonies, suggesting united opposition
June 10 John Hancock's ship, *Liberty*, seized for customs violations; riots result
October 1 Two regiments of British soldiers land in Boston

1769 June Vandalia colony formed in what is now West Virginia
July 16 Mission established at San Diego; first Spanish settlement in California

1770 January 19 Liberty Pole riot in New York City
January 31 Lord North becomes British Prime Minister
March 5 Boston Massacre
April 12 All Townshend duties repealed except for that on tea

1772 June 10 The British ship, *Gaspée,* burned by Americans in Narragansett Bay
November 2 Committees of Correspondence formed by Samuel Adams and Joseph Warren

1773 December 16 Boston Tea Party

1774 March 31 Boston Port Act, first of Coercive Acts, approved by George III
May 10 Louis XVI becomes King of France
May 13 General Thomas Gage arrives in Boston to rule as governor of Massachusetts
May 24 Virginia House of Burgesses expresses sympathy for Boston; declares day of prayer
June 1 Boston harbor closed to trade
June 2 Quartering Act passed by Parliament
June 22 Quebec Act passed by Parliament
August 27 Transylvania colony established in what is now Kentucky
September 1 General Gage seizes powder supplies in Charlestown
September 5 First Continental Congress meets in Philadelphia
September 17 Suffolk Re-

solves drawn up by Joseph Warren

October 5 Massachusetts, outside Boston, organizes a government in defiance of the King; Organizes Minutemen

October 6 End of fighting in Lord Dunmore's War

October 26 First Continental Congress adjourns

November 30 Thomas Paine arrives in Philadelphia from Great Britain

December 13 Colonials seize powder in Portsmouth, New Hampshire

1775 February 26 General Gage sends soldiers to Salem

February 27 New England trade with other colonies banned

March 23 Patrick Henry delivers his "Liberty or Death" speech

April 1 Boonesborough founded by Daniel Boone

April 18–19 The warning ride of Paul Revere and others

April 19 Americans defeat British at Battles of Lexington and Concord

April 23 American siege of Boston begins

May 10 Second Continental Congress meets in Philadelphia. Ethan Allen takes Ticonderoga

May 31 Mecklenburg Resolves adopted by settlers in western North Carolina

June 12 Gage places Boston under martial law

June 14 The Continental army is established

June 15 George Washington appointed commander-in-chief of the Continental army

June 17 Battle of Bunker Hill: British suffer heavy losses; Joseph Warren dies in action

June 22 Congress begins to issue paper money

July 3 Washington takes command of the Continental army

August 23 George III declares colonies in a state of rebellion

September 1 George III refuses to accept petition from Continental Congress

October 10 William Howe replaces Gage as commander-in-chief of British forces in America

October 13 Congress authorizes an American navy

November 13 Richard Montgomery takes Montreal from the British

December 31 Americans defeated at the Battle of Quebec; Montgomery killed; Benedict Arnold wounded

1776 San Francisco founded by Spanish. Spanish also reach mouth of Columbia River

January 1 Washington raises the first striped American flag

January 5 New Hampshire adopts first written state constitution

January 10 Thomas Paine publishes *Common Sense*

January 24 Artillery from Ticonderoga arrives in Boston

March 3 Silas Deane appointed to go to France as commercial agent

March 4 Washington fortifies Dorchester Heights

March 17 Howe evacuates Boston

March 26 British army sails for Halifax from Boston harbor

April 12 North Carolina declares for independence; first colony to do so

April 13 Washington takes army from Cambridge to New York

June 7 Richard Henry Lee offers resolution of independence in the Continental Congress

June 10 France prepares to give the Americans the first loan

June 11 A committee to draft a Declaration of Independence is chosen; Thomas Jefferson at its head

June 12 A committee to draft a plan for a confederation of the colonies is chosen; John Dickinson at its head. A Bill of Rights, drawn by George Mason, is adopted as part of the Virginia State Constitution

June 28 A British naval force repulsed at Charleston, South Carolina. Declaration of Independence presented to Congress

July 2 Congress accepts Declaration of Independence. Howe brings the British army to Staten Island

July 4 John Hancock signs Declaration of Independence

July 12 John Dickinson reports plan for "Articles of Confederation"

August 27 British defeat Americans at the Battle of Long Island

September 6 Abortive peace conference on Staten Island

September 15 British occupy New York City

September 22 Execution of Nathan Hale

October 28 British defeat Americans at the Battle of White Plains

November 16 British take Fort Washington

November 20 British take Fort Lee

November 21 Washington and Greene begin retreat across New Jersey

December Benjamin Franklin in charge of negotiations with France

December 6 Transylvania made part of Virginia as "Kentucky County"
December 8 British occupy Newport, Rhode Island
December 20 Congress, having fled Philadelphia, meets in Baltimore
December 23 First number of Paine's *The American Crisis* appears
December 25 Washington crosses the Delaware River
December 26 Americans victorious at the Battle of Trenton
December 30 Americans occupy Trenton

1777 January 3 Americans win Battle of Princeton
March 4 Congress returns to Philadelphia
June 1 General John Burgoyne starts offensive aimed at cutting the American states in two
June 14 The first flag with both stripes and stars adopted by Congress
July 6 Burgoyne takes Ticonderoga
July 8 Vermont adopts written constitution providing for full male suffrage and the abolition of slavery
July 23 Howe leaves New York in move to take Philadelphia
July 29 Burgoyne takes Fort Edward
August 4 Horatio Gates takes over command of American army opposing Burgoyne
August 6 British and Indians advancing across New York State from the west stopped at the Battle of Oriskany
August 16 Burgoyne's forces defeated at the Battle of Bennington
August 23 British in western New York give up the offensive at the approach of Benedict Arnold
August 25 Howe lands in Maryland
September 11 Howe defeats Washington at the Battle of Brandywine
September 19 The first Battle of Saratoga between Gates and Burgoyne is drawn
September 26 British occupy Philadelphia
September 30 Congress, having fled Philadelphia a second time, meets in York, Pennsylvania
October 3 Howe defeats Washington at Battle of Germantown
October 7 Americans, led by Benedict Arnold, defeat Burgoyne at second Battle of Saratoga
October 17 Burgoyne surrenders
November 15 Congress adopts Articles of Confederation

December Washington goes into winter quarters at Valley Forge

1778 Captain James Cook explores the Oregon coast

February 6 Alliance between France and the United States

February 23 Baron von Steuben arrives at Valley Forge and drills the army

May 8 Clinton replaces Howe as British commander-in-chief

May 12 George Rogers Clark sets out for expedition to northwest

June 18 British evacuate Philadelphia

June 28 Draw at the Battle of Monmouth

July 2 Congress returns to Philadelphia

July 4 Loyalist-Indian massacre at Wyoming Valley

July 5 Clark takes Kaskaskia, later Vincennes

July 10 France declares war on Great Britain

November 11 Loyalist-Indian massacre at Cherry Valley

December 17 British retake Vincennes in the northwest

December 29 British take Savannah, Georgia

1779 January 29 British take Augusta, Georgia

February 25 Clark takes Vincennes again, completes conquest of northwest

June 21 Spain declares war on Great Britain

July 16 Anthony Wayne storms and retakes Stony Point, New York

August Iroquois power destroyed by American forces

September 23 John Paul Jones in the *Bon Homme Richard* destroys the *Serapis* off the Scottish coast

October 9 American attempt to retake Savannah beaten off

October 25 British evacuate Newport, Rhode Island

1780 May 12 British take Charleston, South Carolina. General Lincoln surrenders in great American defeat of the war

July 11 Rochambeau and the French land in Newport; besieged there by British

August 16 Severe American defeat at the Battle of Camden; Gates disgraced

September 23 Benedict Arnold's plot to surrender West Point discovered

October 2 Major André hanged as spy

October 7 American victory at the Battle of Kin's Mountain

December 20 Great Britain declares war on Netherlands

1781 Los Angeles founded by Spanish

January 17 American victory at the Battle of Cowpens

February 20 Robert Morris appointed superintendent of finance

March 1 When colonies promise to give up western claims, Maryland accepts Articles of Confederation; since it is the last state to do so, the Articles come into force

March 15 Narrow American defeat at the Battle of Guilford Courthouse

April 25 Cornwallis heads north for Virginia

July 5 Rochambeau brings his French troops from Newport to New York area to join Washington

August 1 Cornwallis retires to Yorktown

August 30 De Grasse and the French fleet arrive at Yorktown

September 5 De Grasse defeats the British fleet; Washington arrives at Yorktown

September 28 Siege of Yorktown begins

October 19 Cornwallis surrenders at Yorktown

1782 March 20 Lord North resigns as British Prime Minister

April 19 The Netherlands recognizes independence of the United States

July 11 Savannah evacuated by the British

November 10 George Rogers Clark defeats the Shawnees

December 14 Charleston evacuated by the British

1783 April 19 Congress declares Revolutionary War at end

May 13 Society of the Cincinnati formed

June 30 Congress meets at Princeton, New Jersey, after leaving Philadelphia a third time as a result of a soldier mutiny

September 3 Treaty of Paris formally ends the Revolutionary War

November 25 British evacuate New York

December 4 Washington says farewell to his officers at Fraunces Tavern

December 23 Washington resigns as commander-in-chief

1784 State of Franklin organized

April 23 Jefferson's suggestion for organizing the west adopted by Congress (leads to Northwest Ordinance)

June 26 Spain closes Mississippi River to Americans

1785 January 11 Congress meets in New York which remains the capital of the United States for five years

1786 January 21 Virginia legislature calls for meeting of all states at Annapolis to discuss commercial matters

August Shay's Rebellion
September 11 Annapolis Convention meets

1787 February Shay's Rebellion at an end
February 21 Congress calls for Constitutional Convention
May 25 Constitutional Convention opens
May 29 Edmund Randolph presents Virginia Plan
June 15 William Paterson presents New Jersey Plan
July 13 Northwest Ordinance passed by Congress
July 16 Connecticut Compromise accepted by Constitutional Convention
August 22 John Fitch demonstrates steamship on Delaware River
September 17 Constitution signed by members of Constitutional Convention
October 27 First issue of *The Federalist* published
December 7 Delaware ratifies Constitution
December 12 Pennsylvania ratifies Constitution
December 18 New Jersey ratifies Constitution

1788 January 2 Georgia ratifies Constitution
January 9 Connecticut ratifies Constitution
February 6 Massachusetts ratifies Constitution; suggests Bill of Rights
April 28 Maryland ratifies Constitution
May 23 South Carolina ratifies Constitution
June 21 New Hampshire becomes ninth state to ratify Constitution which thus comes into effect
June 25 Virginia ratifies Constitution
July 26 New York ratifies Constitution
October 21 Last meeting of the Continental Congress
November Renewal of Franco-American alliance
December 28 Losantiville founded (later named Cincinnati)

1789 February 4 Electors vote unanimously for George Washington to be first President of the United States; John Adams elected as first Vice President
April 6 First Congress begins sessions
April 21 John Adams sworn in as Vice President in New York
April 30 George Washington sworn in as President in New York
July 14 The Bastille falls in Paris; French Revolution begins
September 11 Alexander Hamilton becomes first Secretary of the Treasury
September 25 Congress submits Bill of Rights to the states

September 26 John Jay becomes first Chief Justice of the Supreme Court
November 21 North Carolina ratifies Constitution

1790 First census shows the population of the United States to be nearly four million
Samuel Slater begins Industrial Revolution in the United States
March 22 Thomas Jefferson becomes first Secretary of State
March 29 Rhode Island ratifies Constitution; all thirteen states now part of the Union
July 16 Congress votes to establish future capital on the Potomac River; capital fixed at Philadelphia till new site is ready
August 9 Robert Gray returns from first American circumnavigation of the world
October 18 American troops defeated by Indians near what is now Fort Wayne

1791 March 3 Excise tax on whisky established
March 4 Vermont enters Union as fourteenth state
November 4 St. Clair defeated on Wabash River by Indians
December 12 Bank of the United States opens
December 15 The Bill of Rights goes into effect as the first ten amendments to the Constitution

1792 April 9 Turnpike opened between Philadelphia and Lancaster; beginning of turnpike era
May 11 Robert Gray of Boston enters Columbia River and names it after his ship
June 1 Kentucky enters Union as fifteenth state
September 21 Revolutionaries proclaim French Republic
December 5 Washington and Adams re-elected

1793 January 21 Louis XVI executed
February 1 France declares war on Great Brit-
March 4 Washington begins his second term
April 6 Reign of Terror begins in France
April 8 Citizen Genêt arrives at Charleston
April 22 Washington issues Neutrality Proclamation
August 23 Washington asks recall of Genêt
December 31 Jefferson resigns as Secretary of State

1794 March 14 Whitney patents cotton gin
July Whisky Rebellion breaks out
July 27 Reign of Terror ends in France
August 20 Anthony Wayne defeats Indians at Battle of Fallen Timbers

November Whisky Rebellion ends
November 19 Jay's Treaty signed by Great Britain and the United States
1795 January 31 Hamilton retires as Secretary of Treasury
August 3 Treaty of Greenville signed with Ohio Indians
August 14 Washington signs Jay's Treaty
October 27 Pinckney's Treaty signed by Spain and the United States
1796 Cleveland founded
April 28 Fisher Ames speaks in support of Jay's Treaty
1796 June 1 Tennessee enters Union as sixteenth state
September 19 Washington's "Farewell Address" published
October 26 Directory established in France
November 15 France suspends diplomatic relations with the United States
December 7 John Adams elected second President of the United States; Thomas Jefferson Vice President
1797 March 4 John Adams inaugurated
May 10 The *United States* launched at Philadelphia; first vessel of the new navy
September 7 The *Constellation* launched at Baltimore
October 18 XYZ affair opens
October 21 The *Constitution* launched at Boston
November 1 Charles Pinckney breaks off negotiations with France, refusing to turn over money
1798 Eli Whitney introduces interchangeable parts
"Hail Columbia" written by Joseph Hopkinson
January 8 Eleventh Amendment to Constitution goes into effect
April 30 The Navy Department is created
June 18 Naturalization Act extends residence requirement for naturalization to fourteen years
June 25 Alien Act
July 14 Sedition Act
November 16 The Kentucky Resolutions
December 24 The Virginia Resolutions
1799 February 9 The *Constellation* captures the French *L'Insurgente*
November 9 Napoleon Bonaparte takes over the French government; becomes First Consul
December 14 Death of George Washington
1800 Summer Washington, D.C., becomes capital of the United States
September 30 End of undeclared war with France

October 1 France forces Spain to cede Louisiana
November 17 Congress convenes in Washington for the first time
December 3 Thomas Jefferson and Aaron Burr in a tie vote for the presidency

1801 January 27 John Marshall becomes Chief Justice of the Supreme Court
February 17 House of Representatives names Thomas Jefferson as third President; Aaron Burr Vice President
March 3 John Adams names last-minute judges
March 4 Thomas Jefferson inaugurated
May 14 Tripoli declares war on the United States

1802 March 27 Treaty of Amiens between France and Great Britain
October 16 Spain closes Mississippi River to American trade

1803 Fort Dearborn (Chicago) founded
February 24 *Marbury v. Madison* establishes principle that the Supreme Court can rule on constitutionality of Federal laws
March 1 Ohio enters Union as seventeenth state
April 30 Louisiana Purchase negotiated
October 31 The Tripolitans capture the *Philadelphia*
December 20 The United States formally takes over Louisiana Territory

1804 February 16 Stephen Decatur destroys the *Philadelphia*
March 12 A New Hampshire Federal judge impeached and, later, convicted
May 14 Lewis and Clark begin exploration of Louisiana Territory
July 11 Alexander Hamilton shot in duel by Aaron Burr
September 25 Twelfth Amendment to Constitution comes into force; President and Vice President to be elected separately
December 2 Napoleon Bonaparte makes himself Emperor Napoleon I of France
December 5 Thomas Jefferson re-elected; George Clinton becomes Vice President

1805 March 1 Justice Samuel Chase acquitted
March 4 Jefferson begins second term
April 27 Eaton takes Tripolitan town of Derna
June 4 Tripolitan war ends in victory for the United States
August 9 Zebulon Pike starts on expedition to explore upper Mississippi River
October 21 Great Britain defeats France at Battle

of Trafalgar; supreme at sea

November 15 Lewis and Clark reach the Pacific Ocean

December 2 Napoleon defeats Russia and Austria at the Battle of Austerlitz; supreme on land

1806 Burr's Conspiracy

September 23 Lewis and Clark back in St. Louis

November 15 Zebulon Pike discovers "Pike's Peak"

1807 February 19 Aaron Burr arrested

June 22 *Chesapeake* forcibly stopped by British warship *Leopard*

July 9 Napoleon signs treaty of friendship with Russia; at peak of power

August 17 Robert Fulton demonstrates steamship on Hudson River

September 1 Aaron Burr acquitted

December 22 Jefferson imposes Embargo Act

1808 March Napoleon invades Spain; beginning of decline

December 7 James Madison elected fourth President; George Clinton remains Vice President

1809 March 1 Embargo Act repealed

March 4 Madison inaugurated

1810 March 16 *Fletcher v. Peck* establishes principle that the Supreme Court can rule on constitutionality of state laws

October 27 West Florida annexed by the United States

1811 March 2 Trade with Great Britain embargoed after Napoleon pretends to lift restrictions on American vessels

May 16 *President* defeats the British ship *Little Belt*

November 4 Twelfth Congress convenes. Henry Clay, leader of the War Hawks, named Speaker of the House

November 7 William Henry Harrison defeats Indians at Battle of Tippecanoe

1812 February 11 Word "gerrymander" first used in reference to manipulation of election districts by Elbridge Gerry

April 30 Louisiana enters Union as eighteenth state

May 11 British Prime Minister Perceval assassinated

June 1 Madison sends war message to Congress

June 18 The United States declares war on Great Britain; "War of 1812" begins

June 22 Napoleon launches invasion of Russia

June 23 Great Britain lifts restrictions against American shipping, not

having heard of the declaration of war
July 17 The British take Fort Machilimackinac
August 13 The *Essex* captures the British ship *Alert*
August 15 Fort Dearborn (Chicago) surrenders to British
August 16 Detroit surrenders to British
August 19 *Constitution* defeats the British ship *Guerrière*
September 14 Napoleon reaches Moscow
October 12 American troops defeated on the Niagara front; British General Isaac Brock dies in action
October 18 *Wasp* captures British *Frolic*
October 25 *United States* captures British *Macedonian*
December 2 Madison reelected; Gerry now Vice President
December 18 Napoleon back in Paris; his army lost in Russia
December 26 British blockade Chesapeake and Delaware
December 29 *Constitution* captures British *Java;* earns name of "Old Ironsides"

1813 January 22 American force surprised and destroyed at Frenchtown
February 24 *Hornet* sinks British *Peacock*
March 4 Madison begins second term
March 30 British blockade entire American coast outside New England
April 27 American troops burn public buildings in York (Toronto)
June 1 British *Shannon* captures *Chesapeake;* James Lawrence dies saying "Don't give up the ship"
June 6 Americans defeated at Battle of Stony Creek
August 30 Fort Mims taken by Creeks; garrison massacred
September 10 Oliver Hazard Perry defeats British at the Battle of Lake Erie
September 18 British evacuate Detroit
October 5 American victory at Battle of Thames River; Tecumseh killed
October 19 Napoleon suffers great defeat in Germany
December 30 British burn Buffalo

1814 March 27 Andrew Jackson defeats Creeks at Horseshoe Bend
April 11 Napoleon abdicates
May 31 British blockade extended to New England
July 4 Winfield Scott de-

feats British at Battle of Chippewa River

July 25 Battle of Lundy's Lane ends in draw

August 19 British land in Maryland

August 24 Americans flee at Battle of Bladensburg; British occupy Washington, burn public buildings

August 27 Madison returns to Washington

August 31 Prevost begins drive down Lake Champlain

September 11 Thomas Macdonough defeats British in Battle of Lake Champlain; ends Prevost's drive

September 14 British bombard Fort McHenry in Baltimore; Francis Scott Key writes words to "Star-Spangled Banner"

September 20 "Star-Spangled Banner" published

October 17 British fleet leaves Chesapeake

November 7 Jackson takes Pensacola

December 15 Hartford Convention meets

December 24 Treaty of Ghent signed ending War of 1812

1815 January 5 Hartford Convention ends

January 8 Jackson wins great victory over British at Battle of New Orleans

March 1 Napoleon returns to France

June 18 Napoleon suffers final defeat at Battle of Waterloo

June 30 Decatur forces an end to Barbary state piracy

1816 Decatur's toast: "My country, right or wrong"

INDEX